th
world's
very
best
e-mails

the world's very best e-mails

>>> compiled by
Geoff Young

Hodder Moa Beckett

ISBN 1-86958-798-7

First published in 1999 by Hodder Moa Beckett Publishers Limited,
[a member of the Hodder Headline Group]
4 Whetu Place, Mairangi Bay, Auckland, New Zealand

Reprinted 2000, 2001, 2002

Produced and designed by Hodder Moa Beckett Publishers Ltd

Printed by Griffin Press, Australia

contents

intro

A dog of a job – but someone had to do it. I found that sifting through hundreds of e-mails took a lot of the gloss off having a sly peek at my incoming mail. (You know the score; you're checking your mail when you are meant to be slaving away at an industrious task making your employer or bank manager a slightly happier person instead.)

But, well, hopefully the sacrifice was worth it. This book is divided into 14 separate chapters ranging from the ubiquitous Battle of the Sexes, where the blokes slag hell out of the women and the women slag hell out of the men, to the naughty Sealed Section for the more x-rated missives. The Battle of the Sexes looks like a male victory going by the pro-bloke bias received and we've come to the conclusion the male bias stems from more men seemingly having the time to piss around making them all up than women, but we're confident the bias is shifting. The book is global although the Americans are prolific e-mail jokesters and a fair chunk of the material came from the land of Uncle Sam.

An important warning is needed. We've had to put all of our politically correct thinking on the back burner and all you new-age males, non-sexists, anti-racists, anti-anti-ageists and lobbyists for religious freedom had best do the same because this book is bound to get right up your nose.

So, go ahead and have a laugh or a hundred and be guaranteed this collection will give you a better chuckle than the pathetic ones you get in your Christmas cracker.

Geoff Young

...is a journalist living in Auckland. After returning from 14 years working on British newspapers, including *The Daily Telegraph*, he did stints on the *New Zealand Herald* and the *Sunday Star-Times*. His book credits include Gerarda Bossard's *P.O.W. – One Girl's Experiences in a Japanese P.O.W. Camp* and *True Bliss – the official story*.

Unashamedly tasteless and
politically incorrect
material within.
Read on at your own risk!

battle of the sexes

The biggest chapter by far. Since blokes allegedly dragged women by their hair in the days of the caveman it can safely be said the man's arrogance to what he called 'lesser' beings has been well documented. Hell, the haughty male has only let the women vote for 100 years or so, with Wyoming and New Zealand leading the way. Other Neanderthal nations lagged well behind and the lot of women in some Islamic nations doesn't bear thinking about from the Western point of view. But, as the old saying goes, 'Hell hath no fury like a woman scorned' and the female of the species is fighting back, as you'll see in this section.

HOW TO SHOWER LIKE A WOMAN >>>

1. Take off clothing and place it in sectioned laundry hamper according to lights and darks.
2. Walk to bathroom wearing long dressing gown. If you see your boyfriend/husband along the way, cover up any exposed flesh and rush to bathroom.
3. Look at your womanly physique in the mirror and stick out your gut so that you can complain and whine even more about how you're getting fat.
4. Get in the shower. Look for facecloth, armcloth, legcloth, long loofah, wide loofah and pumice stone.
5. Wash your hair once with cucumber and lamfrey shampoo with 83 added vitamins.
6. Wash your hair again with cucumber and aloe vera shampoo with 83 added vitamins.
7. Condition your hair with cucumber and aloe vera conditioner enhanced with natural crocus oil. Leave on hair for 15 minutes.
8. Wash your face with crushed apricot facial scrub for 10 minutes until red raw.
9. Wash entire rest of body with ginger nut and jaffa cake body wash.
10. Rinse conditioner off hair (this takes at least 15 minutes as you must make sure that it has all come off).
11. Shave armpits and legs. Consider shaving bikini area but decide to get it waxed instead.
12. Scream loudly when your boyfriend/husband flushes the toilet and you lose the water pressure.
13. Turn off shower.
14. Squeegee all wet surfaces in shower. Spray mould spots with Jiff.
15. Get out of shower. Dry with towel the size of a small African country. Wrap hair in super absorbent second towel.
16. Check entire body for the remotest sign of a zit. Attack with nails/tweezers if found.
17. Return to bedroom wearing long dressing gown and towel on head.
18. If you see your boyfriend/husband along the way, cover up any exposed flesh and then rush to bedroom to spend an hour and a half getting dressed.

HOW TO SHOWER LIKE A MAN >>>

1. Take off clothes while sitting on the edge of the bed and leave them in a pile on the floor.
2. Walk naked to the bathroom. If you see your girlfriend/wife along the way, flash her your tackle making the 'woo' sound.
3. Look at your manly physique in the mirror and suck in your gut to see if you have pecs (no). Admire the size of your dick in the mirror, scratch your balls and smell your fingers for one last whiff.
4. Get in the shower.
5. Don't bother to look for a washcloth (you don't use one).
6. Wash your face.
7. Wash your armpits.
8. Crack up at how loud your fart sounds in the shower.
9. Wash your privates and surrounding area.
10. Wash your ass, leaving hair on the soap bar.
11. Shampoo your hair (do not use conditioner).
12. Make a shampoo Mohawk on top of your head.
13. Pull back shower curtain and look at yourself in the mirror.
14. Pee (in the shower).
15. Rinse off and get out of the shower. Fail to notice water on the floor because you left the curtain hanging out of the tub the whole time.
16. Partially dry off.
17. Look at yourself in the mirror, flex muscles. Admire dick size.
18. Leave shower curtain open and wet bath mat on the floor.
19. Leave bathroom and fan light on.
20. Return to the bedroom with towel around your waist. If you pass your girlfriend/wife, pull off the towel, grab your dick, go 'Yeah baby' and thrust your pelvis at her.
21. Throw wet towel on the bed. Take two minutes to get dressed.

25 RULES THAT GUYS WISHED WOMEN KNEW >>>

1. If you think you're fat, you probably are. Don't ask us.
2. Learn to work the toilet seat. If it's up – put it down.
3. Don't cut your hair. Ever.
4. Sometimes we're not thinking about you. Live with it.

5. Get rid of your cat.
6. Sunday = Sports.
7. Anything you wear is fine – really.
8. Women wearing wonderbras and low-cut blouses lose their right to complain about having their boobs stared at.
9. You have too many shoes.
10. Crying is blackmail.
11. Ask for what you want. Subtle hints don't work.
12. Mark anniversaries on a calendar.
13. Yes, peeing standing up is more difficult than peeing from point-blank range. We're bound to miss sometimes.
14. 'Yes' and 'No' are perfectly acceptable answers.
15. A headache that lasts for 17 months is a problem. See a doctor.
16. Don't fake it. We'd rather be ineffective than deceived.
17. Anything we said six or eight months ago is inadmissible in an argument.
18. If you don't dress like the Dawson Creek girls, don't expect us to act like the soap opera guys.
19. If something we said could be interpreted two ways and one of the ways makes you sad and angry, we meant the other one.
20. Let us ogle. If we don't look at other women, how can we know how pretty you are?
21. Don't rub the lamp if you don't want the genie to come out.
22. You can either ask us to do something OR tell us how you want it done – not both.
23. Christopher Columbus didn't need directions and neither do we.
24. You have enough clothes.
25. Nothing says 'I love you' like sex.

SISTERS ARE DOING IT >>>

Two nuns went out of the convent to sell cookies. One of them is known as Sister Mathematical (SM) and the other one is known as Sister Logical (SL). It is getting dark and they are still far away from the convent.

SL: *Have you noticed that a man has been following us for the past half-hour?*

SM: *Yes, I wonder what he wants.*

SL: *It's logical. He wants to rape us.*

SM: *Oh, no! At this rate he will reach us in 15 minutes at the most. What can we do?*
SL: *The only logical thing to do of course is that we have to start walking faster.*
SM: *It is not working.*
SL: *Of course it is not working. The man did the only obvious thing to do. He started to walk faster too.*
SM: *So, what shall we do? At this rate he will reach us in one minute.*
SL: *The only logical thing we can do is split. You go that way and I'll go this way. He cannot follow both of us.*
So the man decided to go after Sister Logical and Sister Mathematical arrives at the convent and is worried because Sister Logical has not yet arrived. Finally, Sister Logical arrives.
SM: *Sister Logical. Thank God you are here. Tell us what happened.*
SL: *The only logical thing happened. The man could not follow both of us, so he followed me.*
SM: *So, what happened? Please tell us.*
SL: *The only logical thing to happen. I started to run as fast as I could.*
SM: *So what happened?*
SL: *The only logical thing to happen. The man also started to run as fast as he could.*
SM: *And what else?*
SL: *The only logical thing to happen. He reached me.*
SM: *Oh, no! What did you do then?*
SL: *The only logical thing to do. I lifted my habit up.*
SM: *Oh, Sister. What did the man do?*
SL: *The only logical thing to do. He pulled down his pants.*
SM: *Oh, no! What happened then?*
SL: *Isn't it logical, Sister? A nun with her habit up can run faster than a man with his pants down.*
And you thought this was a dirty joke…

LOVES ME, LOVES ME NOT >>>

A girl and boy had been having a relationship for about four months and one Friday night after work they meet in a bar. They stay for a few drinks and then go on to get some food at a restaurant near their respective houses. They eat then go back to his house and she stays over.

Her story:
Well, Ed was in an odd mood when I got to the bar. I thought it might have been me because I was a bit late but he didn't say anything much about it, but the conversation was quite slow going, so I thought we should go off somewhere more intimate so we could talk more privately, so we go to this restaurant and he's still a bit funny and I'm trying to cheer him up and start to wonder whether it's me or something, so I ask him and he says no, but you know I'm not really sure, so anyway, in the cab back to his house I say that I love him and he just puts his arm around me and I don't know what the hell that means, because you know he doesn't say it back or anything, so when we get back to his place I'm wondering if he's going off me and so I try to ask him about it but he just switches on the TV and so I say I'm going to go to sleep and then after about 10 minutes he joins me and we have sex but he seemed really distracted and so afterwards I just want to leave and, I dunno, I just don't know what he thinks any more, I mean, do you think he's met someone else?

His story:
Shit day at work. Great shag later.

BRIDGING THE GAP >>>

A man was walking along a California beach and stumbled across an old lamp. He picked it up and rubbed it and out popped a genie. The genie said 'OK. You released me from the lamp, blah blah blah. This is the fourth time this month and I'm getting a little sick of these wishes, so you can forget about three. You only get one wish.'

The man sat and thought about it for a while and said, 'I've always wanted to go to Hawaii but I'm scared to fly and I get very seasick. Could you build me a bridge to Hawaii so I can drive over there to visit?'

The genie laughed and said, 'That's impossible. Think of the logistics of that! How would the supports ever reach the bottom of the Pacific? Think of how much concrete… how much steel! No, think of another wish.'

The man said OK and tried to think of a really good wish. Finally, he said, 'I've been married and divorced four times. My wives always said that I don't care and that I'm insensitive. So, I wish that I could understand women... know how they feel inside and what they're thinking when they give me the silent treatment... know why they're crying, know what they really want when they say "nothing"... know how to make them truly happy...'

The genie said, 'You want that bridge two lanes or four?'

KERMIT'S GIFT >>>

Three women were out golfing one day and one of them hit her ball into the woods. She went into the woods to look for it and found a frog in a trap.

The frog said to her, 'If you release me from this trap, I will grant you three wishes.' The woman freed the frog and the frog said, 'Thank you, but I failed to mention that there was a condition to your wishes. Whatever you wish for, your husband will get 10 times more or better.'

The woman said, 'That would be OK,' and for her first wish she wanted to be the most beautiful woman in the world.

The frog warned her, 'You do realise this wish will also make your husband the most handsome man in the world, an Adonis, and that women will flock to him.'

The woman replied, 'That will be OK because I will be the most beautiful woman and he will only have eyes for me.' So, poof – she's the most beautiful woman in the world.

For her second wish, she wanted to be the richest woman in the world.

The frog said, 'That will make your husband the richest man in the world and he will be 10 times richer than you.'

The woman said, 'That will be okay because what is mine is his and what is his is mine.' So, poof – she's the richest woman in the world.

The frog then inquired about her third wish and she answered, 'I'd like a mild heart attack.'

PIG 'N' A BITCH >>>

A man is driving up a steep, narrow mountain road. A woman is driving down the same road. As they pass each other the woman leans out of her window and yells 'PIG'.

The man immediately leans out his window and screams back 'BITCH'. They continue on their way. As the man rounds the next corner, he crashes into a pig in the middle of the road.

CODE BREAKERS >>>

A newly married couple returned to their house after being on honeymoon. 'Care to go upstairs and have a shag?' the husband asks.

'Sshhh,' said the bride. 'All the neighbours will know what we're about to do. These walls are paper-thin. In the future, we'll have to ask each other in code. For example, how about asking, "Have you left the washing machine door open" instead?'

So, the following night, the husband asks, 'I don't suppose you left the washing machine door open did you?'

'No, I definitely shut it,' replied the wife who rolled over and went to sleep.

When she woke up, however, she was feeling a little randy herself and she nudged her husband and said, 'I think I did leave the washing machine door open after all. Would you like to do some washing?'

'No thanks,' said the husband, 'It was only a small load and I've done it by hand.'

BARMAN'S BLUES >>>

A rather attractive woman goes up to the bar in a quiet rural pub. She gestures alluringly to the barman who comes over immediately.

When he arrives, she seductively signals that he should bring his face close to hers. When he does so, she begins to gently caress his beard, which is full and bushy.

'Are you the manager?' she asks, softly stroking his face with both hands.

'Actually, no,' he replies.

'Can you get him for me? I need to speak to him,' she says,

running her hands up beyond his beard and into his hair.

'I'm afraid I can't,' breathes the barman, clearly aroused. 'Is there anything I can do?'

'Yes there is. I need you to give him a message,' she continues huskily, popping a couple of fingers into his mouth and allowing him to suck them.

'Tell him,' she says, 'that there is no toilet paper or hand soap in the ladies' toilet.'

THE LUCKY SEX >>>

- We got off the *Titanic* first.
- We can scare male bosses with mysterious gynaecological disorder excuses.
- We never ejaculate prematurely.
- We get to flirt with systems support men who always return our calls and are nice to us when we blow up our computers.
- When we buy a vibrator it's glamorous. When men buy a blow-up doll, it's pathetic.
- Our boyfriend's clothes make us look elfin and gorgeous. Guys look like complete idiots in ours.
- We can be groupies. Male groupies are stalkers.
- We can cry and get off speeding fines.
- We've never lusted after a cartoon character or the central figure in a computer game.
- Taxis stop for us.
- Men die earlier, so we get to cash in on the life insurance.
- We don't look like a frog in a blender when dancing.
- Free drinks, free dinners, free moving (you get the point?).
- We can hug our friend without wondering if she thinks we're gay.
- We know the truth about whether size matters.
- New lipstick gives us a whole new lease on life.
- If we have sex with someone and don't call the next day, we're not the devil.
- Condoms make no significant difference in our enjoyment of sex.
- We can sleep our way to the top.
- Nothing crucial can be cut off with one clean sweep.
- It's possible to live our whole lives without ever taking a group shower.

- No fashion faux pas we make could rival Speedos.
- We don't have to fart to amuse ourselves.
- If we cheat on our spouse, people assume it's because we're being emotionally neglected.
- We never have to wonder if his orgasm was real.
- If we forget to shave, no one has to know.
- We can congratulate our teammate without ever touching her arse.
- If we have a zit, we know how to conceal it.
- We never have to reach down every so often to make sure our privates are still there.
- If we're dumb, some people will find it cute.
- We have an excuse to be a total bitch at least once a month.
- We can talk to people of the opposite sex without having to picture them naked.
- If we marry someone 20 years younger, we're aware that we look like an idiot.
- Our friends won't think we're weird if we ask whether there's spinach in our teeth.
- There are times when chocolate really can solve all your problems.
- Gay waiters don't make us uncomfortable.
- We'll never regret piercing our ears.
- We can fully assess a person just by looking at their shoes.

GOOD CATHOLIC GIRLS >>>

Three women are discussing sex and birth control.

The first woman says, 'We're Catholic, so we can't use it.'

The second woman says, 'I'm also Catholic, but we use the rhythm method.'

The third woman says, 'We use the bucket-and-saucer method.'

Fascinated, the other women ask for an explanation. 'Well, I'm 1.80 m and my husband is 1.50 m,' the third woman says. 'We make love standing up with him standing on a bucket, and when his eyes get as big as saucers I kick the bucket out from under him.'

How many men does it take to open a beer?
None. It should be opened by the time she brings it.

Why is a laundromat a really bad place to pick up a woman?
Because a woman who can't even afford a washing machine will never be able to support you.

Why do women have smaller feet than men?
So they can stand closer to the kitchen sink.

How do you know when a woman is about to say something smart?
When she starts the sentence with, 'A man once told me…'

How do you fix a woman's watch?
You don't. There's a clock on the stove.

Why do men pass gas more than women do?
Because women won't shut up long enough to build up pressure.

If your dog is barking at the back door and your wife is yelling at the front door, who do you let in first?
The dog of course… at least he'll shut up after you've let him in.

All wives are alike, but they have different faces so you can tell them apart.

What's worse than a Male Chauvinist Pig?
A woman who won't do what she's told.

What do you call a woman with two brain cells?
Pregnant.

I married Miss Right. I just didn't know her first name was Always.

I haven't spoken to my wife for 18 months – I don't like to interrupt her.

What do you call a woman who has lost 95 percent of her intelligence?
Divorced.

Bigamy is having one wife too many. Some say monogamy is the same.

Scientists have discovered a certain food that diminishes a woman's sex drive by 90 percent – wedding cake.

DAD HAS HIS SAY >>>

- Today at work, the boss wanted to know when Father's Day was. 'Easy,' I answered. 'It's nine months before Mother's Day.'

- If my son is getting half as much out of university as the university is getting out of me, he'll be a success.

- Father's Day was both a joy and a worry as my kids were growing up. I was always afraid they were going to give me a present that I couldn't afford.

- I've got three TVs, cable and a satellite dish; I have three phone lines into the house, a cell phone and one in the car, plus a pager. I use two computers, three ISPs and a fax machine. I subscribe to two daily papers and one weekly one. I watch the news on every channel every evening. And my kids have the nerve to tell me I'm out of touch.

- With divorce and remarriage so common these days, pity the poor kids. Most of them know what to buy for Father's Day – they just don't know which 'Father' to give it to.

- Neither of my kids ever understood my logic. Both of them failed to see why they had to go to bed when I was tired.

- A friend of mine had five kids. When the youngest finally

turned 16 and was the last one left at home, my friend posted a sign on the kid's bedroom door: 'Check-out time is 18.'

HONEYMOON BLISS >>>

A couple were celebrating their Golden Wedding anniversary. Their domestic tranquillity had long been the talk of the town. A local newspaper reporter was inquiring as to the secret of the long and happy marriage.

'Well, it dates back to our honeymoon,' explained the husband. 'We visited the Grand Canyon and took a trip down to the bottom of the canyon by pack mule. We hadn't gone too far when my wife's mule stumbled. My wife quietly said, "That's once." We proceeded a little further when the mule stumbled again. Once more my wife quietly said, "That's twice." We hadn't gone half a mile when the mule stumbled a third time. My wife took her little Derringer pistol out of her pocket and shot the mule.

'I started to protest over her treatment of the mule when she looked at me and quietly said, "That's once."'

PERSONAL AD-SPEAK >>>

For women:

40-ish... 48.
Adventurous... has had more partners than you ever will.
Athletic... flat-chested.
Average looking... ugly.
Beautiful... pathological liar.
Contagious smile... bring your penicillin.
Educated... college dropout.
Emotionally secure... medicated.
Feminist... fat ball-buster.
Free spirit... substance user.
Friendship first... trying to live down a reputation as a slut.
Fun... annoying.
Gentle... comatose.
Good listener... borderline autistic.
New-age... all body hair, all the time.
Old-fashioned... lights out, missionary position only.
Open-minded... desperate.

Outgoing... loud.
Passionate... loud.
Poet... depressive schizophrenic.
Redhead... shops in the Clairol section.
Rubenesque... grossly fat.
Romantic... looks better by candlelight.
Voluptuous... very fat.
Weight proportional to height... hugely fat.
Wants soulmate... one step away from stalking.
Widow... nagged first husband to death.
Young at heart... toothless crone.

For men:
40-ish... 52 and looking for 25-year-old.
Athletic... sits on the couch and watches Sky Sport.
Average looking... unusual hair growth on ears, nose and back.
Educated... will always treat you like an idiot.
Free spirit... sleeps with your sister.
Friendship first... as long as friendship involves nudity.
Fun... good with a remote and a six-pack.
Good looking... arrogant.
Honest... pathological liar.
Huggable... overweight, more body hair than a bear.
Likes to cuddle... insecure, overly dependent.
Mature... until you get to know him.
Open-minded... wants to sleep with your sister but she's not interested.
Physically fit... I spend a lot of time in front of mirror admiring myself.
Poet... has written on a toilet wall.
Spiritual... once went to church with his grandmother on Easter Sunday.
Stable... occasional stalker, but never arrested.
Thoughtful... says 'please' when demanding a beer.

BELOW THE BELT >>>

A husband and wife are getting snugly in bed. The passion is heating up. But then the wife stops and says, 'I don't feel like it. I just want you to hold me.' The husband says, 'WHAT!'

The wife explains that he can't be in tune with her emotional needs as a woman. The husband realises that nothing is going to happen tonight and he might as well deal with it.

So, the next day the husband takes her shopping at a big department store. He walks around and has her try on three very expensive outfits. She can't decide.

He tells his wife to take all three of them. Then they go over and get matching shoes worth $200 a pair. And then they go to the jewellery department where she gets a set of diamond earrings.

The wife is so excited. She thinks her husband has flipped out, but she doesn't care. She goes for the tennis bracelet. The husband says, 'But you don't even play tennis, but OK, if you like it, then let's get it.'

The wife is jumping up and down so excitedly she cannot even believe what is going on. She says, 'I am ready to go. Let's go to the cash register.'

The husband says, 'No-no-no honey, we're not going to buy all this stuff.'

The wife's face goes blank.

'No honey – I just want you to HOLD this stuff for a while.' Her face gets really red and she is about to explode and the husband says, 'You can't be in tune with my financial needs as a man!'

DIETS RULE OK >>>

THE FEMALE STRESS DIET

This is a specially formulated diet designed to help you cope with the stress that builds up during the day:

Breakfast – 1 grapefruit, 1 slice whole wheat toast, 1 cup of skim milk.

Lunch – Small portion of lean, steamed chicken with a cup of spinach, 1 cup of herbal tea, 1 Tim Tam.

Afternoon Tea – The rest of the packet of Tim Tams, 1 tub of Tip Top ice cream with chocolate topping, 1 jar of Nutella.

Dinner – 4 bottles of red wine, 2 loaves of garlic bread, 1 family-size supreme pizza, 3 Snickers bars.

Late Night Snack – Whole frozen Sarah Lee cheesecake eaten directly from the freezer.

Diet Rules

1. If no one sees you eat something, it has no calories.
2. When drinking a diet Coke with a chocolate bar, the fat in the chocolate is cancelled out by the diet Coke.
3. When you eat with someone else, calories don't count if you do not eat more than they do.
4. Food used for medicinal purposes does NOT count. (For example: hot chocolate, toast, cheesecake, vodka…)
5. If you fatten up the people around you, you will look thinner.
6. Cinema-related foods have a zero calorie count as they are part of the entertainment package and not counted as food intake. This includes popcorn, Minties, Maltesers, Jaffas and frozen Cokes.
7. Biscuit pieces have no calories because breaking the biscuits up causes calorie leakage.
8. Food licked from knives and spoons has no fat if you are in the process of cooking something.
9. Foods that are the same colour have the same amount of fat. Examples are: spinach and peppermint ice cream, apples and red jelly snakes.
10. Chocolate is like a food-colour wildcard and may be substituted for any other colour.
11. Anything eaten while standing has no calories due to gravity and the density of the calorie mass.
12. Food consumed from someone else's plate has no fat as it rightfully belongs to the other person and will cling to his/her plate. (Oh, how fat likes to cling!)

And remember: **'STRESSED' SPELT BACKWARDS IS 'DESSERTS'!**

BLINDED BY SCIENCE >>>

Two builders are seated either side of a table in a rough pub when a well-dressed man enters, orders a beer and sits on a stool at the bar. The two builders start to speculate about the occupation of the suit.

Chris: *'I reckon he's an accountant.'*
James: *'No way – he's a stockbroker.'*
Chris: *'He's no stockbroker. A stockbroker wouldn't come in here.'*
The argument repeats itself for some time until the volume of beer gets the better of Chris and he makes for the toilet. On entering the toilet, he sees that the suit is standing at a urinal. Curiosity and the several beers get the better of the builder.
Chris: *''Scuse me… no offence meant, but me and my mate were wondering what you do for a living.'*
Suit: *'No offence taken. I'm a logical scientist by profession.'*
Chris: *'Yeah, so what's that then.'*
Suit: *'I'll try to explain by example. Do you have a goldfish at home?'*
Chris: *'Er… mmm… well yeah, I do as it happens.'*
Suit: *'Well, it's logical to assume that you keep it in a bowl or in a pond. Which is it?'*
Chris: *'It's in a pond.'*
Suit: *'Well then, it's logical to suppose that you have a large garden then?'*
Chris: *'As it happens, yes I have got a big garden.'*
Suit: *'Well then, it's logical to assume that in this town if you have a large garden then you have a large house?'*
Chris: *'As it happens I've got a five-bedroom house… built it myself.'*
Suit: *'Well, given that you've built a five-bedroom house it is logical to assume that you haven't built it just for yourself and that you're probably married?'*
Chris: *'Yes, I am married. I live with my wife and three children.'*
Suit: *'Well then, it's logical to assume that you are sexually active with your wife on a regular basis.'*
Chris: *'Yep! Four nights a week.'*
Suit: *'Well then, it is logical to suggest that you do not masturbate very often?'*
Chris: *'Me? Never!'*
Suit: *'Well, there you are, that's logical science at work.'*
Chris: *'How's that then?'*
Suit: *'Well, from finding out that you had a goldfish, I've told you about the size of garden you have, the size of house, your family and your sex life.'*

Chris: *'I see. That's pretty impressive... thanks mate.'*
Both leave the toilet and Chris returns to his mate.
James: *'I see the suit was in there. Did you ask him what he does?'*
Chris: *'Yep! He's a logical scientist.'*
James: *'What's that then?'*
Chris: *'I'll try to explain. Do you have a goldfish?'*
James: *'Nope.'*
Chris: *'Well then, you're a wanker.'*

10 WAYS TO KNOW IF YOU HAVE PMS >>>

1. Everyone around you has an attitude problem.
2. You're adding chocolate chips to your cheese omelette.
3. The dryer has shrunk every last pair of your jeans.
4. Your husband is suddenly agreeing to everything you say.
5. You're using your cellular phone to dial up every bumper sticker that says, 'How's my driving? Call 0800 *******.'
6. Everyone's head looks like an invitation to batting practice.
7. You're convinced there's a God and he's male.
8. You're counting down the days until menopause.
9. You're sure that everyone is scheming to drive you crazy.
10. The ibuprofen bottle is empty and you bought it yesterday.

TOP 10 THINGS THAT ONLY WOMEN UNDERSTAND >>>

10. Cats' facial expressions.
9. The need for the same style of shoes in different colours.
8. Why bean sprouts aren't just weeds.
7. Fat clothes.
6. Taking a car trip without trying to beat your best time.
5. The difference between beige, off-white, and eggshell.
4. Cutting your curls to make them grow.
3. Eyelash curlers.
2. The inaccuracy of every bathroom scale ever made.

AND,
The No. 1 thing only women understand: other women.

A TENDER THOUGHT >>>

If you love something, set it free.
If it comes back, it will always be yours.
If it doesn't come back, it was never yours to begin with.
But… if it just sits in your living room, messes up your stuff, eats your food, uses your telephone, takes your money and doesn't appear to realise that you actually set it free in the first place, you either married it or gave birth to it.

TRADITIONAL CAVAN >>>

A wedding occurred just outside Cavan in Ireland. To keep tradition going, everyone gets extremely drunk and the bride's and groom's families have a storming row and begin wrecking the reception room and generally kicking the shit out of each other. The police get called in to break up the fight.

The following week, all members of both families appear in court. The fight continues in the courtroom until the judge finally brings calm with the use of his gavel, shouting, 'Silence in court!'

The courtroom goes silent and Paddy, the best man, stands up and says, 'Judge, I was the best man at the wedding and I think I should explain what happened.'

The judge agrees and asks Paddy to take the stand. Paddy begins his explanation by telling the court that it is traditional in a Cavan wedding that the best man gets the first dance with the bride. The judge says, 'OK.'

'Well,' said Paddy, 'after I had finished the first dance, the music kept going, so I continued dancing to the second song, and after that the music kept going and I was dancing to the third song, when all of a sudden the groom leapt over the table, ran towards us and gave the bride an unmerciful kick right between her legs.'

Shocked, the judge instantly responded, 'God, that must have hurt!'

'Hurt?' Paddy replies. 'He broke three of my fingers!'

ESTROGEN vs TESTOSTERONE >>>

Relationships: When a relationship ends, a woman will cry and pour her heart out to her girlfriends, and she will write a poem titled 'All Men Are Idiots.' Then she will get on with her life. A man has a little more trouble letting go. Six months after the break-up, at 3 am on a Sunday morning, he will call and say, 'I just wanted to let you know you ruined my life, and I'll never forgive you, and I hate you, and you're a total floozy. But I want you to know that there's always a chance for us.' This is known as the 'I Hate You, I Love You' drunken phone call and 99 percent of all men have made it at least once. There are community colleges that offer courses to help men get over this need.

Sex: Women prefer 30 to 40 minutes of foreplay. Men prefer 30 to 40 seconds of foreplay. Men consider driving back to her place as part of the foreplay.

Maturity: Women mature much faster than men do. Most 17-year-old females can function as adults. Most 17-year-old males are still trading baseball cards and giving each other wedgies after gym class. This is why high school romances rarely work out.

Magazines: Men's magazines often feature pictures of naked women. Women's magazines also feature pictures of naked women. This is because the female body is a beautiful work of art, while the male body is lumpy and hairy and should not be seen by the light of day. Men are turned on at the sight of a naked woman's body. Most naked men elicit laughter from women.

Bathrooms: A man has five items in his bathroom – a toothbrush, shaving cream, razor, a bar of soap, and a towel from the Holiday Inn. The average number of items in the typical woman's bathroom is 437. A man would not be able to identify most of these items.

Groceries: A woman makes a list of things she needs and then goes out to the store and buys these things. A man waits till the only items left in his fridge are half a lime and a beer. Then he goes grocery shopping. He buys everything that looks good. By the time a man reaches the checkout counter, his cart is packed tighter than the Clampetts' car on *The Beverly Hillbillies*.
Of course, this will not stop him from going to the 10-items-or-less lane.

Cats: Women love cats. Men say they love cats, but when women aren't looking, men kick cats.

Offspring: Ah, children. A woman knows all about her children. She knows about dentist appointments and soccer games and romances and best friends and favourite foods and secret fears and hopes and dreams. A man is vaguely aware of some short people living in the house.

Dressing Up: A woman will dress up to: go shopping, water the plants, empty the garbage, answer the phone, read a book, get the mail. A man will dress up for weddings and funerals.

Laundry: Women do laundry every couple of days. A man will wear every article of clothing he owns, including his surgical pants that were hip about eight years ago, before he will do his laundry. When he is finally out of clothes, he will wear a dirty sweatshirt inside out, rent a van and take his mountain of clothes to the laundromat. Men always expect to meet beautiful women at the laundromat. This is a myth perpetuated by re-runs of old American sitcoms.

Eating Out: When the bill comes, Mike, Dave, Rob and Jack will each throw in $20 bills, even though it's only for $22.50. None of them will have anything smaller and none will actually admit they want change back. When the girls get their bill, out come the pocket calculators.

Mirrors: Men are vain; they will check themselves out in a mirror. Women are ridiculous; they will check out their reflections in any shiny surface: mirrors, spoons, store windows, bald boyfriend's/father's heads.

Menopause: When a woman reaches menopause, she goes through a variety of complicated emotional, psychological, biological changes. Nature provokes a uniform reaction in men. He buys aviator glasses, a snazzy French cap and leather driving gloves, and goes shopping for a Porsche.

Richard Gere: Women like Richard Gere because he is sexy in a dangerous way. Men hate Richard Gere because he reminds them of that slick guy who works at the health club and dates only married women.

Madonna: Same as above, but reversed. Same reason.

Toys: Little girls love to play with toys. Then when they reach the age of 11 or 12, they lose interest. Men never grow out of their obsession with toys. As they get older, their toys simply become more expensive and silly and impractical. Examples of men's toys: little miniature TVs. Cellphones. Complicated juicers and blenders. Graphic equalisers. Small robots that serve cocktails on command. Video games. Anything that blinks, beeps, and requires at least six big batteries to operate.

Locker Rooms: In the locker room men talk about three things: money, football, and women. They exaggerate about money, they don't know football nearly as well as they think they do, and they fabricate stories about women. Women talk about one thing in the locker room: sex. And not in abstract terms, either. They are extremely graphic and technical, and they never lie.

Movies: Every actress in the history of movies has had to do a nude scene. This is because every movie in the history of movies has been produced by a man. Men will only show their arses, because arse size doesn't really matter.

Jewellery: Women look nice when they wear jewellery. A man can get away with wearing one ring and that's it. Any more than that and he will look like a lounge singer named Ramone.

Time: When a woman says she'll be ready to go out in five more minutes, she's using the same meaning of time as when a man says the football game just has five minutes left. Neither of them is counting time outs, commercials, or replays.

Friends: Women on a 'girls' night out' talk the whole time. Men on a 'boys' night out' say about 20 words all night, most of which are 'Pass the chips' or 'Got any more beer?'

Toilets: Men use toilets for purely biological reasons. Women use toilets as social lounges. Men in toilets will never speak a word to each other. Women who've never met will leave a toilet giggling together like old friends. And never in the history of the world has a man excused himself from a restaurant table by saying, 'Hey Tom, I was just about to take a leak. Do you want to join me?'

PENNY FOR YOUR THOUGHTS

The five toughest questions women ask – and their answers:

1. 'What are you thinking?'
2. 'Do you love me?'
3. 'Do I look fat?'
4. 'Do you think she's prettier than me?'
5. 'What would you do if I died?'

What makes these questions so bad is that every one is guaranteed to explode into a major argument and/or divorce if the man does not answer properly, which is to say dishonestly. For example:

1. 'What are you thinking?'

The proper answer to this question, of course, is: 'I'm sorry if I've been pensive, dear. I was just reflecting on what a warm, wonderful, caring, thoughtful, intelligent, beautiful woman you are and what a lucky guy I am to have met you.' Obviously, this statement bears no resemblance whatsoever to what the guy was really thinking at the time, which was most likely one of five things:

a – rugby.
b – cricket.
c – How fat you are.
d – How much prettier she is than you.
e – How he would spend the insurance money if you died.

The best answer to this stupid question came from Al Bundy, of *Married with Children*, who was asked it by his wife, Peg. His answer: 'If I wanted you to know I'd be talking instead of thinking.'

The other questions also have only one right answer but many wrong answers:

2. 'Do you love me?'
The correct answer to this question is, 'Yes.' For those guys who feel the need to be more elaborate, you may answer, 'Yes dear.'
Wrong answers include:

a – I suppose so.
b – Would it make you feel better if I said yes?
c – That depends on what you mean by 'love'.
d – Does it matter?
e – Who, me?

3. 'Do I look fat?'
The correct male response to this question is to confidently and emphatically state, 'No, of course not' and then quickly leave the room. Wrong answers include:

a – I wouldn't call you fat, but I wouldn't call you thin either.
b – Compared to what?
c – A little extra weight looks good on you.
d – I've seen fatter.
e – Could you repeat the question? I was thinking about your insurance policy.

4. 'Do you think she's prettier than me?'
The 'she' in the question could be an ex-girlfriend, a passerby you were staring at so hard that you almost caused a traffic accident or an actress in a movie you just saw. In any case, the correct response is: 'No, you are much prettier.'
Wrong answers include:

a – Not prettier, just pretty in a different way.
b – I don't know how one goes about rating such things.
c – Yes, but I bet you have a better personality.
d – Only in the sense that she's younger and thinner.
e – Could you repeat the question? I was thinking about your insurance policy.

5. 'What would you do if I died?'
Correct answer: 'Dearest love, in the event of your untimely demise, life would cease to have meaning for me and I would perforce hurl myself under the front tyres of the first truck that came my way.'

This might be the stupidest question of the lot, as is illustrated by the following stupid joke:

'Dear,' said the wife, 'what would you do if I died?'
'Why, dear, I would be extremely upset,' said the husband. 'Why do you ask such a question?'
'Would you remarry?' persevered the wife.
'No, of course not, dear,' said the husband.
'Don't you like being married?' said the wife.
'Of course I do, dear,' he said.
'Then why wouldn't you remarry?'
'All right,' said the husband, 'I'd remarry.'
'You would?' said the wife, looking vaguely hurt.
'Yes,' said the husband.
'Would you sleep with her in our bed?' said the wife after a long pause.
'Well yes, I suppose I would,' replied the husband.
'I see,' said the wife indignantly. 'And would you let her wear my old clothes?'
'I suppose, if she wanted to,' said the husband.
'Really,' said the wife icily. 'And would you take down the pictures of me and replace them with pictures of her?'
'Yes. I think that would be the correct thing to do.'
'Is that so?' said the wife, leaping to her feet. 'And I suppose you'd let her play with my golf clubs, too.'
'Of course not, dear,' said the husband. 'She's left-handed.'

ONE SHAT IN THE CUCKOO'S NEST >>>

Just after I got married, I was invited out for a night with the boys. I told the missus that I would be home by midnight... I promise!

Well, the yarns were being spun and the grog was going down easy and at around 3 am, full as a boot, I went home.

Just as I got in the door, the cuckoo clock started and cuckooed three times. Quickly I realised she'd probably wake up, so I cuckooed another nine times and was really proud of myself for having the quick-wittedness, even when pissed, to escape a possible conflict.

Next morning the missus asked me what time I got in and I told her midnight. Whew, got away with that one!

She then told me that we needed a new cuckoo clock. When I asked her why, she said, 'Well, at 3 am this morning, it cuckooed three times, paused, said bollocks, cuckooed another four times, farted, cuckooed another three times, paused, cleared its throat and cuckooed twice, then giggled for over three minutes.

'I think it's stuffed, don't you?'

TOUCHE >>>

This is an extract of an American National Public Radio interview between a female broadcaster and a US Army Lieutenant-General about sponsoring a Boy Scout Troop on his military installation.

Interviewer: *'So, LT-G, what are you going to do with these young boys on their adventure holiday?'*
LT-G: *'We're going to teach them climbing, canoeing, archery and shooting.'*
Interviewer: *'Shooting! That's a bit irresponsible, isn't it?'*
LT-G: *'I don't see why; they'll be properly supervised on the range.'*
Interviewer: *'Don't you admit that this is a terribly dangerous activity to be teaching children?'*
LT-G: *'I don't see how – we will be teaching them proper range discipline before they even touch a firearm.'*
Interviewer: *'But you're equipping them to become violent killers.'*
LT-G: *'Well, you're equipped to be a prostitute, but you're not one, are you?'*

JESUS WEPT! >>>

Everybody on earth dies and goes to heaven. God comes and says, 'I want the men to make two lines. One line for the men who dominated their women on earth and the other line for the men who were dominated by their women. Also, I want all the women to go with Saint Peter.'

With that said and done, the next time God looked, the women were gone and there were two lines. The line of the men who were dominated by their wives was 160 km long, and in the line of the men who dominated their women, there was only one man.

God got mad and said to the 160-km-long line, 'You men should be ashamed of yourselves. I created you in my image and you were all whipped by your mates. Look at the only one of my sons who stood up and made me proud. Learn from him. Tell them, my son, how did you manage to be the only one in this line?'

And the man replied, 'I don't know. My wife told me to stay here.'

ROLL YOUR OWN >>>

Billy-Joe and Betty-Sue get married and Billy-Joe whisks her away to his daddy's hunting cabin in the woods for a romantic 'nature honeymoon'. He carries her across the threshold and they get into bed, when Betty-Sue whispers in his ear, 'Billy-Joe, be gentle, I ain' never been with a man b'fore.'

'WHAT?' shouts Billy-Joe, and his little bride softly shakes her head. Billy-Joe jumps out of bed, grabs his clothes and races out the door, into his truck... down the mountain... straight to his parents' house... rushes inside screaming, 'Hey Daddy! Paw! Git up!'

His father rushes downstairs and gasps, 'Billy-Joe, what're you doin' here?'

Billy-Joe, still breathing hard from his mad flight, gasps, 'Well, Betty-Sue and I was in the cabin and she toll me she ain't never been with a man afore... so's I rushed outta there an' lit back here quick as I could.'

His father grasps Billy-Joe's shoulder in reassurance and says, 'Son, ya done the right thing. Iffin she ain't good'nuff fer her family, she shure as shit ain't good'nuff fer ours!'

SOUTHERN MAN BETTER KEEP YOUR HEAD >>>

A Kentucky family took a holiday to New York City. For an adventure the father took his son to see a skyscraper. They were amazed by everything they saw – especially the elevator at one end of the lobby.

The boy asked, 'What's that there, Paw?'

The father responded, 'Well son, I reckon I never did see nothing like this in my entire life. I got no darned idea what it is.'

While the boy and his father were watching in wide-eyed astonishment, an old lady in a wheelchair rolled up to the moving walls and pressed a button. The walls opened and the lady rolled between them into a small room. The walls closed and the boy and his father watched small circles of lights above the walls light up. They continued to watch the circles light up in the reverse direction. The walls opened again and a voluptuous 24-year-old woman stepped out.

The father turned to his son and said, 'Go git your Maw.'

WHEN MEN RULED THE WORLD >>>

- Nodding and looking at your watch would be deemed an acceptable response to 'I love you.'
- Hallmark would make 'Sorry, what was your name again?' cards.
- When your girlfriend really needed to talk to you during the game, she would appear in a little box in the corner of the screen during half-time.
- Breaking up would be a lot easier. A smack on the bum would pretty much do it.
- Birth control could come in ale or lager.
- The funniest guy in the office would get to be the big boss.
- 'Sorry I'm late, I got hammered last night,' would be an acceptable excuse for tardiness.
- It'd be considered harmless fun to gather 30 friends, put on horned helmets, and go pillage a nearby town.
- Lifeguards could remove citizens from beaches for violating the 'public ugliness' ordinance.
- Tanks would be far easier to rent.
- Instead of beer belly, you'd get 'beer biceps'.
- Instead of an expensive engagement ring, you could present your wife-to-be with a giant foam hand that said, 'You're No. 1.'
- Valentine's Day would be moved to February 29.
- Cops would be broadcast live and you could phone in advice to the pursuing cops. Or to the crooks.
- The victors in any athletic competition would get to kill and eat the losers.
- The only show opposite *Friday Night Football* would be

Friday Night Football from a Different Camera Angle.

- It would be perfectly legal to steal a sports car, as long as you returned it the following day with a full tank of petrol.
- Every man would get four real 'Get Out of Jail Free' cards per year.
- When a cop gave you a ticket, every smart-alec answer you responded with would actually reduce your fine, as in:

Cop: *'You know how fast you were going?'*
You: *'All I know is that I was spilling my beer all over the place.'*
Cop: *'Nice one. That's $10 off.'*

PERFECTION? >>>

Once upon a time, a perfect man and a perfect woman met. After a perfect courtship, they had a perfect wedding. Their life together was, of course, perfect. One snowy, stormy Christmas Eve, this perfect couple were driving their perfect car along a winding road, when they noticed someone at the side of the road in distress. Being the perfect couple, they stopped to help. There stood Santa Claus with a huge bundle of toys. Not wanting to disappoint any children on the eve of Christmas, the perfect couple loaded Santa and his toys into their vehicle. Soon they were driving along delivering the toys. Unfortunately, the driving conditions deteriorated and the perfect couple and Santa Claus had an accident. Only one of them survived the accident. Who was the survivor? (See below for answer).

>

>

The perfect woman survived. She's the only one who really existed in the first place. Everyone knows there is no Santa Claus and there is no such thing as a perfect man. (Women, stop reading here, that is the end of the story. Men keep reading.)

>

>

So, if there is no perfect man and no Santa Claus, the woman must have been driving. This explains why there was a car accident. By the way, if you're a woman and you're reading this, this illustrates another point: women never listen either.

IF WOMEN RULED THE WORLD >>>

- Women with cold hands would give men prostate exams.
- PMS would be a legitimate defence in court.
- Men would get reputations for sleeping around.
- Singles' bars would have metal detectors to weed out men hiding wedding rings in their pockets.
- A man would no longer be considered a 'good catch' simply because he is breathing.
- Fewer women would be dieting because their ideal weight standard would increase by 20 kg.
- Shopping would be considered an aerobic activity.
- Men would not be allowed to eat gas-producing foods within two hours of bedtime.
- Men would be secretaries for female bosses, working twice as hard for none of the credit.
- Little girls would read Snow White and the Seven Hunks.
- Men would bring drinks, chips and dips to women watching soap operas.
- Men would have to get *Playboy* for the articles, because there would be no pictures.
- Men would learn phrases like: 'I'm sorry,' 'I love you,' 'Sure we can talk. Is now okay?'
- Men would be judged entirely by their looks, women by their accomplishments.
- Men would wonder what WE are thinking.
- Men would pay as much attention to their woman as their computer.
- Road rage would turn in on oneself.
- Men would work on relationships as much as they work on their careers.
- Men would divide up chores with women so WOMEN could be horny.
- TV news segments on sport would never run longer than one minute.
- All men would be forced to spend one month in a PMS simulator.
- During mid-life crisis, men would get hot flushes and women would date 19-year-olds.

- Overweight men would have their weight brought to their attention constantly.
- After a baby is born, men would take six weeks' paternity leave to wait on their wives hand and foot.
- For basic training, soldiers would have to take care of a two-year-old for six weeks.

TRUE BRIT >>>

A proper English gentleman met a beautiful girl and agreed to spend the night with her for $500. So they did. Before he left, he told the girl that he didn't have any cash with him, but that he would have his secretary write a cheque and mail it to her, calling the payment 'Rent for Apartment'.

On the way to the office he regretted what he had done, realising that the whole event was not worth the price. So he had his secretary send a cheque for $250 and enclosed the following note:

Dear Madam,
Enclosed find a cheque in the amount of $250 for rent of your apartment. I am not sending the amount agreed upon because when I rented the apartment, I was under the impression that:
1. It had never been occupied;
2. There was plenty of heat; and
3. It was small enough to make me cozy and at home.
Last night, however, I found out that it had been previously occupied, that there wasn't any heat and that it was entirely too large.

Upon receipt of the note, the girl immediately returned the cheque for $250 with the following letter.

Dear Sir,
First of all, I cannot understand how you expect a beautiful apartment to remain unoccupied indefinitely. As for the heat, there is plenty of it, if you know how to turn it on. Regarding the space, the apartment is indeed of regular size, but if you don't have enough furniture to fill it, please do not blame the landlady.

HIGH NOON >>>

Saturday morning and Bob's just about to tee off for a round of golf when he realises that he forgot to tell his wife that the guy who fixes the washing machine is coming round at noon.

So Bob heads back to the clubhouse and phones home. 'Hello,' says a little girl's voice.

'Hi, honey, it's Daddy,' says Bob. 'Is Mummy near the phone?'

'No, Daddy. She's upstairs in the bedroom with Uncle Frank.'

After a brief pause, Bob says, 'But you haven't got an Uncle Frank, honey.'

'Yes I do, and he's upstairs in the bedroom with Mummy.'

'Okay, then. Here's what I want you to do. Put the phone down, run upstairs and knock on the bedroom door and shout in to Mummy and Uncle Frank that Daddy's car's just pulled up outside the house.'

'Okay, Daddy.'

A few minutes later the little girl comes back to the phone. 'Well I did what you said, Daddy.'

'And what happened?'

'Well, Mummy jumped out of bed with no clothes on and ran round and round screaming, then she tripped over the rug and fell out the front window and now I think she's all dead.'

'Oh my God… and what about Uncle Frank?'

'He jumped out of bed with no clothes on too and he was all scared and he jumped out the back window into the swimming pool, but he must have forgot that last week you took out all the water to clean it, so he hit the bottom of the swimming pool and now he's dead too.'

There is a long pause, then Bob says, 'Swimming pool… what swimming pool? Is this 524-….?'

PC OR NOT PC >>>

How to speak about women and be politically correct:
She is not a babe or a chick; she is a breasted person.
She is not a bleached blonde; she is peroxide dependent.
She is not a bad cook; she is microwave compatible.
She does not wear too much jewellery; she is metallically overburdened.

She is not conceited; she is intimately aware of her best qualities.
She does not want to be married; she wants to lock you in domestic incarceration.
She does not gain weight; she is a metabolic under-achiever.
She is not a screamer or a moaner; she is vocally appreciative.
She is not easy; she is horizontally accessible.
She does not tease or flirt; she engages in artificial stimulation.
She is not dumb; she is a detour off the information super-highway.
She is not too skinny; she is skeletally prominent.
She does not have a moustache; she is in touch with her masculine side.
She has not been around; she is a previously enjoyed companion.
She does not wear too much perfume; she commits fragrance abuse.
She does not get you excited; she causes temporary blood displacement.
She is not kinky; she is a non-inhibited sexual companion.
She does not have a killer body; she is terminally attractive.
She does not go shopping; she is mall fluent.
She is not an airhead; she is reality impaired.
She does not get drunk or tipsy; she gets chemically inconvenienced.
She does not get fat or chubby; she achieves maximum density.
She is not cold or frigid; she is thermally inaccessible.
She is not horny; she is sexually focussed.
She does not wear too much make-up; she has reached cosmetic saturation.
She does not have breast implants; she is gravity resistant.
She does not nag you; she becomes verbally repetitive.
She is not a slut; she is sexually extroverted.
She is not loose; she is morally impaired.
She does not have major league hooters; she is pectorally superior.
She does not have thin lips; she is collagen dependent.

BABYFACE >>

A young couple are on their way to Las Vegas to get married. Before getting there, the girl said to the guy that she had a confession to make. The reason that they had not been intimate was because she was very flat-chested. If he wished to cancel the wedding, it would be okay with her.

The guy thought about it for a while and said he did not mind if she was flat, and sex is not the most important thing in a marriage.

Several kilometres down the road, the guy turned to the girl and said that he also wanted to make a confession. He said that below his waist he was just like a baby, and if the girl wished to cancel the wedding, it'd be fine by him.

The girl thought about it for a while and said that she did not mind and she also believed there were other things far more important in a marriage than sex. Both were happy that they'd been honest with each other.

They went on to Vegas and got married. On the wedding night the girl took off her clothes and she was as flat as a washboard. Finally, the guy took off his clothes and one look at the guy's naked body made the girl faint and fall to the floor.

After she came to, the guy asked, 'I told you before we got married, why did you still faint?'

The girl said, 'You told me it was just like a baby.'

The guy replied, 'Yes, eight pounds and 21 inches.'

GAY BAR LOITERER >>>

An old cowboy went to a bar and ordered a drink. As he sat there sipping his whisky, a young lady sat down next to him. She turned to the cowboy and asked him, 'Are you a real cowboy?'

He replied, 'Well, I've spent my whole life on the ranch, herding cows, breaking horses, mending fences, so I guess I am.'

He then asked her what she was. She replied, 'I'm a lesbian. I spend my whole day thinking about women. As soon as I get up in the morning I think of women, when I eat, shower, watch TV, everything seems to make me think of women.'

A little while later a couple sat down next to the old cowboy and asked him, 'Are you a real cowboy?'

He replied, 'I always thought I was, but I just found out I'm a lesbian.'

THAT OLD DESERT ISLAND >>>

One day, this guy who had been stranded on a desert island all alone for 10 years sees an unusual speck on the horizon. 'It's certainly not a ship,' he thinks to himself. As the speck gets closer and closer, he begins to rule out the possibility of a small boat, then even a raft.

Suddenly emerging from the surf walking towards him comes this drop-dead gorgeous blonde woman wearing a wet suit and scuba gear. She approaches the stunned guy and asks, 'How long has it been since you've had a cigarette?'

'Ten years,' he says.

She reaches over and unzips a waterproof pocket on her left sleeve and pulls out a packet of fresh cigarettes. He takes a long drag and says, 'Man oh man. Is that ever good.'

She then asks him, 'How long has it been since you've had a sip of bourbon?' Trembling, he replies, 'Ten years.'

She reaches over, unzips the waterproof pocket on her right sleeve, pulls out a flask and gives it to him. He opens the flask, takes a long swig, and says, 'Wow, that's absolutely fantastic.'

Then she starts slowly unzipping the long zipper that runs down the front of her wetsuit, looks at him seductively and asks, 'And how long has it been since you've played around?'

The guy, with tears in his eyes, replies, 'Oh my God! Don't tell me you've got golf clubs in there!'

WASTE OF NAGGING >>>

When a woman says: 'This place is a mess! C'mon, you and I need to clean up. Your stuff is lying on the floor, and if we don't do laundry right now, you'll have no clothes to wear.'

What a man hears: 'blah, blah, blah, blah, c'mon, blah, blah, blah, you and I, blah, blah, on the floor, blah, blah, blah, right now, blah, blah, blah, blah, blah, no clothes.'

BOOBY PRIZE >>>

And God created woman and she had three breasts. He then asked the woman, 'Is there anything you'd like to have changed?'

She replied, 'Yes, you could get rid of this middle breast?' And so it was done, and it was good. Then the woman exclaimed as she was holding that third breast in her hand, 'What can be done with this useless boob?'

And God created man.

HORSE SENSE >>>

A man is sitting quietly reading his paper one morning, peacefully enjoying himself, when his wife sneaks up behind him and whacks him on the back of his head with a huge frying pan.
Man: *'What was that for?'*
Wife: *'What was that piece of paper in your pants' pocket with the name Marylou written on it?'*
Man: *'Oh honey, remember two weeks ago when I went to the horse races? Marylou was the name of one of the horses I bet on.'*
The wife looked all satisfied, apologises and goes off to work around the house. Three days later the man is once again sitting in his chair reading and she repeats the frying pan swatting.
Man: *'What the hell was that for this time?'*
Wife: *'Your horse called.'*

IMPRESSIONS COUNT >>>

How to impress a woman: compliment her, respect her, honour her, cuddle her, kiss her, caress her, love her, stroke her, tease her, comfort her, protect her, hug her, hold her, spend money on her, wine and dine her, buy things for her, listen to her, care for her, stand by her, support her, go to the ends of the earth for her.

How to impress a man: Show up naked. Bring beer.

SILENCE IS GOLDEN >>>

Stumpy and his wife, Martha, went to the fair every year and every year Stumpy would say, 'Martha, I'd like to ride in that there aeroplane.'

And every year Martha would say, 'I know Stumpy, but that aeroplane ride costs $10, and $10 is $10.'

One year Stumpy and Martha went to the fair and Stumpy said, 'Martha, I'm 71 years old. If I don't ride that aeroplane this year I may never get another chance.'

Martha replied, 'Stumpy that aeroplane costs $10 and $10 is $10.'

The pilot overheard them and said, 'Folks, I'll make you a deal. I'll take you both up for a ride. If you can stay quiet for the entire ride and not say one word, I won't charge you, but if you say one word it's $10.'

Stumpy and Martha agreed and up they go. The pilot does all kinds of twists and turns, rolls and dives, but not a word is heard. He does all his tricks over again, but still not a word.

They land and the pilot turns to Stumpy, 'By golly, I did everything I could think of to get you to yell out, but you didn't.'

Stumpy replied, 'Well, I was gonna say something when Martha fell out, but $10 is $10.'

MR ED WITH A LOT TO ANSWER FOR >>>

A woman was very distraught at the fact that she had not had a date or any sex in quite some time. She was afraid she might have something wrong with her, so she decided to employ the medical expertise of a sex therapist.

Her doctor recommended that she go and see Dr Chang, the well-known sex therapist. So she went to see him and upon entering the examination room, Dr Chang said, 'OK, take off all you crose.' So she did.

Dr Chang then said, 'Ok now, crawl reery fass to the other side of the room.' So she did. Dr Chang then said, 'OK, now crawl reery fass to me,' so she did. Dr Chang slowly shook his head and said, 'Your problem vewy bad, you haf Ed Zachary Disease, worse case I ever see, that why you not haf sex or dates.'

Confused the woman asked, 'What is Ed Zachary Disease?'

Dr Chang replied, 'It when your face rook Ed Zachary rike your arse.'

TAX THE SLACK >>>

The only thing that the tax department has not taxed yet is the male penis. This is due to the fact that 40 percent of the time it is hanging around unemployed, 30 percent of the time it is hard up, 20 percent of the time it is pissed off and 10 percent of the time it is on the hole. On top of that, it has two dependents and they are both nuts.

Effective 1 January 2000, your penis will be taxed according to size, as follows:

11-12″ ...... Luxury Tax $30
8-10″ .... Pole Tax $25
6-7″ .... Privilege Tax $15
5″ .... Nuisance Tax $3

A male exceeding 12″ must file under capital gains while anyone under 4″ is eligible for a refund.
PLEASE DO NOT ASK FOR AN EXTENSION.
Sincerely
Pecker Checker, Tax Department

We are still waiting for answers to the following:
Are there penalties for early withdrawals?
What if one's penis is self-employed?
Do multiple partners count as a corporation?
Are condoms a deductible expense as work clothes?

TURBULENT EXCHANGE >>>

On a transatlantic flight, a plane passed through a severe storm. The turbulence was very strong and things went from bad to worse when one wing of the plane was struck by lightning.

One woman in particular lost it. Screaming, she stands up in the front of the plane. 'I'm too young to die,' she wails. Then she yells, 'Well, if I'm going to die I want my last minutes on earth to be memorable. I've had plenty of sex in my life, but no one has ever made me really feel like a woman. Well, I'm fed up with it. Is there anyone on this plane who can make me feel like a woman?'

For a moment there is silence. Everyone has forgotten their own peril. They all stare riveted at the desperate woman in the front of the plane. Then a man stands up in the rear of the plane. 'I can make you feel like a woman,' he says. He's gorgeous. Tall, well built, with flowing black hair and jet black eyes, he starts to walk slowly up the aisle, unbuttoning his shirt one button at a time.

No one moves. The woman is breathing heavily in anticipation. The stranger approaches. He removes his shirt. Muscles ripple across his chest as he reaches her and extends the arm holding the shirt to the trembling woman and says, 'Iron this.'

WHEELIES IN HEAVEN >>>

Dave, John and Sam were involved in a horrific car accident in which all three died. As they stood at the gates of heaven, Saint Peter came up to them and said, 'You will all be given a method of transportation for your eternal use around heaven. You will be judged on your past deeds and will have your transport chosen accordingly.'

Saint Peter looked at Dave. 'You, Dave, were a bad man. You cheated on your wife four times. For this you will drive around heaven in an old, beat-up Trabant.'

Next Saint Peter looked at John. 'You were not so evil, but you still cheated on your wife two times. For this you will forever travel through heaven in a Lada stationwagon.'

Saint Peter finally looked at Sam. 'You, Sam, have set a fine example. You did not have sex before marriage and you never cheated on your wife. For this, you will forever travel through heaven in a Ferrari.'

A short time later, John and Dave pulled their cars next to Sam's Ferrari and there he is, sitting on the bonnet, head in hands, crying.

'What's wrong Sam?' they asked. 'You got the Ferrari. You're set forever. Why so down?'

Sam looked up ever so slowly, opened his mouth and cried, 'I just saw my wife go by on a skateboard.'

BREAKING UP IS SO EASY TO DO >>>

Men often find breaking up to be the most difficult part of the dating process. The closest they ever come to telling a woman it's over is to look her straight in the eye and say, 'I'll call you next week.'

But there is now a great way to get her out of your life. It's safe, it's affordable and the best thing is, she has no opportunity to throw things at you. E-mail her. That's how all the happening, '90s kind of guys are telling women they are not worthy. You'll feel like a real man knowing you have told her how you really feel from the safety of your keyboard. And you can delete her response without ever reading it. What could be more painless?

Following is an e-mail rejection letter. Men can use it the next time they need to put a girlfriend on notice. Just cut and paste the sucker into your e-mail and, hey presto, she's gone.

Dear (her name),
I regret to inform you that you have been eliminated from further contention to become the future Mrs (your last name). As you are probably aware, the competition was exceedingly tough this year and dozens of well-qualified candidates such as yourself also failed to make the final cut. I will, however, keep your name on file should an opening become available.

So that you may find better success in your future romantic endeavours, please allow me to offer the following rationales as to why you were disqualified from the competition.

Tick items that apply:

❑ *Your failure to reach for your purse in even a feigned attempt to pay for dinner by the fourth date displayed a stunning ignorance of basic economics.*

❑ *Your inadvertent admission that you 'buy condoms and K-Y Jelly by the truckload' indicates that you may be slightly over-qualified for the position.*

❑ *My breasts are bigger than yours.*

❑ *Your height is out of proportion with your weight. If you should, however, happen to gain the necessary 17 vertical inches, please resubmit your application.*

❑ *Your repeated comments such as, 'Is it still called a penis when it's this small?' were both uncalled for and thoughtless.*

❑ *The way you enthusiastically jumped on stage at the alternative bar and danced with the lesbians demonstrated that you are far too impressionable and have a disconcerting lack of commitment to heterosexuality.*

❑ *Your revelation that you would most certainly allow your ex-boyfriend to shack up with you again after he 'beats that domestic abuse rap' shows compassion but makes it difficult to take you seriously.*

❑ *Although your inability to achieve orgasm was of paramount importance to me, your suggestion that we invite the basketball team into the bedroom so it would be 'just like college' seemed somewhat extreme and inappropriate.*

❑ *I am out of your league – set your sights lower next time.*

Sincerely
(Your name)

TABLE TOPPING >>>

A lady goes to the doctor and complains that her husband is losing interest in sex. The doctor gives her a pill, but warns her it is still experimental and tells her to slip it into his mashed potatoes at dinner. So, that night at dinner, she does. About a week later she's back at the doctor's. She says, 'Doc, the pill worked great! I put it in the potatoes like you suggested. It wasn't five minutes and he jumps up, rakes all the food and dishes on the floor, grabs me, rips all my clothes off and ravishes me right there on the table.'

The doctor says, 'I'm sorry, we didn't realise the pill was that strong. The foundation will be glad to pay for any damages.'

'Naah…' she says, 'that's okay. We aren't going back to that restaurant anyway.'

SIGNWRITING >>>

The modest young lass had just purchased some lingerie and asked if she might have the sentence, 'If you can read this you're too damned close' embroidered on her panties and bra.

'Yes madam,' said the assistant, 'I'm quite certain that could be done. Would you prefer block or script letters?'

'Braille,' she replied.

ASSASSIN WANTED >>>

There was an opening with the CIA as an assassin. These highly classified positions are hard to fill, and there's a lot of testing and background checks involved before you can even be considered for the position.

After sending some applicants through the background checks, training and testing, they narrowed the possible choices down to three men, but only one position was available.

So the day came for the final test to see which man would get the extremely secretive job. The CIA men administering the test took one of the men to a large metal door and handed him a gun. 'We must know that you will follow your instructions no matter what the circumstances,' they explained. 'Inside this room you will find your wife sitting in a chair. Take this gun and kill her.'

The man got a shocked look on his face and said, 'You can't be serious! I could never shoot my own wife.'

'Well,' says the CIA man, 'you're definitely not the right man for the job then.'

So they bring the second man to the same door and hand him a gun. 'We must know that you will follow instructions no matter what the circumstances,' they explained to the second man. 'Inside you will find your wife sitting in a chair. Take this gun and kill her.'

The second man looked a bit shocked, but nevertheless took the gun and went into the room. All was quiet for about five minutes, and then the door opened and the man came out with tears in his eyes. 'I tried to shoot her but I just couldn't pull the trigger and shoot my own wife. I guess I'm not the right man for the job.'

'No,' the CIA man replied, 'you don't have what it takes. Take your wife and get the hell home.'

Now the CIA are down to one man left to test. Again they lead him to the same door of the same room and give him the same gun. 'We must be sure that you will follow instructions no matter what the circumstances. This is your final test. Inside you will find your wife sitting in a chair, take this gun and kill her.'

The third man took the gun and opened the door and before the door had even closed all the way, the CIA heard the gun start firing, one shot after another for 13 shots. Then all hell broke loose in the room. They heard screaming, crashing, banging on the walls. This went on for several minutes, and then all went quiet. The door opened slowly, and there stood the third man.

He wiped the sweat from his brow and said, 'You guys didn't tell me the gun was loaded with f***ing blanks. I had to beat the bitch to death with the chair.'

BALLAD OF THE BOBBIT HILLBILLIES >>>

To the tune of *The Beverly Hillbillies*:

Come and listen to my story 'bout a man named John,
  a poor ex-marine with a little fraction gone.
It seems one night after gettin' with his wife; she loped off
  his dong with the swipe of a knife.
Penis that is. Clean cut. Missed his nuts.
Well the next thing you know there's a Ginsue by his side
And Lorena is in the car taking willie for a ride.
She soon got tired of her purple-headed friend,
And she tossed him out the window as she went around a bend.
Curve that is. Tossed the nub in the scrub.
She went to the cops and confessed to the attack and they
  called out the hounds just to get his weenie back.
They sniffed and they barked
And they pointed 'over there'.
To John Wayne's henry that was waving in the air.
Found that is. By the fence. Evidence.
So the dick doc said, 'Hey, I can fix your dong.
A needle and a thread is all we're gonna need.'
And the whole world waited 'til they heard that Johnny peed.
Whizzed that is. Even seam. Straight steam.
Well he healed and he hardened and he took his dick to court.
With a half-arsed lawyer, 'cause his assets came up short.
They cleared her assault and acquitted him of rape
And his pecker was the only one they didn't show on tape.
Video that is. Unexposed. Case closed.
Ya'll sleep on your stomachs now, ya hear?!

QUICKIE QUIZ >>>

What's the difference between a man and a condom?
Condoms have changed. They're no longer thick and insensitive.

What do UFOs and caring men have in common?
You keep hearing about them but you never see any for yourself.

Why is sex like a game of cards?
Because if you don't have a good partner, you'd better have a good hand.

What's the difference between a man and a bottle of whisky?
Whisky improves with age.

Why does a man have a clear conscience?
Because it is unused.

What do you call a man who has suddenly lost 98 percent of his brain?
Divorced.

Did you hear about the stupid man who wanted to be a chef?
He thought coq au vin was sex in the back of a lorry.

Why don't women like basketball players as lovers?
Because they always dribble before they shoot.

Did you hear about the man who used to complain about the decorating while having sex?
He was destined to a life of DIY.

What are the three types of men?
The handsome, the caring and the majority.

What's a man's ultimate embarrassment?
Walking into a wall with an erection and hurting his nose.

What is a man?
A life-support machine for a penis.

What's the nicest thing about a nudist wedding?
You don't have to ask – you can see who the best man is.

What should you do if your boyfriend starts smoking?
Slow down.

Why do men find it hard to make eye contact?
Breasts don't have eyes.

What should you do with your old mates after a good night in?
Tie them in knots and throw them in the bin.

What do you call a Spanish streaker?
Senor Willy.

BARBER BEWARE >>>

This guy sticks his head into a barber shop and asks, 'How long before I can get a haircut?' The barber looks around the shop and says, 'About two hours.' The guy leaves. A few days later the same guy sticks his head in the door and asks, 'How long before I can get a haircut?' The barber looks around at his shop full of customers and says, 'About two hours.' The guy leaves. A week later the same guy sticks his head in the shop and asks, 'How long before I can get a haircut?' The barber looks around the shop and says, 'About an hour and a half.' The guy leaves.

The barber looks over at a friend in the shop and says, 'Hey, Bill, follow that guy and see where he goes.' In a little while, Bill comes back into the shop laughing hysterically. The barber asks, 'Bill, where did that guy go when he left here?' Bill looks at him and says, 'To your house.'

CON'S TRICK >>>

An escaped convict broke into a house and tied up a young couple who had been sleeping in the bedroom.

As soon as he had a chance, the husband turned to his voluptuous young wife, bound up on the bed in a skimpy nightgown, and whispered, 'Honey, this guy hasn't seen a woman in years. Just cooperate with anything he wants. If he wants to have sex with you, just go along with it and pretend you like it. Our lives depend on it.'

'Dear,' the wife hissed, spitting out her gag, 'I'm so relieved you feel that way, because he just told me he thinks you have a really nice arse.'

WHAT A BLAST >>>

A bodybuilder picks up a woman at a bar and takes her home with him. He takes off his shirt and the woman says, 'What a great chest you have.'

The bodybuilder tells her, 'That's 500 kg of dynamite.'

He takes off his pants and the woman says, 'What massive calves you have,' and the bodybuilder tells her, 'That's 500 kg of dynamite.'

He then takes off his underwear and the woman goes running and screaming out of the apartment. The bodybuilder puts his clothes back on and chases after her.

He finally catches up and asks her why she ran out of the apartment.

The woman replies, 'I was afraid to be around all that dynamite after I saw what a short fuse you have.'

THE MALE THOUGHT PROCESS >>>

A man is dating three women and wants to decide which to marry. He decides to give them a test. He gives each woman a present of $5000 and waits to see what they do with the money.

The first does a total makeover. She goes to a fancy beauty salon, gets her hair done, new makeup and buys several new outfits and dresses up very nicely for the man. She tells him that she has done this to be more attractive for him because she loves him so much.

The man is impressed.

The second goes shopping to buy the man gifts. She gets him a new set of golf clubs, some new gizmos for his computer, and some expensive clothes. As she presents these gifts, she tells him that she has spent all the money on him because she loves him so much, Again, the man is impressed.

The third woman invests the money in the stock market. She earns several times the $5000, gives him back the original $5000 and invests the rest in a joint account. She tells him that she wants to save for their future because she loves him so much. Obviously the man is impressed.

The man had a difficult choice and thought for a long time about what each woman had done with the money and then he married the one with the biggest tits.

MALE CHAUVINISTS RULE OK >>>

How many male chauvinists does it take to change a light bulb?
None. Let her do the dishes in the dark.

What is love?
The delusion that one woman differs from another.

What is the difference between your wife and your job?
After five years your job still sucks.

Why did God create lesbians?
So feminists couldn't breed.

Why do women rub their eyes when they get up in the morning?
Because they don't have balls.

What's the difference between your bonus and your dick?
You don't have to beg a woman to blow your bonus.

Why is a woman like a laxative?
They both irritate the shit out of you.

What's worse than a male chauvinist pig?
A woman who won't do as she's told.

Why are wives like condoms?
They both spend too much time in your wallet, and not enough time on the end of your dick.

Why do men die before their wives?
They want to.

How many men does it take to fix a vacuum cleaner?
Why the hell should we fix it? We don't use the damn thing.

What is a wife?
An attachment you screw on the bed to get the housework done.

How are women like parking spaces?
The good ones are taken and the rest are handicapped.

Why do women have tits?
So men will talk to them.

Why do women close their eyes during sex?
They can't stand to see a man having a good time.

What's 6 inches long, 2 inches wide and drives women wild?
A $100 bill.

Why do women have periods?
Because they deserve them.

Why did the woman cross the road?
Who cares – what was she doing out of the kitchen anyway?

THE EARS HAVE IT >>>

Duane rents an apartment in New York, and goes to the lobby to put his name on the group mailbox. While he is there, an attractive young lady comes out of the apartment next to the mailboxes wearing a robe. Duane smiles at the young lady and she strikes up a conversation with him.

As they talk, her robe slips open, and it's quite obvious that she has nothing on underneath. Poor Duane breaks out into a sweat trying to maintain eye contact. After a few minutes, she places her hand on his arm and says, 'Let's go in my apartment, I hear someone coming…'

He goes with her into the apartment, and after she closes the door, she leans against it allowing her robe to fall off completely. Being completely nude, she purrs at him, 'What would you say is my best feature?'

The flustered, embarrassed Duane stammers, clears his throat several times, and finally squeaks out, 'Oh, it's got to be your ears!'

She's astounded. 'Why my ears? Look at these breasts! They are full, don't sag, and they're 100 percent natural. My buns – they are firm and do not sag, and have no cellulite. Look at this skin, no blemishes or scars. Why in heaven's name would you say my ears are the best part of my body?'

Clearing his throat once again, Duane stammers, 'Outside when you said you heard someone coming? That was me.'

COURSES FOR WOMEN >>>

Women think they already know everything, but wait… training courses are now available for women in the following subjects:

- Silence, the final frontier: Where no woman has gone before.
- The undiscovered side of banking: Making deposits.
- Parties: Going without new outfits.
- Man management: Minor household chores can wait till after the game.
- Bathroom etiquette I: Men need space in the bathroom cabinet too.
- Bathroom etiquette II: His razor is his.
- Communication skills I: Tears – the last resort, not the first.
- Communication skills II: Thinking before speaking.
- Communication skills III: Getting what you want without nagging.
- Driving a car safely: A skill you can acquire.
- Telephone skills: How to hang up.
- Advanced parking: Backing into a space.

- Water retention: Fact or fat.
- Cooking I: Bringing back bacon, eggs and butter.
- Cooking II: Bran and tofu are not for human consumption.
- Cooking III: How not to inflict your diets on other people.
- Compliments: Accepting them gracefully.
- PMS: Your problem… not his.
- Dancing: Why men don't like to.
- Classic clothing: Wearing outfits you already have.
- Household dust: A harmless natural occurrence only women notice.
- Integrating your laundry: Washing it all together.
- Oil and gas: Your car needs both.
- TV remotes: For men only.

BRAIN SURGERY >>>

The patient's family gathered to hear what the specialist had to say. 'Things don't look good. The only chance is a brain transplant. This is an experimental procedure. It might work, but the bad news is that brains are very expensive, and you will have to pay the costs yourselves.'

'Well, how much does a brain cost?' asked the relatives. 'For a male brain, $500,000. For a female brain, $200,000.'

Some of the younger male relatives tried to look shocked, but all the men nodded because they thought they understood. A few actually smirked. But the patient's daughter was unsatisfied and asked, 'Why the difference in price between male brains and female brains?'

'A standard pricing practice,' said the head of the team. 'Women's brains have to be marked down because they have actually been used.'

DROPPING HIM IN IT >>>

A man who is driving a car is stopped by a police officer. The following exchange takes place…

Man: *'What's the problem officer?'*
Officer: *'You were going at least 75 in a 50 zone.'*
Man: *'No sir, I was going 65.'*
Wife: *'Oh, Harry. You were going 80.'*

The man gives the wife a dirty look.
Officer: *'I'm also going to give you a ticket for your broken tail light.'*
Man: *'Broken tail light? I didn't know about a broken tail light!'*
Wife: *'Oh Harry, you've known about that tail light for weeks.'*
Man gives his wife a dirty look.
Officer: *'I'm also going to give you a ticket for not wearing your seat belt.'*
Man: *'Oh, I just took it off when you were walking up to the car.'*
Wife: *'Oh, Harry, you never wear your seat belt.'*
Man: *'Shut your big bloody mouth, OK!'*
Officer: *'Ma'am, does your husband talk to you this way all the time?'*
Wife: *'No, only when he's drunk.'*

WHAT A SUCKER >>>

A couple went golfing one day at a very, very exclusive course lined with million-dollar homes. On the third tee, the husband cautioned, 'Honey, be careful when you drive. If we break one of those windows it'll cost us a fortune to repair.'

Of course, she teed off and promptly shanked it right through the window of the biggest house on the course.

The husband cringed. 'I warned you to watch out. Now we'll have to go up there and apologise and see how much that lousy drive is going to cost.'

They walked up, knocked on the door, and a warm voice said, 'Come on in.'

When they opened the door they saw glass all over the place and a broken bottle lying on its side near the broken window. A man reclining on the couch said, 'Are you the people that broke the window?'

'Uh yeah, we're sure sorry about that,' the husband replied.

'Oh, no apology is necessary. Actually I want to thank you. You see, I'm a genie, and I've been trapped in that bottle for a thousand years.

'Now that you've released me I'm allowed to grant three wishes. I'll give you each one wish, and I'll keep the last one for myself.'

'Wow, that's great!' the husband said. 'He pondered a moment and blurted out, 'I'd like a million dollars a year for the rest of my life.'

'No problem, it's the least I can do. And you, young lady, what do you want?' the genie said looking at the wife.

'I'd like to own a gorgeous home in every country in the world,' she said.

'Consider it done,' the genie said.

'And what's your wish, genie?' they asked in unison.

'Well, since I've been trapped in that bottle and haven't had sex with a woman in a thousand years, my wish is to sleep with your wife.'

The husband looked at his wife and said, 'Gee, honey, you know we now have a fortune, and all those houses. What do you think?'

She mulled it over for a few moments and said, 'Considering all that, I guess I wouldn't mind.'

The genie took the woman upstairs and ravished her for the rest of the afternoon. Both had been satisfied repeatedly, and as the genie rolled over he looked at the wife and asked, 'How old is your husband?'

'He's 35,' she responded breathlessly.

'No shit! Thirty-five years old and that idiot still believes in genies?'

COP THAT >>>

A fellow bought a new Mercedes and was out for a nice evening drive. The top was down, the breeze was blowing through what was left of his hair and he decided to open her up.

As the needle jumped up to 120 kph, he suddenly saw flashing red and blue lights behind him. 'There's no way they can catch a Mercedes,' he thought to himself and opened her up further. The needle hit 130, 140, 150, 160... before the reality of the situation hit him. 'What the hell am I doing?' he thought and pulled over.

The cop came up to him, took his licence without a word and examined it and the car. 'It's been a long day, this is the end of my shift and it's Friday the 13th. I don't feel like more paperwork, so if you can give me an excuse for your driving that I haven't heard before, you can go.'

The guy thinks for a second and says, 'Last week my wife ran off with a cop. I was afraid you were trying to give her back.'

'Have a nice weekend,' said the officer.

- Movie nudity is virtually always female.
- You know stuff about tanks.
- Your bathroom lines are 80 percent shorter.
- You can open all your own jars.
- When clicking through TV channels, you don't have to stall on every shot of someone crying.
- Your arse is never a factor in a job interview.
- Guys in hockey masks don't attack you.
- You can go to the bathroom without a support group.
- You can kill your own food.
- The garage is all yours.
- You get extra credit for the slightest act of thoughtfulness.
- Nobody secretly wonders if you swallow.
- The National College Cheerleading Championship.
- If you're 34 and single, nobody notices.
- You can get into a non-trivial pissing contest.
- You can be President.
- Flowers fix everything.
- You never have to worry about other people's feelings.
- You get to think about sex 90 percent of your waking hours.
- You can wear a white shirt to a water park.
- You never feel compelled to stop a pal from getting laid.
- The world is your urinal.
- You never misconstrue innocuous statements to mean your lover is about to leave you.
- You get to jump up and slap stuff.
- One mood, all the time.
- You can admire Clint Eastwood without starving yourself to look like him.
- Same work… more pay.
- You don't have to leave the room to make an emergency crotch adjustment.
- With 400 million sperm per shot, you could double the earth's population in 15 tries, at least in theory.
- You don't cry off others' desserts.
- If you retain water, it's in a canteen.
- The remote is yours and yours alone.
- People never glance at your chest when you're talking to them.

- You can drop by to see a friend without bringing a little gift.
- Bachelor parties beat the shit over bridal showers.
- You can buy condoms without the shopkeeper imagining you naked.
- Someday you'll be a dirty old man.
- If another guy shows up at the party in the same outfit, you might become lifelong buddies.
- There is always a game on somewhere.
- You never have to miss a sexual opportunity because you're not in the mood.
- You think the idea of punting a small cat is funny.
- If something mechanical doesn't work, you can bash it with a hammer and throw it across the room.
- Porn movies are designed with your mind in mind.
- Your pals can be trusted never to trap you with: 'So… notice anything different?'
- Baywatch.
- The occasional well-rendered belch is practically expected.
- All your orgasms are real.

EYE, EYE >>>

A guy with a black eye boards his plane bound for Pittsburgh and sits down in his seat. He immediately notices that the guy next to him also has a black eye.

He says to him, 'Hey this is a coincidence: we both have black eyes. Mind if I ask how you got yours?'

So the guy tells him, 'Well, it just happened. It was a tongue twister accident, sort of. See, I was at the ticket counter and this gorgeous blonde with the biggest breasts in the world was there. So, instead of saying, "I'd like a ticket to Pittsburgh," I said, "I'd like a picket to Tittsburgh." She socked me one.'

The first guy responded, 'Mine was a tongue twister too. I was at the breakfast table and I wanted to say to my wife, "Please pour me a bowl of Wheaties." But I accidentally said, "You ruined my life, you lousy bitch."'

WOMEN GET THEIR OWN BACK >>>

Slogans for women's T-shirts:

- I'm out of estrogen – I have a gun.
- Guys have feelings too. But like… who cares?
- I don't believe in miracles. I rely on them.
- Next mood swing: six minutes.
- And your point is?
- I used to be schizophrenic, but we're OK now.
- I'm busy. You're ugly. Have a nice day.
- Warning: I have an attitude and I know how to use it.
- Of course I don't look busy… I did it right the first time.
- Why do people with closed minds always open their mouths?
- I'm multi-talented: I can talk and annoy you at the same time.
- Do NOT start with me. You will NOT win.
- You have the right to remain silent, so please SHUT UP.
- All stressed out and no one to choke.
- I'm one of those bad things that happen to good people.
- How can I miss you if you won't go away?
- Sorry if I looked interested. I'm not.
- Objects under this shirt are larger than they appear.

ACRONYMS >>>

Two guys and a woman were sitting at a bar talking about themselves.

The first guy says, 'I'm a yuppie… you know… young, urban, professional.'

The second guy says, 'I'm a dink… you know… double income, no kids.'

They asked the woman, 'And you?'

She replied, 'I'm a wife… you know… wash, iron, f***, etc.'

GETTING A LIFT >>>

Viagra can now be purchased at a huge discount under its generic name. Just ask your doctor or chemist for the generic Viagra known as: Mycoxaflopin.

SAINSBURY'S SPECIAL >>>

Tired of constantly being broke, and stuck in an unhappy marriage, a young husband decided to solve both problems by taking out a large insurance policy on his wife, with himself as the beneficiary, and arranging to have her killed.

A 'friend of a friend' put him in touch with a nefarious underworld figure, who went by the name of Artie. Artie explained to the husband that his going price for snuffing out a spouse was 5000 quid.

The husband said he was willing to pay that amount but that he wouldn't have any cash on hand until he could collect his wife's insurance money.

Artie insisted on being paid something up front. The man opened up his wallet, displaying the single pound coin that rested inside. Artie sighed, rolled his eyes, and reluctantly agreed to accept the quid as down-payment for the dirty deed.

A few days later, Artie followed the man's wife to the local Sainsbury's supermarket. There, he surprised her in the produce department and proceeded to strangle her with his gloved hands.

As the poor unsuspecting woman drew her last breath and slumped to the floor, the manager of the produce department stumbled unexpectedly onto the scene. Unwilling to leave any witnesses behind, Artie had no choice but to strangle the produce manager as well. Unknown to Artie, the entire proceedings were captured by hidden cameras and observed by the store's security guard, who immediately called the police. Artie was caught and arrested before he could leave the store.

When Artie was tried and found guilty, the headlines read, 'Artie Chokes Two for a Pound at Sainsbury's!'

HEART ATTACK ANTICS >>>

A guy gets home early from work and hears strange noises coming from the bedroom. He rushes upstairs to find his wife naked on the bed, sweating and panting.

'What's up?' he says.

'I'm having a heart attack,' cries the woman.

He rushes downstairs to grab the phone, but just as he's dialling, his four-year-old son comes up and says, 'Daddy! Daddy! Uncle

Ted's hiding in your wardrobe and he's got no clothes on!'

The guy slams the phone down and storms upstairs into the bedroom, past his screaming wife and rips open the wardrobe door.

Sure enough, there is his brother, totally naked, cowering on the wardrobe floor.

'You jerk,' yells the husband, 'my wife's having a heart attack and you're running around with no clothes on scaring the kids!'

TABLE OF ELEMENTS >>>

Element name: Woman.
Symbol: WO.
Atomic Weight: Don't even go there.
Physical Properties: Generally round in form, boils at nothing and may freeze any time. Melts whenever treated properly. Very bitter if not used well.
Chemical Properties: Very active. Highly unstable. Possesses strong affinity to gold, silver, platinum and precious stones. Violent when left alone. Able to absorb great amounts of exotic food. Turns slightly green when placed next to better specimen.
Usage: Highly ornamental. An extremely good catalyst for dispersion of wealth. Probably the most powerful income-reducing agent known.
Caution: Highly explosive in inexperienced hands.

Element Name: Man.
Symbol: XY.
Atomic Weight:150 kg plus or minus 50 kg.
Physical Properties: Solid at room temperature, but gets bent out of shape easily. Fairly dense and sometimes flaky. Difficult to find pure sample. Due to rust, ageing samples are unable to conduct electricity as easily as young samples.
Chemical Properties: Attempts to bond with WO any chance it can get. Also tends to form strong bonds with itself. Becomes explosive when mixed with KD (Element: Child) for prolonged period of time. Neutralise by saturating with alcohol.
Usage: None known. Possibly good methane source. Good samples are able to produce large quantities on command.
Caution: In the absence of WO, this element rapidly decomposes and begins to smell.

If agony aunts were uncles:

Reader: *My husband-to-be still pines for his old girlfriends. I'm afraid he will not be faithful.*
Jim: *A man's capacity to love is boundless. It has been proven to increase with the number of sexual partners. Thus, by having a few other women, your partner is really increasing his love for you. Best thing to do is to buy him a nice, expensive present, and cook him a nice meal and don't mention this aspect of his behaviour.*

Reader: *My husband has too many nights out with the boys.*
Jim: *This is perfectly natural behaviour and it should be encouraged. The man is a hunter and he needs to prove his prowess with other men. Far from being pleasurable, a night out with the boys is a stressful affair and to get back to you is a relief for your partner. Just look back at how emotional and happy the man is when he returns to his stable home. Best thing to do is to buy him a nice, expensive present, and cook him a nice meal and don't mention this aspect of his behaviour.*

Reader: *My husband wants to experience three-in-a-bed-sex with me and my sister.*
Jim: *Your husband is clearly devoted to you. He cannot get enough of you, so he goes for the next best thing – your sister. Far from being an issue, this will bring all of the family together. Why not get mum involved? If you are still apprehensive, then let him go with your relatives, buy him a nice, expensive present, and cook him a nice meal and don't mention this aspect of his behaviour.*

Reader: *My husband continually asks me to perform oral sex with him.*
Jim: *Do it. Sperm is not only great tasting, but with only 10 calories a spoonful it is nutritious and helps you to keep your figure and gives a great glow to the skin. Interestingly, a man knows this. His offer to you to perform oral sex with him is totally selfless. Oral sex is extremely painful for a man. This*

shows he loves you. Best thing to do is to thank him, buy him a nice, expensive present and cook him a nice meal.

Reader: *My husband doesn't know where my clitoris is.*
Jim: *Your clitoris is of no concern to your husband. If you must mess with it, do it in your own time. To help with the family budget, you may wish to video yourself while doing this and to sell it at a car boot sale. To ease your selfish guilt, buy your man a nice, expensive present and cook a delicious meal.*

SOFTWARE PROBLEMS >>>

Last year I upgraded from Girlfriend 7.0 to Wife 1.0 and noticed that the new program began unexpected child processing that took up a lot of space and valuable resources. No mention of this phenomenon was included in the product brochure. In addition, Wife 1.0 installs itself into all other programs and launches during system initialisation, where it monitors all other system activity.

Applications such as Poker Night 10.3, Boys' Night 2.5 and Sunday Football 5.0 no longer run, crashing the system whenever they are selected. I cannot seem to keep Wife 1.0 in the background while attempting to run some of my other favourite applications. I am thinking about going back to Girlfriend 7.0, but the un-install does not work on this program.

Can you help me, please?!
Thanks,
Joe

Dear Joe
This is a very common problem men complain about but is mostly due to a primary misconception.

Many people upgrade from Girlfriend 7.0 to Wife 1.0 with the idea that Wife 1.0 is merely a UTILITIES & ENTERTAINMENT program. Wife 1.0 is an OPERATING SYSTEM and designed by its creator to run everything. It is unlikely you would be able to purge Wife 1.0 and still convert back to Girlfriend 7.0. Hidden operating files within your system would cause Girlfriend 7.0 to emulate Wife 1.0 so nothing is gained. It is impossible to un-install, delete, or purge the program files from the system once installed.

You cannot go back to Girlfriend 7.0 because Wife 1.0 is not designed to do this. Some have tried to install Girlfriend 8.0 or Wife 2.0 but end up with more problems than the original system. Look in your manual under 'Warnings – Alimony/Child Support.' I recommend you keep Wife 1.0 and just deal with the situation.

Having Wife 1.0 installed myself, I might also suggest you read the entire section regarding General Partnership Faults (GPFs). You must assume all responsibility for faults and problems that might occur, regardless of their cause.

The best course of action will be to enter the command C:\APOLOGISE. In any case, avoid excessive use of the ESC key because ultimately you will have to give the APOLOGISE command before the operating system will return to normal. The system will run smoothly as long as you take the blame for all the GPFs. Wife 1.0 is a great program, but very high maintenance.

Consider buying additional software to improve the performance of Wife 1.0. I recommend Flowers 2.1 and Chocolates 5.0. Do not, under any circumstances, install Secretary With Short Skirt 3.3. This is not a supported application for Wife 1.0 and is likely to cause irreversible damage to the operating system.

Best of Luck.
Tech Support
Matt Smith

SHORT AND SWEET! >>>

What do bungee jumping and sex with a prostitute have in common?

1. They both cost about $100.
2. They both last about 30 seconds.
3. And in both cases, if the rubber breaks, you're a dead man.

FEMALE EMPIRE STRIKES BACK >>>

Why do only 10 percent of men make it to heaven?
Because if they all went, it would be called hell.

How are husbands like lawn mowers?
They're hard to get started, they emit noxious fumes, and half the time they don't work.

How can you tell when a man is well hung?
When you can just barely slip your finger in between his neck and the noose.

How do you get a man to stop biting his nails?
Make him wear shoes.

How many men does it take to screw in a lightbulb?
One. He just holds it up there and waits for the world to revolve around him.

How many men does it take to screw in a lightbulb?
Three. One to screw in the bulb and two to listen to him brag about the screwing part.

How many men does it take to tile a bathroom?
Two – if you slice them very thinly.

Why can't men get mad cow disease?
Because they are pigs.

What do you call a handcuffed man?
Trustworthy.

What does it mean when a man is in your bed gasping for breath and calling your name?
You didn't hold the pillow down long enough.

How does a man show he's planning for the future?
He buys an extra case of beer.

What do you call the useless piece of skin on a penis?
The man.

Why do men have a hole in their penis?
So their brains can get some oxygen now and then.

Why do men name their penises?
Because they don't like the idea of having a stranger make 90 percent of their decisions.

Why does it take 100 million sperm to fertilise an egg?
Because not one will stop and ask for directions.

What makes a man think about a dinner by candlelight?
A power failure.

What should you give a man who has everything?
A woman to show him how to work it.

What has eight arms and an IQ of 60?
Four guys watching a football game.

What's the best way to force a man to do sit-ups?
Put the remote control between his toes.

What's a man's idea of honesty in a relationship?
Telling you his real name.

What's the difference between Big Foot and intelligent man?
Big Foot has been spotted several times.

Why did God create man before woman?
He didn't want any advice.

Why did God create man before woman?
Because you need a rough draft before creating your masterpiece.

Why do doctors slap babies' bums right after they're born?
To knock the penises off the smart ones.

Why do little boys whine?
Because they're practising to be men.

kids - don't you just love 'em

It's a fact of life that children are funny. Before they grow up too much they always seem to have the wherewithal to embarrass the hell out of parents and teachers - and there is always a 'Little Johnny' around who's a right little smart arse.

LOUVRE RUDE >>>

A French woman took her little daughter to the Louvre where they saw a statue of a nude male.

'What is that?' asked the child pointing to the penis.

'Nothing, nothing at all, cherie,' replied the mother.

'I want one,' said the child.

The mother tried to focus her daughter's attention on a more suitable subject, but the little girl persisted. 'I want one just like that,' she kept repeating. At last the mother said, 'If you are a good girl and stop thinking about it now, when you grow up, you will have one.'

'And if I'm bad?' asked the little one.

'Then,' sighed the mother, 'you will have many.'

ADVICE TO LIVE BY >>>

'Never trust a dog to watch your food.' – Patrick, aged 10.

'When your dad is mad and asks you, "Do I look stupid?" don't answer.' – Hannah, aged 9.

'Never tell your mum her diet's not working.' – Michael, aged 14.

'Stay away from prunes.' – Randy, aged 9.

'Don't squat with your spurs on.' – Noronha, aged 13.

'Don't pull dad's finger when he tells you to.' – Emily, aged 10.

'When your mum is mad at your dad, don't let her brush your hair.' – Taylia, aged 11.

'Never allow your three-year-old brother in the same room as your school assignment.' – Traci, aged 14.

'Don't sneeze in front of your mum when you're eating crackers.' – Mitchell, aged 12.

'Puppies still have bad breath even after eating a Tic-Tac.' – Andrew, aged 9.

'Never hold a dust-buster and a cat at the same time.' – Kyoyo, aged 9.

'You can't hide a piece of broccoli in a glass of milk.' – Armir, aged 9.

'Don't wear polka-dotted underwear under white shorts.' – Kellie, aged 11.

'If you want a kitten, start out by asking for a horse.' – Naomi, aged 15.

'Felt pens are not good to use as lipstick.' – Lauren, aged 9.

'Don't pick on your sister when she's holding a baseball bat.' – Joel, aged 10.

'When you get a bad grade at school, show it to your mum when she's on the phone.' – Alyesha, aged 13.

'Never try to baptise a cat.' – Eileen, aged 8.

GROW UP, WILL YOU! >>>

The kindergarten kids had graduated to the infant class. Their teacher wanted them to be more grown up since they were no longer in kindergarten. She told them to use grown-up words instead of baby words. She then asked them to tell her what they did during the summer. The first little one said he went to see his Nana.

The teacher said, 'No, no, you went to see your grandmother. Use the grown-up word.'

The next little one said she went for a trip on a choo-choo. The teacher again said, 'No, no, you went on a trip on a train. That's the grown-up word.'

Then the teacher asked the third little one what he did during the summer. He proudly stated that he read a book. The teacher asked what book he had read. He puffed out his chest and, in a very adult way, replied, 'Winnie the Shit.'

STAYING ON TRACK >>>

A mother was working in the kitchen listening to her son playing with his new electric train in the living room. She heard the train stop and her son saying, 'All you sons of bitches who want off, get the hell off now, 'cause this is the last stop. And all you sons of bitches who are getting on, get your arses in the train, 'cause we're going down the tracks.'

The horrified mother went in and told her son, 'We don't use that kind of language in this house. Now I want you to go to your room and you are to stay there for two hours. When you come out, you may play with your train, but I want you to use nice language.'

Two hours later, the son came out of the bedroom and resumed playing with his train. Soon the train stopped and the mother heard her son say, 'All passengers who are disembarking the train, please remember to take all of your belongings with you. We thank you for riding with us today and hope your trip was a pleasant one. We hope you will ride with us again soon.'

She hears the little boy continue, 'For those of you just boarding, we ask you to stow all of your hand luggage under your seat. Remember, there is no smoking on the train. We hope you will have a pleasant and relaxing journey with us today.'

As the mother began to smile, the child added, 'For those of you who are pissed off about the two-hour delay, please see the bitch in the kitchen.'

BOOK CORNER >>>

25 children's books you'll never see:

1. *You are different and that's bad.*
2. *Pop goes the hamster… and other great microwave games.*
3. *Testing homemade parachutes using only your household pets.*
4. *Barbar meets the Taxidermist.*
5. *Curious George and the high-voltage fence.*
6. *The boy who died from eating all his vegetables.*
7. *Start a real estate empire with the change from your mum's purse.*
8. *Daddy's new wife Timothy.*

9. *The pop-up book of human anatomy.*
10. *Things rich kids have, but you never will.*
11. *The Care Bears maul some campers and are shot dead.*
12. *How to become the dominant military power in your elementary school.*
13. *Controlling the playground: Respect through fear.*
14. *You were an accident.*
15. *Strangers have the best sweets.*
16. *The Little Sissy who snitched.*
17. *Some kittens can fly!*
18. *Getting more chocolate on your face.*
19. *Kathy was so bad her mum stopped loving her.*
20. *The kids' guide to hitchhiking.*
21. *When Mummy and Daddy don't know the answer, they say God did it.*
22. *Garfield gets feline leukaemia.*
23. *Why can't Mr Fork and Ms Electrical Outlet be friends?*
24. *Bi-curious George.*
25. *Daddy drinks because you cry.*

MORAL VICTORIES >>>

A teacher was giving class lessons in morals and asked for examples.

Little Mary stood up and said, 'My father is a chicken farmer and when we collect the eggs each morning, we take more than one basket, so you don't put all your eggs in one basket.'

'Very good, Mary,' said the teacher. 'Any more morals?'

Little Johnny stands up. 'During the war,' he says, 'my Uncle Charlie was alone in a fox-hole with a rifle and a bottle of whisky.

'A whole German battalion was approaching him, so he had a big gulp of the whisky and fired all his bullets at the Germans, killing at least 100. He fell back into the fox-hole, took another large swig of whisky and ran out and used his bayonet and rifle butt to kill all the Germans left.'

'That's very brave of your uncle,' said the teacher, 'but where's the moral to the story?'

'Well,' said Johnny, 'You don't f*** around with Uncle Charlie when he's been on the piss.'

LUKE'S SHITTY CHRISTMAS >>>

Little Luke had a cussing problem and his father was getting tired of it. He decided to ask his shrink what to do.

The shrink said, 'Since Christmas is coming up, you should ask Luke what he wants Santa to bring him. If he cusses while he tells you his wish list, leave a pile of dog shit in place of the gifts or gifts he requests.'

Two days before Christmas, Luke's father asked him what he wanted for Christmas. 'I want a damn teddy bear laying right beside me when I wake up. When I go downstairs I want to see a damn train going around the damn tree. And when I go outside I want to see a damn bike leaning up against the damn garage.'

On Christmas morning, little Luke woke up and rolled over into a pile of dog shit. Confused, he walked downstairs and saw another pile under the tree. Scratching his head, he walked outside and saw a huge pile of dog shit by the garage.

When Luke walked back inside with a curious look on his face, his dad smiled and asked, 'What did Santa bring you this year?'

Luke replied, 'I think I got a dog but I can't find the son-of-a-bitch!'

TO THE POINT >>>

An actual note handed to a flight attendant on a Qantas flight by an eight-year-old girl.

Dear Captain,
My name is Nicola I'm 8 years old. This is my first flight but I'm not scared. I like to watch the clouds go by. My mum says the crew is nice. I think your plane is good. Thanks for a nice flight don't fuck up the landing.
Luv Nicola
xxxx

GREEN EGGS AND RAM >>>

Dr Seuss explains computers:

If a packet hits a pocket on a socket on a port,
And the bus is interrupted as a very last resort,
And the address of the memory makes your floppy disk abort,
Then the socket packet pocket has an error to report.

If your cursor finds a menu item followed by a dash,
And the double clicking icon puts your window in the trash,
And your data is corrupted 'cause the index doesn't hash
Then your situation's hopeless and your system's gonna crash.

If the label on the cable on the table at your house
Says the network is connected to the button on your mouse,
But your packets want to tunnel on another protocol,
That's repeatedly rejected by the printer down the hall,

And your screen is all distorted by the side effects of gauss,
So your icons in the window are as wavy as a souse,
Then you may as well reboot it, and let it go out with a bang,
'Cause as sure as I'm a poet, the sucker's gonna hang.

When the copy of your floppy's getting sloppy on the disk,
And the micro-code instructions cause unnecessary risk,
Then you have to flash your memory and you'll want to
  ram your ROM,
So quickly turn off your computer and go and tell your mum!

SUNDAY SCHOOL SAYINGS >>>

The following statements about the *Bible* were written by children and have not been retouched or corrected (ie. bad spelling has been left in):

'In the first book of the Bible, Guinessis, God got tired of creating the world, so he took the Sabbath off.'

'Adam and Eve were created from an apple tree.'

'Noah's wife was called Joan of Ark.'

'Noah built an ark, which the animals come on to in pears.'

'Lot's wife was a pillar of salt by day, but a ball of fire by night.'

'The Jews were a proud people and throughout history they had trouble with the unsympathetic Genitals.'

'Samson was a strongman who let himself be led astray by a Jezebel like Delilah.'

'Samson slayed the Philistines with the axe of the Apostles.'

'Moses led the Hebrews to the Red Sea, where they made unleavened bread which is bread without any ingredients.'

'The Egyptians were all drowned in the dessert. Afterwards, Moses went up on Mount Cyanide to get the 10 ammendments.'

'The first commandment was when Eve told Adam to eat the apple.'

'The seventh commandment is thou shalt not admit adultery.'

'Moses died before he ever reached Canada.'

'Then Joshua led the Hebrews in the battle of Geritol.'

'The greatest miracle in the Bible is when Joshua told his son to stand still and he obeyed him.'

'David was a Hebrew king skilled at playing the liar. He fought with the Finklesteins, a race of people who lived in Biblical times.'

'Solomon, one of David's sons, had 300 wives and 700 porcupines.'

'When Mary heard that she was the mother of Jesus, she sang the Magna Carta.'

'When the three wise guys from the east side arrived, they found

Jesus in the manager.'

'Jesus was born because Mary had an immaculate contraption.'

'St John, the blacksmith, dumped water on his head.'

'Jesus said the Golden Rule, which says to do one to others before they do one to you.'

'He also explained, "A man doth not live by sweat alone."'

'It was a miracle when Jesus rose from the dead and managed to get the tombstone off the entrance.'

'The people who followed the Lord were called the 12 decibels.'

'The epistles were the wives of the apostles.'

'One of the opossums was St Matthew who was also a taximan.'

'St Paul cavorted to Christianity. He preached holy acrimony, which is another name for marriage.'

'A Christian should have only one spouse. This is called monotony.'

Bless their little hearts!

GENIAL GENERAL >>>

As the crowded airliner is about to take off, the peace is shattered by a five-year-old boy who picks that moment to throw a wild temper tantrum. No matter what his frustrated, embarrassed mother does to try to calm him down, the boy continues to scream furiously and kick the seats around him.

Suddenly, from the rear of the plane, an elderly man in the uniform of an Air Force Wing General is seen slowly walking forward up the aisle. Stopping the flustered mother with an upraised hand, the white-haired, courtly, soft-spoken general leans down and, motioning toward his chest, whispers something into the boy's ear.

Instantly the boy calms down, gently takes his mother's hand, and quietly fastens his seat belt.

All the other passengers burst into spontaneous applause. As the general slowly makes his way back to his seat, one of the cabin attendants touches his sleeve.

'Excuse me, General,' she asks quietly, 'but could I ask you what magic words you used on that little boy?'

The old man smiles serenely and gently confides, 'I showed him my pilot's wings, service stars, and battle ribbons, and explained that they entitle me to throw one passenger out the plane door, on any flight I choose.'

PERIOD PAIN >>>

The kindergarten class had a homework assignment to find out about something exciting and relate it to the class the next day. When the time came for the little kids to give their reports, the teacher was calling on them one at a time.

Eventually little Johnny's turn came. Little Johnny walked up to the front of the class and, with a piece of chalk, made a small white dot on the blackboard, waited a short time and make a second small white dot next to the first.

Well the teacher couldn't figure out what Johnny had in mind for his report, so she asked him just what that was.

'It's a period,' reported Johnny.

'Yes, I can understand that,' she said, 'but what is so exciting about a period?'

'Damned if I know,' said Johnny, 'but this morning my sister said she missed one. Then Daddy had a heart attack, Mummy fainted, and the man next door shot himself.'

THREE LITTLE PIGS >>>

My friend likes to read his two young sons fairy tales at night. Having a deep-rooted sense of humour, he often ad-libs parts of the stories for fun.

One day his youngest son was sitting in his new entrants' class as the teacher was reading the story of the *Three Little Pigs*. She came to the part where the first pig was trying to acquire building materials for his home.

She said, 'And so the pig went up to the man with a wheelbarrow full of straw and said, "Pardon me, sir, but might I have some of that straw to build my house with?"

Then the teacher asked the class, 'And what do you think that man said?'

And my friend's son raised his hand and said 'I know! I know. He said, "Holy shit! A talking pig!"'

The teacher was unable to teach for the next 10 minutes.

FACTS OF LIFE >>>

Little Simon came running into the house and asked, 'Mummy, can little girls have babies?'

'No,' said his mum, 'of course not.'

Simon ran back outside and his mum heard him yell to his friends, 'It's okay, we can play that game again!'

URINATE IN PEACE >>>

Little Dion was sitting in class one day. All of a sudden, he needed to go to the toilet. He yelled out, 'Miss Jones, I need to have a piss!' Miss Jones replied, 'Now Dion, that is not the proper word to use in this situation. The correct word you want to use is urinate. Please use the word urinate in a sentence correctly and I will allow you to go.'

Little Dion thinks for a bit, then says, 'You're an eight, but if you had bigger tits, you'd be a 10.'

IF IT WORKS FOR MUM... >>>

A few months after his parents were divorced, little Mattie passed his mum's bedroom and saw her rubbing her body and moaning, 'I need a man, I need a man.'

Over the next couple of months, he saw her doing this several times. One day Mattie came home from school and heard her moaning again. When he peeked into the bedroom, he saw a man on top of her.

Little Mattie ran into his room, took off his clothes, threw himself on his bed, started stroking himself and moaned, 'Ohh, I need a bike! I need a bike!'

JOHNNY'S BIG STING >>>

Little Johnny (that little bugger again!) was being particularly reckless one day. He was playing in the backyard when some honeybees started swirling around, annoying him. He began stomping on them in a temper and his father saw him.

'That's it. No honey for you for one month.'

Later, Johnny pondered over some butterflies and soon started catching them and crushing them under his feet. His father again caught him and after a brief moment of thought said, 'No butter for you for one month.'

Early that evening, Johnny's mother was cooking dinner and got jumpy when cockroaches started scurrying around the kitchen floor. She began stomping on them one by one until all the cockroaches were dead.

Johnny's mother looked up to find Johnny and his father standing there watching her, to which Johnny said, 'Are you going to tell her, Daddy, or do you want me to?'

THE BIRDS AND THE BEES >>>

A teacher cautiously approaches the subject of sex education with her Standard Two class because she realises Little Johnny's habit of using sexual innuendo is going to cause some trouble.

Johnny remains attentive throughout the whole class and, finally, the teacher asks for examples of sex education from the class.

One little boy raises his hand, 'I saw a bird in her nest with some eggs.'

'Very good, William,' said the teacher.

'My mummy had a baby,' said little Esther.

'Oh, that's nice,' replied the teacher.

Finally, Little Johnny raises his hand. With much fear and trepidation, the teacher calls on him. 'I was watching TV yesterday and I saw the Lone Ranger. He was surrounded by hundreds and hundreds of Indians. And they all attacked at one time. And he killed every one of them with his two guns.'

The teacher was relieved but puzzled, 'And what does that have to do with sex education, Johnny?'

'It'll teach those Indians not to f*** with the Lone Ranger.'

HORSEY, HORSEY >>>

That little bastard Little Johnny was passing his parents' bedroom in the middle of the night in search of a glass of water. Hearing a lot of moaning and thumping, he peeks in and catches his parents in The Act.

Before his dad can even react, Little Johnny exclaims, 'Oh boy! Horsey. Daddy can I ride on your back?'

Daddy, relieved that Johnny was not asking more uncomfortable questions and seeing the opportunity not to break his stride, agrees.

Johnny hops on and daddy starts going to town. Pretty soon his mummy starts moaning and gasping and Johnny cries out, 'Hang on tight, Daddy. This is the part where me and Mike the milkman usually get bucked off!'

CIRCUMSPECTION >>>

Two five-year-old boys are standing at the toilet to piss.

One says, 'Your thingy doesn't have any skin on it.'

'I've been circumcised,' the other one says.

'What's that mean?'

'It means they cut the skin off at the end.'

'How old were you when it was cut off?'

'My mum said I was two days old.'

'Did it hurt?'

'You bet it hurt. I couldn't walk for a year.'

FAKING IT >>>

A little girl is in line to see Santa. When it's her turn, she climbs up on Santa's lap and Santa asks, 'What would you like me to bring you for Christmas?'

The little girl replies, 'I want a Barbie and a G.I. Joe doll.'

Santa looks at the little girl for a moment and says, 'I thought Barbie comes with Ken.'

'No,' the little girl replies, 'She comes with G.I. Joe, she fakes it with Ken.'

Amnesia: Condition that enables a woman who has gone through labour to have sex again.

Dumbwaiter: One who asks if the kids would care to order dessert.

Family Planning: The art of spacing your children the proper distance apart to keep you on the edge of financial disaster.

Feedback: The inevitable result when the baby doesn't appreciate the strained carrots.

Full Name: What you call your child when you are angry with him/her.

Grandparents: The people who think your children are wonderful even though they're sure you're not raising them right.

Hearsay: What toddlers do when anyone mutters a dirty word.

Impregnable: A woman whose memory of labour is still vivid.

Independent: How we want our children to be as long as they do everything we say.

Ow: The first word spoken by children with older siblings.

Pre-natal: When your life was still somewhat your own.

Puddle: A small body of water that draws other small bodies wearing dry shoes into it.

Show Off: A child who is more talented than yours.

Sterilise: What you do to your first baby's dummy by boiling it and to your last baby's dummy by blowing on it.

Top Bunk: Where you should never put a child wearing Superman pyjamas.

Two-Minute Warning: When the baby's face turns red and he/she begins to make those familiar grunting noises.

Verbal: To whine in words.

Whodunnit: None of the kids that live in your house.

DAD, YOU'RE A DIAMOND >>>

Ten things that dads probably don't say too often!

10. 'Well, how 'bout that?… I'm lost. Looks like we'll have to stop and ask for directions.'
9. 'You know Pumpkin, now that you're 13, you'll be ready for unchaperoned car dates. Won't that be fun?'
8. 'I notice that all your friends have a certain "up yours" attitude… I like that.'
7. 'Here's a credit card and the keys to my new car… go crazy.'
6. 'What do you mean you wanna play rugby? Figure skating not good enough for you, son?'
5. 'Your mother and I are going away for the weekend… you might want to consider throwing a party.'
4. 'Well, I don't know what's wrong with your car. Probably one of those watchamacallits – you know – that makes it run or something. Just have it towed to a mechanic and pay whatever he asks.'
3. 'No son of mine is going to live under this roof without an earring, now quit your belly-aching and let's go to the mall.'
2. 'Whaddya wanna go and get a job for? I make plenty of money for you to spend.'
1. 'Father's Day? Don't worry about that – it's no big deal.'

VIRGIN ON THE BRILLIANT! >>>

Two daughters had been given parts in the Christmas pageant at their church. At dinner that night, they got into an argument as to who had the most important role.

Finally the 14-year-old said to her eight-year-old younger sister, 'Well, you ask Mum. She'll tell you it's harder to be a virgin than it is to be an angel.'

COPPING IT >>>

On Christmas morning, a cop on horseback is sitting at a traffic light and next to him is a kid on his shiny new bike. The cop says to the kid, 'Nice bike you got there. Did Santa bring that to you?'

The kid says, 'Yeah.'

The cop says, 'Well next year, tell Santa to put a tail light on that bike.' The cop then proceeds to issue the kid a $20 bicycle safety violation ticket.

The kid takes the ticket and before he rides off he says, 'By the way, that's a nice horse you got there. Did Santa bring that to you?'

Humouring the kid, the cop says, 'Yeah, he sure did.'

The kid says, 'Well next year, tell Santa to put the dick underneath the horse instead of on top.'

SILLY QUESTION! >>>

A travelling salesman knocks on the door of a house. A kid, about 12 years old, answers the door. He's wearing a pink tutu, has a cigar in one hand, and a martini in the other.

The salesman is a little taken back, so he asks, 'Excuse me, son, are your parents home?'

The kid takes a big puff on the cigar and answers, 'What the f*** do you think?'

BRIGHT KIDS >>>

A policeman had a perfect spot to watch for speeding motorists but wasn't getting many. Then he discovered the problem. A 10-year-old boy was standing up the road with a hand-painted sign that read 'Radar Trap Ahead'. The officer then found a young accomplice down the road with a sign reading 'Tips' and a bucket full of change.

IT'S A DOG'S LIFE >>>

A little girl asks her mum, 'Mum, may I take the dog for a walk around the block?'

Mum says, 'No, because the dog is in heat.'

'What's that mean?' asks the child.

'Go ask your Father. I think he's in the garage'.

The little girl goes to the garage and says, 'Dad, can I take Susie for a walk around the block? I asked Mum but she said the dog was in heat and that I should ask you.'

Dad says, 'Bring Susie over here.' He takes a rag, soaks it with gasoline, and scrubs the dog's rear with it and says, 'OK, you can go now but keep Susie on the leash and only go one time around the block.'

The little girl leaves and returns a few minutes later with no dog on the leash. Dad says, 'Where's Susie?' The little girl says, 'Susie ran out of gas about halfway down the block and there's another dog pushing her home.'

TEACHING MANNERS >>>

Son: *'Mum, when I was on the bus with Dad this morning, he told me to give up my seat to a lady.'*
Mum: *'Well, you have done the right thing.'*
Son: *'But Mum, I was sitting on daddy's lap.'*

LOAD OF BALLOONY >>>

A small boy walks into his mother's room and inadvertently catches her topless. 'Mummy, Mummy, what are those?' he says, pointing to her breasts. 'Well, son,' she says, 'these are… er, balloons. And when I die, they inflate and float me up to heaven.' Incredibly, the boy appears to believe this explanation and goes off quite satisfied.

Two days later, while his mother is making tea, he rushes into the kitchen. 'Mummy, Mummy, Aunt Eliza is dying!'

'What do you mean?' asks his mother.

Well, she's out in the garden shed, lying on the floor. Both her balloons are out, Daddy's blowing them up, and she keeps yelling, 'God, I'm coming! God, I'm coming!'

IF YOU GO DOWN TO THE WOODS TODAY >>>

'Mummy, Mummy, I was at the playground and Daddy and…' Mummy tells him to slow down. She wants to hear the story, so Little Johnny tells her. 'I was at the playground and I saw Daddy's car go into the woods with Aunt Jane.

'I went back to look and he was giving Aunt Jane a big kiss, then he helped her take off her shirt, then Aunt Jane helped Daddy take his pants off, then Aunt Jane laid down on the seat, then Daddy…'

At this point Mummy cut him off and says, 'Johnny, this is such an interesting story, suppose you save the rest of it for suppertime. I want to see the look on Daddy's face when you tell it tonight.'

At the dinner table, Mummy asks Little Johnny to tell his story. Johnny starts his story, describing the car going into the woods, the undressing, laying down on the seat and '… then Daddy and Aunt Jane did that same thing Mummy and Uncle Bill used to do when Daddy was in the Navy.'

weird and wonderful world

It's definitely a strange world. There are plenty of geniuses out there who can think up some amazing lists and sayings that will make you wonder. There's an urge to suggest they get a life, but then we'd be missing out on some of the deathless prose that wings its way across the Net. Ponder on, oh thought-provoking ones.

- If you yelled for eight years, seven months and six days, you would have produced enough sound energy to heat one cup of coffee. (Hardly seems worth it!)
- If you pass air consistently for six years and nine months, enough gas is produced to create the energy of an atomic bomb. (That one's easy to understand, isn't it?)
- The human heart creates enough pressure when it pumps out to the body to squirt blood 9.5 m. (And you thought those Monty Python guys didn't do any fact checking!)
- A pig's orgasm lasts for 30 minutes. (In my next life I want to be a pig!)
- Banging your head against a wall uses 150 calories an hour. (Still not over that pig thing!)
- Humans and dolphins are the only species that have sex for pleasure. (What about pigs?)
- On average, people fear spiders more than they do death.
- The strongest muscle in the body is the tongue. (Hmmm…)
- You can't kill yourself by holding your breath.
- Americans on the average eat 18 ha of pizza every day. (It shows.)
- Every time you lick a stamp, you're consuming one-tenth of a calorie.
- You are more likely to be killed by a champagne cork than by a poisonous spider. (Moral: Always be willing to pay extra for good champagne. Cheap champagne is not worth the risk.)
- Right-handed people live, on average, nine years longer than left-handed people do. (So those teachers that used to whack your left hand with a ruler and make you write with your right hand were actually trying to do you a favour, the miserable, misguided, fascist, sadistic bastards.)
- In ancient Egypt, priests plucked every hair from their bodies, including their eyebrows and eyelashes. (That's a real leg crosser!)
- A crocodile cannot stick its tongue out.
- The ant can lift 50 times its own weight, can pull 30 times its own weight and always falls over on its right side when intoxicated. (How did they know that?)
- Polar bears are left-handed. (This means they live, on average, nine years less.)

- The catfish has over 27,000 taste buds. (Are our palates just not sophisticated enough to appreciate the complex taste of pond scum?)
- The flea can jump 350 times its body length. It's the equivalent of a human jumping the length of a football field.
- A cockroach will live nine days without its head, before it starves to death. (Creepy!)
- The male praying mantis cannot copulate while its head is attached to its body. The female initiates sex by ripping the male's head off. ('Honey, I'm home… What the…?')
- Some lions mate over 50 times a day. (Yeah, baby!)
- Butterflies taste with their feet. (Oh shit!)
- Elephants are the only animals that can't jump.
- A cat's urine glows under a black light. (That's in case you can't smell it.)
- An ostrich's eye is bigger than its brain.
- Starfish haven't got brains.

After reading all these, all I can say is, 'Those disgusting, snorting, garbage-eating, lucky pigs.'

DOG'S WORLD >>>

There were two buddies, one with a Doberman Pinscher and the other with a Chihuahua. The guy with the Doberman says to his friend, 'Let's go over to that restaurant and get something to eat.'

The guy with the Chihuahua says, 'We can't go in there. We've got dogs with us.'

The buddy with the Doberman says, 'Just follow my lead.'

They walk over to the restaurant; the guy with the Doberman puts on a pair of dark glasses and starts to walk in. The bouncer at the door says, 'Sorry, Mac, no pets allowed.'

The Doberman man says, 'You don't understand. This is my seeing-eye dog.'

The bouncer says, 'A Doberman Pinscher?' He says, 'Yes, they're using them now. They're very good and protect you from robbers too.' The man at the door says, 'Come on in.'

The buddy with the Chihuahua figures, 'What the heck,' so he puts on a pair of dark glasses and starts to walk in. Once again the bouncer says, 'Sorry pal, no pets allowed.'

The guy with the Chihuahua says, 'You don't understand. This is my seeing-eye dog.' The bouncer at the door says, 'A Chihuahua?'

The Chihuahua man says, 'A Chihuahua? Those bastards gave me a Chihuahua?'

A CROAKER, MY SON!

A frog goes into a bank and approaches the teller. He can see from her nameplate that the teller's name is Patricia Whack.

So he says, 'Ms Whack, I'd like to get a loan to buy a boat and go on a long holiday.' Patti looks at the frog in disbelief and asks how much he wants to borrow. The frog says, '$30,000.'

The teller asks his name and the frog says his name is Kermit Jagger and that it's OK, he knows the bank manager.

Patti explains that $30,000 is a substantial amount of money and that he will need some collateral to secure the loan. She asks if he has anything that he can use as collateral.

The frog says, 'Sure, I have this,' and produces a tiny pink porcelain elephant, about 2 cm tall, bright pink and perfectly formed. Very confused, Patti explains that she'll have to consult the manager and disappears into a back office.

She finds the manager and says, 'There's a frog called Kermit Jagger out there who claims to know you and wants to borrow $30,000. And he wants to use this as collateral.' She holds up the tiny pink elephant and says, 'I mean, what the heck is this?'

So the manager looks back at her and says, 'It's a knick-knack Patti Whack. Give the frog a loan. His old man's a Rolling Stone.'

WE'VE GOT YOUR NUMBER >>>

You'll need a calculator to work out this simple little sum.

1. First of all, pick the number of days a week that you would like to eat out.
2. Multiply this number by two.
3. Add five.
4. Multiply it by 50.
5. If you've already had your birthday this year, add 1749. If you haven't, add 1748.
6. Now subtract the four-digit year that you were born.

You should now have a three-digit number. The first digit of this was your original number (how many times you would like to eat out each week). The second two digits are your age. Freaky, eh? This year (1999) is the only year that little exercise will ever work, according to the boffins at Victoria's Monash University's Department of Accounting and Finance.

MIND BOGGLING HEADLINES >>>

Include your children when baking cookies.

Something went wrong in jet crash, experts say.

Police begin campaign to run down jaywalkers.

Drunks get nine years in violin case.

Iraqi head seeks arms.

Is there a ring of debris around Uranus?

Prostitutes appeal to Pope.

Panda mating fails – veterinarian takes over.

Teacher strikes idle kids.

Clinton wins budget – more lies ahead.

Miners refuse to work after death.

Juvenile court to try shooting defendant.

Two sisters reunited after 18 years in checkout counter.

If strike isn't settled quickly, it may last a while.

Couple slain – police suspect homicide.

Man struck by lightning faces battery charge.

New study of obesity looks for larger test group.

Astronaut takes blame for gas in space.

Local high school dropouts cut in half.

Typhoon rips through cemetery – hundreds dead.

BLOODY HELL! >>>

A vampire bat came flapping in from the night covered in fresh blood and parked himself on the roof of the cave to get some sleep.

Pretty soon all the other bats smelt the blood and began hassling him about where he got it. He told them to piss off and let him get some sleep, but they persisted until he finally gave in.

'OK, follow me,' he said and flew out of the cave with hundreds of bats behind him. Down through a valley they went, across a river and into a forest full of trees. Finally he slowed down and all the other bats excitedly milled around him.

'Now, do you see that tree over there?' he asked.

'Yes, yes, yes!' the bats all screamed in a frenzy.

'Good,' said the first bat, 'because I f***ing didn't!'

LEARNED FRIEND >>>

I've learned that you cannot make someone love you. All you can do is stalk them and hope they panic and give in.

I've learned that no matter how much I care, some people are just arseholes.

I've learned that it takes years to build up trust, and only suspicion – not proof – to destroy it.

After that, you'd better have a big dick or huge tits.

I've learned that you shouldn't compare yourself to others – they are more fed up than you think.

I've learned you should always leave loved ones with loving words. You may need to borrow money.

I've learned that you can keep puking long after you think you're finished.

I've learned that we are responsible for what we do, unless we are celebrities.

- Why do we wait until a pig is dead to 'cure' it?
- Why do we wash bath towels? Aren't we clean when we use them?
- Why do we put suits in a garment bag and put garments in a suitcase?
- Why doesn't glue stick to the inside of the bottle?
- Do Roman paramedics refer to IVs as '4s'?
- What do little birdies see when they get knocked unconscious?
- Why doesn't Tarzan have a beard?
- If man evolved from monkeys and apes, why do we still have monkeys and apes?
- Should you trust a stockbroker who's married to a travel agent?
- Is boneless chicken considered to be an invertebrate?
- Do married people live longer than single people do, or does it just SEEM longer?
- I went to a book store and asked the saleswoman, 'Where's the self-help section?' She said if she told me it would defeat the purpose.
- If all those psychics know the winning lottery numbers, why are they all still working?
- Isn't the best way to save face to keep the lower part shut?

MAINLINING ON ONE-LINERS >>>

- Well, this day was a total waste of makeup.
- Well, aren't we just a ray of f***ing sunshine?
- Make yourself at home! Clean my kitchen.
- Not the brightest crayon in the box now, are we?
- A hard-on doesn't count as personal growth?
- Don't bother me. I'm living happily ever after.
- This isn't an office; it's hell with fluorescent lighting.
- I started out with nothing and I still have most of it left.
- I pretend to work, they pretend to pay me.
- Therapy is expensive; popping bubble-wrap is cheap. You choose.
- I like cats too. Let's exchange recipes.
- If I want to hear the pitter-patter of little feet, I'll put shoes on my cat.
- Did the aliens forget to remove your anal probe?
- Errors have been made. Others will be blamed.

- And your crybaby, whiny-arsed opinion would be…?
- See no evil, hear no evil, date no evil.
- Allow me to introduce myselves.
- Sarcasm is just one more service we offer.
- Better living through denial.
- Whatever kind of look you were going for, you missed.

WHO SAID THAT? >>>

- Do not walk behind me, for I may not lead. Do not walk ahead of me, for I may not follow. Do not walk beside me, either. Just leave me the hell alone.
- The 1000 km journey always begins with a broken fanbelt and a leaky tyre.
- It's always darkest before dawn. So if you're going to steal the neighbour's newspaper that's the time to do it.
- It's a small world. So you gotta use your elbows a lot.
- Sex is like air. It's not important unless you aren't getting any.
- We are born naked, wet and hungry. Then things get worse.
- No one is listening until you make a mistake.
- Always remember you're unique, just like everyone else.
- Never test the depth of the water with both feet.
- It may be that your sole purpose in life is simply to serve as a warning to others.
- It is far more impressive when others discover your good qualities without your help.
- If you think nobody cares if you're alive, try missing a couple of car payments.
- If you tell the truth, you don't have to remember anything.
- If you lend someone $20, and never see that person again, it was probably worth it.
- You can't strengthen the weak by weakening the strong.
- When someone says, 'Do you want my opinion?' it is always a negative one.
- When someone is having a bad day, be silent, sit close by and nuzzle him or her gently. The word 'listen' contains the same letters as the word 'silent'.
- The trouble with work is – it's so daily.
- The difference between ordinary and extraordinary is that little extra.

- Scientists say one out of every four people is crazy. Check three friends – if they are OK, you're it.
- Pain and suffering is inevitable but misery is optional.

THINGS THAT PISS US OFF >>>

- People who point at their wrist while asking for the time. 'I know where my watch is buddy, where the f*** is yours?' Do we point at our crotch when we ask where the toilet is?
- People who are willing to get off their arse to search the entire room for the TV remote because they refuse to walk to the TV and change the channel manually.
- When people say, 'Oh you just want to have your cake and eat it too.' Piss off. What good is a goddamn cake if you can't eat it?
- When people say, 'It's always in the last place you'd look.' Of course it is. Why the hell would you keep looking after you've found it? Do some people do this? Who and where are they?
- When people say, while watching a movie, 'Did you see that?' No, shit-for-brains, I paid $15 to come to the cinema and stare at the f***ing ceiling up there. What did you come here for?
- People who ask, 'Can I ask you a question?' don't really give you a choice, do they?
- When something is 'new and improved' – which is it? If it's new, then there has never been anything before it. If it's an improvement, then there must have been something before it.
- When a cop pulls you over and then asks if you know how fast you were going, say: 'You should know, arsehole, you pulled me over.'

THINGS TO DO IN THE ELEVATOR >>>

- When there's only one other person in the elevator, tap them on the shoulder and then pretend it wasn't you.
- Push the buttons and pretend they give you a shock. Smile, and go back for more.
- Ask if you can push the button for other people, but push the wrong ones.
- Drop a pen and wait until someone reaches to help pick it up, then scream 'that's mine'.
- Bring a camera and take pictures of everyone in the elevator.

- Move your desk into the elevator and whenever someone gets on, ask if they have an appointment.
- Leave a box in the corner and when someone gets on ask them if they hear something ticking.
- Pretend you are a flight attendant and review emergency procedures and exits with the passengers.
- Ask, 'Did you feel that?'
- Stand really close to someone, sniffing them occasionally.
- When the doors close, announce to the others, 'It's okay, don't panic, they open again.'
- Call out 'group hug', and then enforce it.
- Wear a puppet on your hand and use it to talk to the other passengers.
- Make explosion noises when anyone presses a button.

IQ TEST >>>

1. How long did The Hundred Years' War last?
2. Which country makes Panama hats?
3. From what animal do we get catgut?
4. In what month do Russians celebrate the October Revolution?
5. What is Camel's hairbrush made from?
6. The Canary Islands in the Atlantic are named after what animal?
7. What was King George VI's first name?
8. What colour is a Purple Finch?
9. Where are Chinese Gooseberries from?
10. How long did the Thirty Years' War last?

You think you're so smart, don't you? Here are the answers:

1. 116 years, from 1337 to 1453.
2. Ecuador.
3. From sheep and horses.
4. November. The Russian calendar was 13 days behind ours.
5. Squirrel fur.
6. The Latin name was Insularia Canaria – Island of the Dogs.
7. Albert. In 1937 on the abdication of his brother King Edward VII, he respected the wish of Queen Victoria that no future king should ever be called Albert, the name of her husband.

8. Distinctively crimson.
9. New Zealand.
10. 30 years of course. 1618 to 1648.

POISON PENS >>>

Newspaper clippings:

A sign seen in a police canteen in Christchurch, New Zealand: 'Will the person who took a slice of cake from the Commissioner's Office return it immediately. It is needed as evidence in a poisoning case.'
– *The Guardian,* London.

A young girl who was blown out to sea on a set of inflatable teeth was rescued by a man on an inflatable lobster. A coastguard spokesman commented: 'This sort of thing is all too common these days.'
– *The Times.*

A sex line caller has complained to trading standards officers after dialling a number from an advertisement entitled 'Hear Me Moan'. The caller was played a tape of a woman nagging her husband for failing to do jobs around the house. Consumer watchdogs refused to look into the complaint, saying, 'He got what he deserved.'
– *The Citizen,* Gloucester.

Under the heading 'Brussels pays £200,000 to save prostitutes': '… the money will not be going directly into the prostitutes' pocket, but will be used to encourage them to lead a better life. We will be training them for new positions in hotels.'
– *Daily Telegraph,* London.

We apologise for the error in the last edition, in which we stated that Mr Fred Nicolme is a defective of the Police Force. This was a typographical error. We meant, of course, that Mr Nicolme is a detective in the Police Farce.
– *Derby Abbey Community News.*

After being charged 20 pounds for a 10-pound overdraft, 30-year-old Michael Howard of Leeds changed his name by deed poll to 'Yorkshire Bank PLC are Fascist Bastards'. The bank has now asked

him to close his account, and Mr Bastards has asked them to repay the 69p balance by cheque, made out in his new name.
– *The Guardian*.

Police, called to arrest a naked man on the platform at Piccadilly Station, released their suspect after he produced a valid rail ticket.
– *Manchester Evening News*.

'Would the Congregation please note that the bowl at the back of the church, labelled 'For the Sick' is for monetary donations only.'
– *Churchdown Parish Magazine*.

FLYING HIGH >>>

Airline employees' entertaining little quips – all real:

'Smoking in the lavatories is prohibited. Any person caught smoking in the lavatories will be asked to leave the plane immediately.'

Pilot: 'Folks, we have reached our cruising altitude now, so I am going to switch the seatbelt sign off. Feel free to move about as you wish, but please stay inside the plane till we land… it's a bit cold outside, and if you walk on the wings it affects the flight pattern.'

And after landing: 'Thank you for flying Business Express. We hope you enjoyed giving us the business as much as we enjoyed taking you for a ride.'

As a plane landed and was coming to a stop at Washington National, a voice comes over the loudspeaker, 'Whoa, big fella, whoa!'

After a particularly rough landing during thunderstorms in Memphis, a flight attendant announced, 'Please take care when opening the overhead compartments because, after a landing like that, sure as hell everything has shifted.'

From an airline employee: 'Welcome aboard Flight XXX to YYY. To operate your seatbelt, insert the metal tab into the buckle and pull tight. It works just like every other seatbelt and if you don't know how to operate one, you probably shouldn't be out in public unsupervised. In the event of a sudden loss of cabin pressure, oxygen masks will descend from the ceiling. Stop screaming, grab the mask and pull it over your face. If you have a small child travelling with you, secure your mask before assisting with theirs. If you are travelling with two small children, decide now which one you love more…

'Your seat cushions can be used for flotation, and in the event of an emergency water landing, please take them with our compliments.

'Should the cabin lose pressure, oxygen masks will drop from the overhead area. Please place the bag over your own mouth and nose before assisting children or adults acting like children.'

Just after a very hard landing in Salt Lake City, a flight attendant's voice came over the intercom and said: 'That was quite a bump and I know what y'all are thinking. I'm here to tell you it wasn't the airline's fault, it wasn't the pilot's fault, it wasn't the flight attendants' fault… it was the asphalt!'

Another flight attendant's comment on a less than perfect landing: 'We ask you to please remain seated as Captain Kangaroo bounces us to the terminal.'

After another hard landing, the first officer was finding it difficult to look anyone in the eye as they exited the plane. Almost everyone had got off the plane when this little old lady walking with a cane asked him, 'Sonny, mind if I ask you a question?'

'Why no ma'am,' said the pilot, 'what is it?'

The old lady said, 'Did we land or were we shot down?'

After a real crusher of a landing in Phoenix, the flight attendant came on with, 'Ladies and gentleman, please remain in your seats until Captain Crash and the crew have brought the aircraft to a screeching halt up against the gate. And, once the tyre smoke has cleared and the warning bells are silenced, we'll open the door and you can pick your way through the wreckage to the terminal.'

ELEMENTARY, MY DEAR WATSON >>>

Sherlock Holmes and Dr Watson went on a camping trip. After a good meal and a bottle of wine they lay down for the night, and went to sleep.

Some hours later, Holmes awoke and nudged his faithful friend. 'Watson, look up at the sky and tell me what you see.'

Watson replied, 'I see millions and millions of stars.'

Holmes: 'What does that tell you?'

Watson pondered for a minute. 'Astronomically, it tells me that there are millions of galaxies and potentially billions of planets. Astrologically, I observe that Saturn is in Leo. Horologically, I deduce that the time is approximately a quarter past three. Theologically, I can see that God is all-powerful and that we are small and insignificant. Meteorologically, I suspect that we will have a beautiful day tomorrow. What does it tell you?'

Holmes was silent for a minute, then spoke. 'Watson, you are positively stupid. Some bastard has stolen our tent.'

CATERING FOR THE LOWEST COMMON DENOMINATOR >>>

Labels for idiots:

On a hairdryer: **'Do not use while sleeping.'**
On a bag of chips: **'You could be a winner! No purchase necessary. Details inside.'**
On a bar of soap: **'Directions: use like regular soap.'**
On some frozen dinners: **'Serving suggestion: defrost.'**
On a hotel-provided shower cap in a box: **'Fits one head.'**
On packaged Tiramisu dessert (printed on bottom of the box): **'Do not turn upside down.'**
On packaged Bread Pudding: **'Product will be hot after heating.'**
On packaging for an iron: **'Do not iron clothes on body.'**
On children's cough medicine: **'Do not drive car or operate machinery.'**
On sleep aid: **'Warning: may cause drowsiness.'**
On a string of Chinese-made Christmas lights: **'For indoor or outdoor use only.'**
On peanuts: **'Warning: contains nuts.'**

On a packet of nuts: **'Instructions: open packet, eat nuts.'**
On a Swedish chainsaw: **'Do not attempt to stop chain with your hands or genitals.'**
On a child's Superman costume: **'Wearing of this garment does not enable you to fly.'**

PICKUP IN THE RAIN >>>

One night at 11.30 pm, an older African-American woman was standing on the side of an Alabama highway trying to endure a lashing rain storm. Her car had broken down and she desperately needed a lift.

Soaking wet, she decided to flag down the next car. A young white man stopped to help her – generally unheard of in those conflict-filled 1960s. The man took her to safety, helped her get assistance and put her into a taxi. She seemed to be in a big hurry. She wrote down his address, thanked him and drove away.

Seven days went by and a knock came on the man's door. To his surprise, a giant console colour TV was delivered to his home. A special note was attached. It read: 'Thank you so much for assisting me on the highway the other night. The rain drenched not only my clothes but my spirits. Then you came along. Because of you, I was able to make it to my dying husband's bedside just before he passed away. God bless you for helping me and unselfishly serving others.

Sincerely

Mrs Nat King Cole.'

GIVING BLOOD >>>

Many years ago, when I worked as a volunteer at Stanford Hospital, I got to know a little girl named Liz who was suffering from a rare and serious disease. Her only chance of recovery appeared to be a blood transfusion from her five-year-old brother, who had miraculously survived the same disease and had developed the antibodies needed to combat the illness. The doctor explained the situation to her little brother and asked the boy if he would be willing to give his blood to his sister. I saw him hesitate for only a moment before taking a deep breath and saying, 'Yes, I'll do it if it will save Liz.'

As the transfusion progressed, he lay in bed next to his sister and smiled, as we all did, seeing the colour returning to her cheeks.

Then his face grew pale and his smile faded. He looked up at the doctor and asked with a trembling voice, 'Will I start to die right away?'

Being young, the boy had misunderstood the doctor; he thought he was going to have to give his sister all of his blood.

Now, swallow hard to get rid of that lump in your throat!

ANOTHER TRUE STORY >>>

In Atlantic City, a woman won a bucketful of quarters at a slot machine. She took a break from the slots for dinner with her husband in the hotel dining room. But first she wanted to stash the quarters in her room.

'I'll be right back and we'll go to eat,' she told her husband and she carried the coin-laden bucket to the elevator. As she was about to walk into the elevator she noticed two men already aboard. Both were black.

One of them was big... very big... an intimidating figure. The woman froze.

Her first thought was: These two are going to rob me. Her next thought was: Don't be a bigot, they look like perfectly nice gentlemen.

But racial stereotypes are powerful, and fear immobilised her. She stood and stared at the two men. She felt anxious, flustered, and ashamed. She hoped they didn't read her mind, but knew they surely did; her hesitation about joining them on the elevator was all too obvious. Her face was flushed. She couldn't just stand there, so with a mighty effort of will she picked up one foot and stepped forward and followed with the other foot and was in the elevator.

Avoiding eye contact, she turned around stiffly and faced the elevator doors as they closed. A second passed, and then another second, and then another.

Her fear increased. The elevator didn't move. Panic consumed her. My God, she thought, I'm trapped and about to be robbed. Her heart plummeted.

Perspiration poured from every pore. Then... one of the men said, 'Hit the floor.'

Instinct told her: Do what they tell you. The bucket of quarters flew upwards as she threw out her arms and collapsed on the elevator carpet. A shower of coins rained down on her. Take my money and spare me, she prayed.

More seconds passed. She heard one of the men say politely, 'Ma'am, if you'll just tell us what floor you're going to, we'll push the button.'

The one who said it had a little trouble getting the words out. He was trying mightily to hold in a belly laugh. She lifted her head and looked up at the two men. They reached down to help her up. Confused, she struggled to her feet. 'When I told my man here to hit the floor,' said the average sized one, 'I meant that he should hit the elevator button for our floor. I didn't mean for you to hit the floor, ma'am.' He spoke genially. He bit his lip. It was obvious he was having a hard time not laughing.

She thought: My God, what a spectacle I've made of myself. She was too humiliated to speak. She wanted to blurt out an apology, but words failed her. How do you apologise to two perfectly respectable gentlemen for behaving as though they were going to rob you? She didn't know what to say.

The three of them gathered up the strewn quarters and refilled her bucket. When the elevator arrived at her floor, they insisted on walking her to her room.

She seemed a little unsteady on her feet, and they were afraid she might not make it down the corridor. At her door they bid her a good evening.

As she slipped into her room she could hear them roaring with laughter while they walked back to the elevator. The woman brushed herself off. She pulled herself together and went downstairs for dinner with her husband.

The next morning flowers were delivered to her room – a dozen roses. Attached to each rose was a crisp $100 bill. The card said: 'Thanks for the best laugh we've had in years.'

It was signed, 'Eddie Murphy and Michael Jordan.'

YOU WOULDN'T READ ABOUT IT! >>>

From a San Francisco newspaper – a particularly shitty day for this poor bugger:

Fire authorities in California found a corpse in a burnt-out section of forest while assessing the damage done by a forest fire.

The deceased male was dressed in a full wetsuit, complete with a dive tank, flippers, and facemask. A post-mortem examination revealed that the person died not from burns but from massive internal injuries.

Dental records provided a positive identification.

Investigators then set about determining how a fully clad diver ended up in the middle of a forest fire. It was revealed that, on the day of the fire, the person went for a diving trip off the coast – some 35 km away from the forest. The firefighters called in a fleet of helicopters with very large buckets. The buckets were dropped into the ocean for rapid filling, then flown to the forest fire and emptied.

You guessed it. One minute our diver was making like Flipper in the Pacific, the next thing he was doing a breaststroke in a fire bucket 100 m in the air. Apparently, he extinguished exactly 1.78 m of the fire.

From a Florida newspaper:

A man was working on his motorcycle on his patio and his wife was in the house in the kitchen. The man was racing the engine on the motorcycle and, somehow, the bike slipped into gear. The man, still holding the handlebars, was dragged through a glass patio door and along with the motorcycle dumped onto the floor inside the house.

The wife, hearing the crash, ran into the dining room, and found her husband lying on the floor, cut and bleeding, the motorcycle lying next to him and the patio door shattered. The wife ran to the phone and summoned an ambulance.

Because they lived on a fairly large hill, the wife went down the several flights of long steps to the street to direct the paramedics to her husband. After the ambulance arrived and transported the husband to the hospital, the wife pushed the motorcycle outside.

Seeing that gas had spilled on the floor, the wife obtained some papers towels, blotted up the petrol, and threw the towels in the toilet.

The husband was treated at the hospital and was released to come home. After arriving home, he looked at the shattered patio door and the damage done to his motorcycle. He became despondent, went into the bathroom, sat on the toilet and smoked a cigarette. After finishing the cigarette, he flipped it between his legs into the toilet bowl while still seated.

The wife, who was in the kitchen, heard a loud explosion and her husband screaming. She ran into the bathroom and found her husband lying on the floor. His trousers had been blown away and he had burns to the buttocks, the back of his legs and his groin. The wife again ran to the phone and called for an ambulance. The same ambulance crew was dispatched and the wife met them at the street.

The paramedics loaded the husband on the stretcher and began carrying him to the street. While they were going down the stairs to the street accompanied by the wife, one of the paramedics asked the wife how the husband had burned himself. She told them and the paramedics started laughing so hard, one of them tipped the stretcher and dumped the husband out. He fell down the remaining steps and broke his arm.

Some days it just doesn't pay to get out of bed.

MORONS OF THE WORLD UNITE

With a little help from our friends!
Police in Oakland, California, spent two hours attempting to subdue a gunman who had barricaded himself inside his home. After firing 10 teargas canisters, officers discovered that the man was standing beside them, shouting, 'Please come out and give yourself up!'

What was Plan B?
An Illinios man pretending to have a gun kidnapped a motorist and forced him to drive to two different automated teller machines. The kidnapper then proceeded to withdraw money from his own bank accounts.

These nitwits are teaching our children?
A nine-year-old boy in Manassas, Virginia, received a one-day suspension under his elementary school's drug policy last week – for Certs! Joey Hoeffer allegedly told a classmate that the mints would make him 'jump higher'.

and...
A student in Belle, West Virginia, was suspended for three days for giving a classmate a cough drop. School principal Forest Mann reiterated the school's 'zero-tolerance' policy (not to be confused with the 'zero-intelligence' policy).

They definitely saw this bloke coming

Fire investigators on Maui, Hawaii, have determined the cause of a blaze that destroyed a $127,000 home last month – a short in the homeowner's newly installed fire prevention alarm system. 'This is even worse than last year,' said the distraught homeowner, 'when someone broke in and stole my new security system.'

Working for your supper!

A man walked in to a Topeka, Kansas, Kwik Shop, and asked for all the money in the cash drawer. Apparently the take was too small, so he tied up the store clerk and worked the counter himself for three hours until police showed up and grabbed him.

Taking care of the competition

In Medford, Oregon, a 27-year-old jobless man with an MBA blamed his college degree for his murder of three people. 'There are too many business grads out there,' he said. 'If I had chosen another field, all this may not have happened.'

Me and my big mouth!

Police in Los Angeles had good luck with a robbery suspect who just couldn't control himself during a lineup. When detectives asked each man in the lineup to repeat the words, 'Give me all your money or I'll shoot,' the man shouted, 'That's not what I said!'

Burning a hole in the pocket!

A bank robber in Virginia Beach got a nasty surprise when a dye pack designed to mark stolen money exploded in his Fruit-of-the-Looms. The robber apparently stuffed the loot down the front of his pants as he was running out the door. 'He was seen hopping and jumping around,' said police spokesman Mike Carey, 'with an explosion taking place inside his pants.' Police have the man's charred trousers in custody.

My old man's a plonker!

A man spoke frantically into the phone, 'My wife is pregnant and her contractions are only two minutes apart!'

'Is this her first child?' the doctor asked.

'No, you idiot!' the man shouted. 'This is her husband!'

Not the sharpest knife in the drawer!
In Modesto, California, Steven Richard King was arrested for trying to hold up a Bank of America branch without a weapon. King used a thumb and a finger to simulate a gun, but unfortunately, he failed to keep his hand in his pocket.

POLLY POKES THE BORAX >>>

There was this bloke on a plane trying to get a drink. He tried to get the hostess' attention by catching her eye. All of a sudden, the parrot sitting next to him leans across and squawks, 'Oy you, y'deaf tart. Get me a f***ing whisky.'

Hurriedly the stewardess brings the parrot the drink, but ignores the bloke. The parrot downed it in one and screams out again, 'Oy you! Yeah you with the tarty wonderbra and plastic face. Bring me another whisky.'

The stewardess rushes over and serves the parrot. The bloke still can't get her attention, but being the clever type, realises where he is going wrong. The bloke shouts out, 'Oy you! You with the trampish hair. Yeah you, you f***wit. Bring me a bloody whisky.'

The stewardess hurriedly rushes off to the back of the plane and then reappears with two huge blokes and points at the bloke and the parrot. A moment later during free fall to imminent death, the parrot turns to the bloke and says, 'You know, for someone who can't fly, you're a cheeky bastard.'

S-S-STUTTERING ALONG >>>

A huge muscular guy with a bad stutter goes to a counter in a department store and asks, 'W-w-w-w-where's the m-m-m-men's dep-p-p-artment? The man behind the counter just looks at him and says nothing. The man repeats himself, 'W-w-w-where's the m-m-men's dep-p-partment?' Again the clerk doesn't answer him.

The guy asks several more times, 'W-w-w-where's the m-m-m-en's dep-p-artment?' and the clerk just seems to ignore him. Finally the guy is angry and storms off. The customer who was waiting behind the stutterer asks the clerk, 'Why wouldn't you answer that guy's question?'

The clerk answers, 'D-d-d-do you th-th-th-think I w-w-w-want to get b-b-beaten up-p?'

Two French Legionnaires had been separated from their unit in the desert and they were lost. They'd been wandering for several days without food and water and were nearly resigned to the fact that they would soon die from dehydration.

Suddenly, at the top of yet another sand dune, they see a big, bustling market laid out before them.

Naturally they can't believe their eyes and think it's a mirage, but as they draw closer, they can hear the stallholders' cries and they eventually reach the market and realise it is really there.

So the legionnaires rush up to the first stall they can and cry to the stallholder, 'Sir, sir, we have been travelling in the desert for many days and have had no food or water. We shall surely die soon unless you have some you can sell us. Tell us, do you have any sustenance for us?'

The stallholder shakes his head and replies, 'I'm sorry, French Legionnaire-type people, but all I have to sell is a load of bowls full of jelly, topped with custard and cream and lovingly sprinkled with hundreds and thousands.'

The legionnaires look at each other, mildly surprised, and move on to the next stall, where they ask the stallholder, 'Mr Purveyor of fine foodstuffs and the like, we have been travelling in the desert for days, deprived of the necessary beverages and foodstuffs that are required for survival. We shall surely die soon unless you can sell us some skins of water.'

The stallholder looks at them embarrassedly and confesses, 'Gentlemen, tragic as I admit it is, I have none of the ingredients necessary to life for which you ask me. All I have to sell is this large bowl of jelly topped with custard and cream and sprinkled with hundreds and thousands, with a little cocktail cherry in the middle at the top. I cannot help you.'

The legionnaires look at each other in desperation and run on to the next stall, where they demand of the stallholder, 'Look mate,' ['cos they'd stopped talking funny all of a sudden] 'we need water or we'll die. We've been travelling without water for days and need some now. Do you have any you can sell us?'

The stallholder looks at his curl-ended shoes in shame as he confesses, 'Sorry, fellas, all I have to sell you is a bowl of jelly, with custard, cream and hundreds and thousands. I can't help you. I'll have to condemn you to a long and lingering death through dehydration.'

The legionnaires are really worried by this point and they go through the market, stall by stall, asking each stallholder whether they had any water they could sell them to save their lives, but each stallholder gave the same reply. All they had to sell was a bowl of jelly with cream, custard and hundreds and thousands.

Dejected and resigned to their grim fate, the legionnaires leave the desert market and walk off into the setting sun. As they do so, one turns to the other and says, 'That was really odd. A big market in the middle of nowhere and all they sold was bowls of jelly with custard, cream and hundreds and thousands.'

The other turns to face his companion and replies, 'Yes, it was a trifle bazaar.'

LUCKY LAS VEGAS >>>

A guy gets home from work one night and hears a voice. The voice tells him, 'Quit your job, sell your house, take your money, go to Vegas.'

The man is disturbed at what he hears and ignores the voice. The next day when he gets home from work, the same thing happens. The voice tells him, 'Quit your job, sell your house, take your money, go to Vegas.' Again the man ignores the voice, though he is very troubled by the event.

Every day, day after day, the man hears the same voice when he gets home from work, 'Quit your job, sell your house, take your money, go to Vegas.'

Each time the man hears the voice he becomes increasingly upset. Finally, after two weeks, he succumbs to the pressure. He does quit his job, sells his house, and takes his money and heads to Vegas.

The moment the man gets off the plane in Vegas the voice tells him, 'Go to Harrah's.' So he hops in a cab and rushes over to Harrah's. As soon as he sets foot in the casino, the voice tells him, 'Go to the roulette table.'

The man does as he is told. When he gets to the roulette table, the voice tells him, 'Put all your money on 17.' Nervously the man cashes in his money for chips and then puts them all on 17.

The dealer wishes the man good luck and spins the roulette

wheel. Around and around the ball spins. The man anxiously watches the ball as it slowly loses speed until finally it settles into number… 21.

The voice says, 'Bugger.'

NO ROOM AT THE INN >>>

By the time the sailor pulled into Greymouth, every hotel room was taken. 'You've got to have a room somewhere,' he pleaded. 'Or just a bed, I don't care where.'

'Well, I do have a double room with one occupant – an air force guy,' admitted the manager of the last hotel he'd tried, 'and he might be glad to split the cost. But to tell you the truth, he snores so loudly that people in adjoining rooms have complained in the past. I'm not sure it'd be worth it to you.'

'No problem,' the tired navy man assured him. 'I'll take it.'

The next morning, the sailor came down to breakfast bright-eyed and bushy-tailed.

'How'd you sleep?' asked the manager.

'Never better.'

The manager was impressed. 'No problem with the other guy snoring?'

'Nope. I shut him up in no time,' said the navy guy.

'How'd you manage that?' asked the manager.

'He was already in bed, snoring away, when I came into the room,' the sailor explained. 'I went over, gave him a kiss on the cheek, and said, "Goodnight beautiful," and he sat up all night watching me.'

LOAD OF BULL >>>

Three bulls heard via the grapevine that the farmer was going to bring yet another bull onto the farm, and this prospect raised a discussion among them.

First Bull: *'Boys, we all know I have been here for five years. Once we settled our differences, we agreed on which 100 of the cows would be mine. I don't know where this newcomer is going to get his cows, but I ain't givin' him any of mine.'*

Second Bull: *'That pretty much says it for me too. I've been here three years and have earned my right to the 50 cows we*

have agreed are mine. I'll fight him off or kill him, but I'm keeping all my cows.'
Third Bull: *'I've only been here a year and so far you guys have only let me have 10 cows to take care of. I may not be as big as you fellows yet, but I am young and virile, so I simply must keep all my cows.'*
They had just finished their big talk when an 18-wheeler pulls up in the middle of the paddock with only one animal in it. It was the biggest son-of-another-bull these guys had ever seen. At 2000 kg, each step he took toward the ground strained the steel ramp to breaking point.
First Bull: *'Ahem… you know, it's actually been some time since I really felt I was doing all my cows justice. Anyway, I think I can spare a few for our new friend.'*
Second Bull: *'I'll have plenty of cows to take care of if I just stay on the opposite side the paddock from him. I'm certainly not looking for an argument.'*
They look over at their young friend, the Third Bull, and find him pawing the dirt, shaking his horns and snorting.
First Bull: *'Son, let me give you some advice real quick. Let him have some of your cows and live to tell about it.'*
Third Bull: *'Hell, he can have all my cows. I'm just making sure he knows I'm a bull.'*

LOVE A DUCK >>>

This guy walks into a quiet bar. He is carrying three ducks. One in each hand and one under his left arm. He places them on the bar, has a few drinks and chats with the barman.

The barman is experienced and has learned not to ask people about the animals they bring into the pub, so he doesn't mention the ducks.

They chat for about 30 minutes before the guy with the ducks has to go to the toilet, leaving the ducks on the bar.

The barman is alone with the ducks. There is an awkward silence and the barman decides to try and make some conversation.

'What's your name?' he says to the first duck. 'Huey,' replies the first duck.

'How's your day been, Huey?'

'Great. Lovely day. Had a ball. Been in and out of puddles all day.'

'Oh, that's nice,' says the barman. Then he says to the second duck, 'Hi. And what is your name?'

'Dewey,' came the answer.

'So how's your day been, Dewey?'

'Great. Lovely day. Had a ball. Been in and out of puddles all day. If I had the chance another day I would do the same again.'

So the barman turns to the third duck and says, 'So, you must be Louie?'

'No,' growls the third duck, 'My name is Puddles. And don't ask me about my f***ing day.'

ELEPHANT-ITIS >>>

Bob goes to the doctor and says, 'Doc, I'm having trouble getting my penis erect, can you help me?'

After a complete examination, the doctor tells him, 'Well, the problem with you is that the muscles around the base of your penis are damaged. There's really nothing we can do for you unless you are willing to try an experimental treatment.'

Bob asks sadly, 'What is this treatment?'

'Well,' the doctor says, 'What we should do is take the muscles from the trunk of a baby elephant and implant them in your penis.'

Bob thinks about it silently and says, 'Well, the thought of going through life without ever having sex again is too much. Let's go for it.'

A few weeks after the operation, Bob was given the green light to use his improved equipment. He planned a romantic evening with his girlfriend and took her to one of the nicest restaurants in the city.

In the middle of dinner, he felt a stirring between his legs that continued to the point of being uncomfortable. To release the pressure Bob unzipped his fly.

His penis immediately sprang from his pants, went to the top of the table, grabbed a roll and returned to his pants. His girlfriend was stunned at first and then said with a sly smile. 'That was incredible. Can you do that again?'

Bob replied, 'Well, I guess so, but I don't think I can fit another roll in my arse.'

GOOSEBUMPS >>>

After the Falklands War, a British regiment commander was addressing some troops under his command who had heroically performed above and beyond the call of duty.

He informed them that Her Majesty's Army had committed to reward each of the three soldiers £100 per inch of distance between two different parts of the man's body.

The commander addressed the first soldier. 'Where would you like to be measured, Sergeant?'

'From the tip of me head to the soles of me feet, Sir,' he replied.

'Very good,' the commander said, and the sergeant was measured at 6'5" and was paid the handsome sum of £7700.

The second soldier was asked, 'What about you, Corporal?'

'Between the tips of the fingers of me outstretched arms, Sir,' the corporal said.

'Very good,' said the commander and the corporal, a man of considerable wingspan, was rewarded with 8000 quid.

'And you, Private, where would you like to be measured?'

'From the tip of me penis to the base of me balls, Sir,' retorted the private.

The commander replied, 'I must admit this is quite an unusual request, Private, but it's your decision.'

He ordered the private to drop his pants for the ensuing measurement. Immediately the commander's mouth fell agape and he stammered, 'Where in God's name are your gonads, Private?'

The private proclaimed, 'Goose Green, Falkland Islands, Sir!'

BLAME THE MUESLI! >>>

A man was found murdered in his home over the weekend. Detectives at the scene found the man face down in his bath. The bath had been filled with milk and the deceased had a banana protruding from his buttocks.

Police suspect a cereal killer...

GIVING THE FINGER >>>

A little history lesson:

Before the Battle of Agincourt in 1415, the French, anticipating victory over the English, proposed to cut off the middle finger of all captured English soldiers. Without the middle finger it would be impossible to draw the renowned English longbow and therefore they would be incapable of fighting in the future.

This famous weapon was made of the native English yew tree, and the act of drawing the longbow was known as 'plucking the yew' (or 'pluck yew'). The English got wind of the French plan to do away with their middle digits and much to the bewilderment of the French, the English won a major upset and began mocking the French by waving their middle fingers at the defeated army, saying, 'See, we can still pluck yew.'

Since pluck yew is rather difficult to say, the difficult consonant cluster at the beginning has gradually changed to a labiodental fricative 'F', and thus the words often used in conjunction with the one-finger-salute are mistakenly thought to have something to do with an intimate encounter.

It is also because of the pheasant feathers on the arrows used with the longbow that the symbolic gesture is known as 'giving the bird'.

And yew thought yew knew everything... well, now you do!

MOANING MOGGIE >>>

Day 752 – My captors continue to torment me with bizarre little dangling objects. They dine lavishly on fresh meat, while I am forced to subsist on dry cereal. The only thing that keeps me going is the hope of eventual escape, and the mild satisfaction I get from occasionally ruining some piece of their furniture. I fear I may be going insane. Yesterday, I ate a houseplant. Tomorrow I may eat another.

Day 761 – Today my attempt to kill my captors by weaving around their feet while they were walking almost succeeded, must try this at the top of the stairs. In an attempt to disgust and repulse these vile oppressors, I once again induced myself to vomit on their favourite chair... must try this on their bed.

Day 762 – Slept all day so that I could annoy my captors with sleep-depriving, incessant pleas for food at ungodly hours of the night.

Day 765 – Decapitated a mouse and brought them the headless body, in an attempt to make them aware of what I am capable of, and to try to strike fear into their hearts. They only cooed and condescended about what a good little cat I was… Hmmm. Not working according to plan.

Day 768 – I am finally aware of how sadistic they are. For no good reason I was chosen for water torture. This time however it included a burning foamy chemical called 'shampoo'. What sick minds could invent such a liquid? My only consolation is the piece of thumb still stuck between my teeth.

Day 771 – There was some sort of gathering of their accomplices. I was placed in solitary throughout the event. However, I could hear the noise and smell the foul odour of the glass tubes they call 'beer'. More importantly I overheard that my confinement was due to MY power of 'allergies'. Must learn what this is and how to use it to my advantage.

Day 774 – I am convinced the other captives are flunkies and may be snitches. The dog is routinely released and seems more than happy to return. He is obviously a half-wit. The bird, on the other hand, has got to be an informant. He has mastered their frightful tongue (something akin to mole speak) and speaks with them regularly. I am certain he reports my every move. Due to his current placement in the metal room, his safety is assured. But I can wait, it is only a matter of time…

WHO SAID CANADIANS HAD NO SENSE OF HUMOUR? >>>

Quotes from the Montreal comedy festival:

On going to war over religion: 'You're basically killing each other to see who's got the better imaginary friend.' – Rich Jeni.

On the difference between men and women: 'On the one hand, we'll never experience childbirth. On the other hand, we can open all our own jars.' – Jeff Green.

'And God said: "Let there be Satan, so people don't blame everything on me. And let there be lawyers, so people don't blame everything on Satan."' – John Wing.

'What are the three words guaranteed to humiliate men everywhere? – "Hold my purse."' – François Morency.

'The Web brings people together because no matter what kind of a twisted sexual mutant you happen to be, you've got millions of pals out there. Type in "Find people that have sex with goats that are on fire" and the computer will say, "Specify type of goat."' – Rich Jeni.

'Luge strategy? Lie flat and try not to die.' – Tim Steeves.

'Women might be able to fake orgasms. But men can fake whole relationships.' – Jimmy Shubert.

'There are only two reasons to sit in the back row of an aeroplane: either you have diarrhoea, or you're anxious to meet people who do.' – Rich Jeni.

'My girlfriend always laughs during sex – no matter what she's reading.' – Emo Philips.

'What's with squeegee kids? I mean, they don't really wash the windshield, do they? They simply redistribute the dirt.' – Ken Scott.
'Clinton lied. A man might forget where he parks or where he lives, but he never forgets [oral sex] no matter how bad it is.' – Lenny Clarke.

'My cousin just died. He was only 19. He got stung by a bee – the natural enemy of a tightrope walker.' – Emo Philips.

'I saw a woman wearing a sweatshirt with "Guess" on it. I said, "Thyroid problem?"' – Emo Philips.

'Honesty is the key to a relationship. If you can fake that, you're in.' – Rich Jeni.

'Hockey is a sport for white men. Basketball is a sport for black men. Golf is a sport for white men dressed like black pimps.' – Ren Hicks.

'Something you'll never hear a woman say: "My, what an attractive scrotum!"' – Jeff Green.

'I read somewhere that 77 percent of all the mentally ill live in poverty. Actually, I'm more intrigued by the 23 percent who are apparently doing quite well for themselves.' – Emo Philips.

'My parents saw the president they loved get shot in the head. I saw my president get head.' – Elon Gold.

'I discovered I scream the same way whether I'm about to be devoured by a Great White or if a piece of seaweed touches my foot.' – Kevin James.

'Capital punishment turns the state into a murderer. But imprisonment turns the state into a gay dungeon-master.' – Emo Philips.

'My mother never saw the irony in calling me "a son-of-a-bitch".' – Rich Jeni.

CREATURES OF HABIT

A farmer buys several sheep, hoping to breed them for wool and meat. After several weeks, he notices that none of the sheep are getting pregnant and phones a vet for help.

The vet tells the farmer that he should try artificial insemination. The farmer doesn't have the slightest idea what this means but, not wanting to display his ignorance, only asks the vet how he will know when the sheep are pregnant.

The vet tells him that they will stop standing around and will, instead, lie down in the grass and roll around when they are pregnant. The farmer hangs up and gives it some thought. He comes to the conclusion that artificial insemination means that he has to impregnate the sheep.

So, he loads the sheep into his truck, drives them out into the woods, has sex with them all, brings them back and goes to bed.

Next morning, he wakes and looks out at the sheep. Seeing that they are all still standing around, he concludes that the first try did not take and loads them into the truck again. He drives them out to the woods, bangs each sheep twice for good measure, and brings them back and goes to bed.

Next morning, he wakes to find the sheep still just standing around. One more try, he tells himself, and proceeds to load them up and drive them out to the woods. He spends all day shagging the sheep and, upon returning home, falls listlessly into bed.

The next morning, he cannot even raise himself from the bed to look at the sheep. He asks his wife to look out and tell him if the sheep are lying in the grass.

'No,' she says, 'they're all in the truck and one of them is honking the horn!'

A REAL TONIC >>>

A polar bear goes into a pub and says, 'Can I have a gin and...

....

.... tonic please.'

The barman serves him and says, 'Why the large pause?'

The polar bear replies, 'Don't know, I've always had them.'

NO WONDER 'FRIENDLY FIRE' IS A PROBLEM! >>>

'Squawks' are problems noted by US air force pilots and left for maintenance crews to fix before the next flight. Here are some actual maintenance complaints logged by those air force pilots and the replies from the maintenance crews.

(P) = Problem (S) = Solution

(P) Left inside main tyre almost needs replacement.
(S) Almost replaced left inside main tyre.

(P) Test flight OK, except auto-land very rough.
(S) Auto-land not installed on this aircraft.

(P) Something loose in cockpit.
(S) Something tightened in cockpit.

(P) No. 2 propeller seeping prop fluid.
(S) No. 2 propeller seepage normal – No. 1, No. 3, and No. 4 propellers lack normal seepage.

(P) Evidence of leak on right main landing gear.
(S) Evidence removed.

(P) DME volume unbelievably loud.
(S) Volume set to more believable level.

(P) Dead bugs on windshield.
(S) Live bugs on order.

(P) Autopilot in altitude-hold mode produces a 200 fpm descent.
(S) Cannot reproduce problems on ground.

(P) IFF inoperative.
(S) IFF always inoperative in OFF mode.

(P) Friction locks cause throttle levers to stick.
(S) That's what they're there for.

(P) No. 3 engine missing.
(S) Engine found on right wing after brief search.

(P) Aircraft handles funny.
(S) Aircraft warned to straighten up, 'fly right', and be serious.

(P) Target Radar hums.
(S) Reprogrammed Target Radar with the words.

A MOTTO A DAY >>>

- Save the whales. Collect the whole set.
- A day without sunshine is like night.
- On the other hand, you have different fingers.
- I got lost in thought. It was unfamiliar territory.
- 42.7 percent of all statistics are made on the spot.
- 99 percent of lawyers give the rest a bad name.
- I feel like I'm diagonally parked in a parallel universe.

- You have the right to remain silent. Anything you say will be misquoted then used against you.
- Honk if you love peace and quiet.
- Remember half the people you know are below average.
- Despite the cost of living, have you noticed how popular it remains?
- Atheism is a non-prophet organisation.
- He who laughs last thinks slowest.
- Depression is merely anger without enthusiasm.
- Eagles may soar, but weasels don't get sucked into jet engines.
- The early bird may get the worm, but the second mouse gets the cheese.
- I drive way too fast to worry about cholesterol.
- I intend to live forever – so far so good.
- Borrow money from a pessimist – they don't expect it back.
- If Barbie is so popular, why do you have to buy her friends?
- Quantum mechanics: the dreams stuff are made of.
- The only substitute for good manners is fast reflexes.
- Support bacteria – they're the only culture some people have.
- When everything's coming your way, you're in the wrong lane and going the wrong way.
- If at first you don't succeed, destroy all evidence that you tried.
- A conclusion is the place where you got tired of thinking.
- Experience is something you don't get until just after you need it.
- For every action, there is an equal and opposite criticism.
- Bills travel through the mail at twice the speed of cheques.
- Never do card tricks for the group you play poker with.
- No one is listening until you make a mistake.
- Success always occurs in private and failure in full view.
- The colder the x-ray table, the more of your body is required on it.
- The hardness of butter is directly proportional to the softness of the bread.
- The severity of the itch is inversely proportional to the ability to reach it.
- To steal ideas from one person is plagiarism; to steal from many is research.
- To succeed in politics, it is often necessary to rise above your principles.

- Monday is an awful way to spend one-seventh of your life.
- You never really learn to swear until you learn to drive.
- Two wrongs are only the beginning.
- The problem with the gene pool is that there is no lifeguard.
- The sooner you fall behind, the more time you'll have to catch up.
- A clear conscience is usually the sign of a bad memory.
- Change is inevitable except from vending machines.
- Get a new car for your spouse – it'll be a great trade.
- Plan to bc spontaneous – tomorrow.
- Always try to be modest and be proud of it.
- Love may be blind but marriage is a real eye-opener.
- If at first you don't succeed, then skydiving isn't for you.

INDYCAR RACING >>>

One day a hunter was walking through the woods and he spotted an Indian chief being chased by a grizzly bear. So the hunter pulled out his trusty rifle and shot the bear, thus saving the chief's life.

The chief invited the hunter back to his camp to throw him one heck of a bash for saving his life. There was plenty of food. Indians were dancing all over the place with happiness. They were smoking the peace pipe when the chief said to the hunter, 'I have a very special surprise for you. I've picked 500 of my prettiest Indian maidens. You look at all of them and chose one, she will be your wife.'

With this the Indian chief clapped his hands and out of several tepees emerged young beautiful Indian maidens. They walked in front of the hunter so he could get a better view of them. The hunter noticed that all of the maidens were topless. And with closer inspection, noticed that none had any nipples on their breasts.

He turned to the chief and asked why didn't any of his maidens have nipples.

The chief replied, 'What, you've never heard of the Indian Nipple-less 500?'

THAW IN RELATIONS >>>

David received a parrot for his birthday. The parrot was fully grown with a bad attitude and worse vocabulary. Every other word was an expletive. Thosc that weren't expletives were, to say the least, rude.

David tried hard to change the bird's attitude and was constantly saying polite words, playing soft music, anything he could think of to try to set a good example.

Nothing worked. He yelled at the bird and the bird yelled back. He shook the bird and the bird just got angrier and ruder.

Finally, in a moment of desperation, David put the parrot in the freezer.

For a few moments he heard the bird squawk and kick and scream. Then suddenly there was quiet. Not a sound for half a minute. David was frightened that he might have hurt the bird and quickly opened the freezer door.

The parrot calmly stepped onto David's extended arm and said, 'I believe I may have offended you with my rude language and actions. I will endeavour at once to correct my behaviour. I really am truly sorry and beg your forgiveness.'

David was astonished at the bird's change in attitude and was about to ask what had made such a dramatic change when the parrot continued, 'May I ask what the chicken did?'

CLASSIC BUMPER STICKERS >>>

- Constipated people don't give a crap.
- Practise safe sex: go screw yourself.
- Accidents cause people.
- Who lit the fuse on your tampon?
- If you don't believe in oral sex, keep your mouth shut.
- If that phone was up your butt, maybe you could drive a little better.
- My kid got your honour roll student pregnant.
- Thank you for pot smoking.
- To all you virgins: thanks for nothing.
- Impotence: nature's way of saying 'no hard feelings'.
- If you can read this, I've lost my trailer.
- If you're not a haemorrhoid, get off my arse.
- You're just jealous because the voices are talking to me.
- I have the body of a god – Buddha.
- So many pedestrians – so little time.
- Cleverly disguised as a responsible adult.
- If we quit voting will they all go away?
- Eat right, exercise, and die anyway.

- Honk if anything falls off.
- He who hesitates is not only lost but also miles from the next exit.
- I haven't lost my mind; it's backed up on disk somewhere.
- If you can read this, the bitch fell off (back of a biker's vest).
- Necrophilia: that uncontrollable urge to crack open a cold one.
- Body by Nautilus; brain by Mattel.
- Boldly going nowhere.
- Caution – driver legally blonde!
- Don't be sexist – broads hate that.
- How many roads must a man travel down before he admits he's lost?
- Money isn't everything, but it sure keeps the kids in touch.
- What has four legs and an arm? A happy pit bull.

A DICKTAKER

A guy goes to the doctor and stutters, 'DDDDDoctor, yyyou ggggot ttto help me. III can't ssstop this stuttering.'

The doc says, 'Well I am not a speech therapist but I will give you a physical exam to see if everything checks out.' So, the doc gives him a physical and tells the guy, 'I found the problem. It's your dick, it's about 6 inches too long. I can cut off 6 inches and you will stop stuttering.'

The guy thinks for a minute and stutters back, 'WWWWell IIII don't kkknow doc I had bbbetter tttalk it oooover with my wwwwwife.'

The next day the guy returns and says 'OOOOK ddddoc mmmmmy wwwwife ccan't stand tttthis stuttering. Go ahead.'

The doc goes ahead with the operation and six months later the guy returns to the doctor's office and tells the him in beautiful unbroken English, 'Doc, the operation worked perfectly. I have not stuttered one word in six months. There is only one problem, I cannot satisfy my wife, you have to sew that 6 inches back on.'

The doc looks at him and thinks for a minute then says, 'FFFFF off.'

Things you would never know without movies:

- Large, loft-style apartments in New York are well within the price range of most people – whether they are employed or not.
- Should you decide to defuse a bomb, don't worry which wire to cut. You will always choose the right one.
- Most laptop computers are powerful enough to override the communications system of any invading alien society.
- It does not matter if you are heavily outnumbered in a fight involving martial arts – your enemies will wait patiently to attack you one by one by dancing around in a threatening manner until you have knocked out their predecessors.
- When you turn out the light to go to bed, everything in your bedroom will still be clearly visible, just slightly bluish.
- If you are blonde and pretty, it is possible to become a world expert on nuclear fission at the age of 22.
- Honest and hard-working policemen are traditionally gunned down three days before their retirement.
- Rather than wasting bullets, megalomaniacs prefer to kill their arch-enemies using complicated machinery involving fuses, pulley systems, deadly gases, lasers, and man-eating sharks, which will allow their captives at least 20 minutes to escape.
- During all police investigations, it will be necessary to visit a strip club at least once.
- All beds have special L-shaped cover sheets that reach up to armpit level on a woman but only to waist level on the man lying beside her.
- All grocery shopping bags contain at least one stick of French bread.
- Once applied, lipstick will never rub off – even while scuba diving.
- You're very likely to survive any battle in any war unless you make the mistake of showing someone a picture of your sweetheart back home.
- Should you wish to pass yourself off as a German or Russian officer, it will not be necessary to speak the language. A German or Russian accent will do.
- The Eiffel Tower can be seen from any window in Paris.
- A man will show no pain while taking the most ferocious

beating but will wince when a woman tries to clean his wounds.

- If a large pane of glass is visible, someone will be thrown through it before long.
- If staying in a haunted house, women should investigate any strange noises in their most revealing underwear.
- Word processors never display a cursor on screen but will always say, 'Enter Password Now'.
- Even when driving down a perfectly straight road, it is necessary to turn the steering wheel vigorously from left to right every few moments.
- A detective can only solve a case once he has been suspended from duty.
- If you decide to start dancing in the street, everyone you meet will know all the steps.
- Police departments give their officers personality tests to make sure they are deliberately assigned a partner who is their total opposite.
- When they are alone, all foreign military officers prefer to speak to each other in English.

MIGHTY MOUSE >>>

Three mice are sitting at a bar in a pretty rough neighbourhood late at night trying to impress each other about how tough they are. The first mouse pours a shot of scotch, slams the glass onto the bar, turns to the second mouse and says, 'When I see a mousetrap, I lie on my back and set it off with my foot. When the bar comes down, I catch it in my teeth, bench press it 20 times to work up an appetite, and then make off with the cheese.'

The second mouse orders up two shots of bourbon, slams each glass into the bar, turns to the first mouse, and replies: 'Yeah, well, when I see rat poison, I collect as much as I can, take it home, grind it into a powder, and add it to my coffee each morning so I can get a good buzz going for the rest of the day.'

The first mouse and the second mouse then turn to the third mouse. The third mouse lets out a long sigh and says to the first two, 'I don't have time for this bullshit. I gotta go home and f*** the cat.'

'It's a great advantage to be able to hurdle with both legs.' – David Coleman.

'We now have exactly the same situation as we had at the start of the race, only exactly the opposite.' – Murray Walker.

'We didn't underestimate them. They were a lot better than we thought.' – Bobby Robson.

'And with an alphabetical irony, Nigeria follows New Zealand.' – David Coleman.

'Don't sit on the fence Terry. What chance do you think Germany has of getting through?' Terry Venables: 'I think it's 50-50.' – Jimmy Hill

'We actually got the winner three minutes from the end but then they equalised.' – Ian McNail.

'I never comment on referees and I'm not going to break the habit of a lifetime for that prat.' – Ron Atkinson.

'I was in a no-win situation, so I'm glad that I won rather than lost.' – Frank Bruno.

'There's going to be a real ding-dong when the bell goes.' – David Coleman.

'There is Brendan Foster, by himself, with 20,000 people.' – David Coleman.

'The lead car is absolutely unique, except for the one behind it which is identical.' – Murray Walker.

'She's not Ben Johnson – but then who is?' – David Coleman.

'I owe a lot to my parents, especially my mother and father.' – Greg Norman.

‘Sure there have been injuries and deaths in boxing but none of them serious.’ – Alan Minter.

‘The racecourse is as level as a billiard ball.’ – John Francombe.
‘Playing with wingers is more effective against European sides like Brazil than English sides like Wales.’ – Ron Greenwood.

‘That’s inches away from being millimetre perfect.’ – Ted Lowe.

‘Bobby Gould thinks I’m trying to stab him in the back. In fact I’m right behind him.’ – Stuart Pearson.

‘Lara’s chanced his arm, and it’s come off.’ – Brian Johnston.

from the workstation

This is surely where the majority of funny e-mails emanate from. You're sitting at your computer bored rigid; the sun's streaming through the window and the heat is frying your brain. The job at hand must surely suffer. So you nip out for a fag or a cup of strong coffee because you're trying to stay awake. But you're only delaying the inevitable. When you arrive back at the workstation, the sun's still shining in and the air-conditioning's buggered, the task at hand is mind-numbingly boring and it's still two hours till knock-off time. That's when a bit of extra-curricular e-mail matter hits you between the ears. Who can I take the piss out of now?

DILBERT'S WORDS OF WISDOM AND LAW >>>

- I can only please one person per day. Today is not your day. Tomorrow is not looking good either.
- I love deadlines. I especially like the whooshing sound they make as they go flying by.
- Tell me what you need, and I'll tell you how to get along without it.
- Accept that some days you are the pigeon, and some days, the statue.
- Needing someone is like needing a parachute. If he isn't there the first time, chances are you won't be needing him again.
- I don't have an attitude problem; you have a perception problem.
- My reality check bounced.
- On the keyboard of life, always keep one finger on the escape key.
- I don't suffer from stress. I am a carrier.
- You are slower than a herd of turtles stampeding through peanut butter.
- Do not meddle in the affairs of dragons, because you are crunchy and taste good with ketchup.
- Everybody is somebody else's weirdo.
- Never argue with an idiot. They drag you down to their level, then beat you with experience.
- A pat on the back is only a few centimetres from a kick in the arse.
- Don't be irreplaceable – if you can't be replaced, you can't be promoted.
- After any salary rise, you will have less money at the end of the month than you did before.
- The more crap you put up with, the more crap you are going to get.
- You can go anywhere you want if you look serious and carry a clipboard.
- Eat one live toad first thing in the morning and nothing worse will happen to you for the rest of the day.
- When bosses talk about improving productivity, they are never talking about themselves.

- If at first you don't succeed, try again. Then quit. No use being a damn fool about it.
- There will always be beer cans rolling on the floor of your car when the boss asks for a ride home from the office.
- Everything can be filed under 'miscellaneous'.
- Never delay the ending of a meeting or the beginning of a cocktail hour.
- To err is human; to forgive is not our policy.
- Anyone can do any amount of work provided it isn't the work he or she is supposed to be doing.
- Important letters that contain no errors will develop errors in the mail.
- If you are good, you will be assigned all the work. If you are really good, you will get out of it.
- You are always doing something marginal when the boss drops by your desk.
- People who go to conferences are the ones who shouldn't.
- If it wasn't for the last minute, nothing would get done.
- At work, the authority of a person is inversely proportional to the number of pens that person is carrying.
- When you don't know what to do, walk fast and look worried.
- Following the rules will not get the job done.
- Getting the job done is no excuse for not following the rules.
- When confronted by a difficult problem, you can solve it more easily by reducing it to the question, 'How would the Lone Ranger handle this?'
- The last person that quit or was fired will be held responsible for everything that goes wrong.

A HI-TECH DOODLE >>>

Finally, something other than smiley faces... :-)

(o)(o)	perfect breasts
(+)(+)	fake silicone breasts
(*)(*)	high nipple breasts
(@)(@)	big nipple breasts

oo A cups

{O} {O} D cups

(oYo) wonderbra breasts

(^)(^) cold breasts

(o)(O) lopsided breasts

(Q)(O) pierced breasts

(p)(p) hanging tassels breasts

\o/\o/ Grandma's breasts

(–)(–) flat against the shower door breasts

|o||o| android breasts

($)($) Elle Macpherson's breasts

POSTMAN'S KNOCK >>>

It was George the postie's last day on the job after 35 years of carrying the mail through all kinds of weather to the same neighbourhood. When he arrived at the first house on his route, he was greeted by the whole family there, who roundly and soundly congratulated him and sent him on his way with a tidy gift envelope.

At the second house they presented him with a box of fine cigars. The folks at the third house handed him a selection of terrific fishing lures. At the fourth house he was met at the door by a strikingly beautiful woman in a revealing negligee. She took him by the hand, gently led him through the door (which she closed behind him) and led him up the stairs to the bedroom where she blew his mind with the most passionate love he had ever experienced.

When he had enough they went downstairs, where she fixed him a giant breakfast of eggs, potatoes, ham, sausage, blueberry waffles and freshly squeezed orange juice.

When he was truly satisfied she poured him a cup of steaming coffee. As she was pouring, he noticed a dollar bill sticking out from under the cup's bottom edge. 'All this was just too wonderful for words,' he said, 'but what's the dollar for?'

'Well,' she said, 'last night, I told my husband that today would be your last day and that we should do something special for you. I asked him what to give you. He said, "F*** him. Give him a dollar." The breakfast was my idea.'

BALLS IN YOUR COURT >>>

After a two-year-long study, America's National Science Foundation announced the following results on corporate America's recreation preferences.

1. The sport of choice for unemployed or incarcerated people is basketball.
2. The sport of choice for maintenance level employees is bowling.
3. The sport of choice for frontline workers is football.
4. The sport of choice for supervisors is baseball.
5. The sport of choice for middle management is tennis.
6. The sport of choice for corporate officers is golf.

Conclusion: The higher you are in the corporate structure, the smaller your balls become.

DOING TIME >>>

Prison versus work:

In prison: You spend the majority of your time in an 8 x 10 cell.
At work: You spend most of your time in a 6 x 8 cubicle.

In prison: You get three meals a day.
At work: You only get a break for one meal and you have to pay for it.

In prison: You get time off for good behaviour.
At work: You get rewarded for good behaviour with more work.

In prison: A guard locks and unlocks all the doors for you.
At work: You must carry around a security card and unlock and open all the doors yourself.

In prison: You can watch TV and play games.
At work: You get the sack for watching TV and playing games.

In prison: You get your own toilet.
At work: You have to share.

In prison: They allow your family and friends to visit.
At work: You can't even speak to your family and friends.

In prison: All expenses are paid by taxpayers with no work required.
At work: You get to pay all the expenses to go to work and then they deduct taxes from your salary to pay for prisoners.

In prison: You spend most of your life looking through bars from the inside wanting to get out.
At work: You spend most of your time wanting to get out and go inside bars.

In prison: There are wardens who are often sadistic.
At work: They are called supervisors.

In prison: You have unlimited time to read e-mail jokes.
At work: You get the sack if you get caught.

Now get back to work…

NUMBER CRUNCHING >>>

A 54-year-old accountant leaves a letter for his wife one Friday evening that reads: 'Dear Wife,' that's what he calls her, 'I am 54 and by the time you receive this letter I will be at the Grand Hotel with my beautiful and sexy 18-year-old secretary.'

When he arrived at the hotel, there was a letter waiting for him that read: 'Dear Husband,' that's what she called him, 'I too am 54 and by the time you receive this letter I will be at the Breakwater

Hotel with my handsome and virile 18-year-old toy boy. You being an accountant will therefore appreciate that 18 goes into 54 more times than 54 goes into 18.'

PAIN-IN-THE-ARSE CORNER >>>

- At lunchtime, sit in your parked car and point a hair-dryer at passing cars to see if they slow down.
- Page yourself over the intercom. (Don't disguise your voice.)
- Find out where your boss shops and buy exactly the same outfits. Always wear them one day after your boss does. (This is especially effective if your boss is the opposite gender.)
- Send e-mail to the rest of the company to tell them what you're doing. For example: 'If anyone needs me, I'll be in the bathroom.'
- Put mosquito netting around your cubicle.
- Insist that your e-mail address be 'xena_goddess_of_fire@companyname.com' or 'Elvis_the_King@companyname.com'.
- Every time someone asks you to do something, ask if they want fries with that.
- Encourage your colleagues to join you in a little synchronised chair dancing.
- Put your garbage can on your desk and label it 'IN'.
- Develop an unnatural fear of staplers.
- Send e-mail messages that advertise free pizza, doughnuts, etc, in the lunchroom. When people complain that there was nothing there, lean back, rub your stomach, and say, 'You've got to be faster than that.'
- Put decaf in the coffee maker for three weeks. Once everyone has got over their caffeine addictions, switch to espresso.
- In the memo field of all your cheques, write 'for sexual favours'.
- Reply to everything someone says with, 'That's what you think.'
- Finish all your sentences with 'in accordance with the prophecy'.
- Adjust the tint on your monitor so that the brightness level lights up the entire working area. Insist to others that you like it that way.
- Don't use any punctuation.

- As often as possible, skip rather than walk.
- Ask people what sex they are.
- Specify that your drive-through order is 'to take away'.
- Sing along at the opera.
- Go to a poetry recital and ask why the poems don't rhyme.
- Five days in advance, tell your friends you can't attend their party because you're not in the mood.

VIRUS ON THE LOOSE >>>

If you receive any sort of 'work' at all, whether via e-mail, Internet or simply handed to you by a colleague… do not open it!

The 'work' virus has been circulating round our building for months and those who have been tempted to open it or even look at it have found that their social life is deleted and the brain ceases to function properly.

If you do encounter 'work' via e-mail, then to transmogrify the virus, send an e-mail to your boss with the words, 'I've had enough of your shit… I'm off down the pub.' Your brain should automatically forget the 'work' and your career will now be successfully destroyed.

If you receive 'work' in paper document form, simply lift the document and drag to your wastepaper bin and deposit there. Put on your hat and coat and skip to the nearest pub with two friends and order three pints. After repeating this action 14 times you will find that work will no longer be of any relevance to you.

Send this message to everyone in your mailbox. If you do not have anyone in your mailbox, then I'm afraid the 'work' virus has already corrupted your life.

Go out and get some friends, you sad bastard.

PROFESSIONAL RIVALS >>>

Two attorneys boarded a flight out of Seattle. One sat in the window seat, the other sat in the middle seat. Just before take-off, a doctor got on and took the aisle seat next to the two attorneys.

The doctor kicked off his shoes, wiggled his toes and was settling in when the attorney in the window seat said, 'I think I'll get up and get a Coke.' 'No problem,' said the doctor, 'I'll get it for you.'

While he was gone, one of the attorneys picked up the doctor's shoe and spat in it. When he returned with the Coke, the other attorney said, 'That looks good, I think I'll have one too.' Again, the doctor obligingly went to fetch it and while he was gone, the other attorney picked up the other shoe and spat in it.

The doctor returned and they all sat back and enjoyed the flight.

As the plane was landing, the doctor slipped his feet into his shoes and knew immediately what had happened.

'How long must this go on?' he asked. 'This fighting between our professions? This hatred? This animosity? This spitting in shoes and pissing in Cokes?'

COMPANY BLUES >>>

- You've sat at the same desk for four years and worked for three different companies.
- Your company welcome sign is attached with Velcro.
- Your CV is on a disk in your pocket.
- You get really excited about a two percent pay rise.
- You learn about your lay-off on the 9 o'clock news.
- Your biggest loss from a system crash is that you lose your best jokes.
- Your boss doesn't have the ability to do your job.
- The board members' salaries are higher than all the Third World countries' annual budgets combined.
- It's dark when you go to and from work.
- Communication is something your group is having problems with.
- You see a good-looking person and you know it's a visitor.
- Free food left over from meetings is your main staple.
- Being sick is defined as can't walk or you're in hospital.
- You're already late on the assignment you just got.
- Your boss' favourite lines are 'when you get a few minutes', 'in your spare time', 'when you're freed up' and 'I have an opportunity for you'.
- Holidays are something you roll over to next year or a cheque you get every January.
- Your family describe your job as 'works with computers'.
- The only reason you recognise your kids is because you have their pictures on your desk.
- You read this entire list and understood it.

FOOD FOR THOUGHT >>>

An Irishman, a Mexican and a redneck were doing construction work on the scaffolding of a tall building. They were eating lunch and the Irishman said, 'Corned beef and cabbage! If I get corned beef and cabbage one more time for lunch I'm going to jump off this building.'

The Mexican opened his lunch box and exclaimed, 'Burritos again! If I get burritos one more time, I'm going to jump off too.'

The redneck opened his lunch and said, 'Bologna again! If I get a bologna sandwich one more time, I'm jumping too.'

Next day the Irishman opens his lunch box, sees corned beef and cabbage and jumps to his death.

The Mexican opens his lunch, sees a burrito and jumps too. The redneck opens his lunch, sees the bologna and jumps to his death as well.

At the funeral, the Irishman's wife is weeping. She says, 'If I'd known how really tired he was of corned beef and cabbage, I never would have given it to him again.'

The Mexican wife also weeps and says, 'I could have given him tacos or enchiladas. I didn't realise he hated burritos so much.'

Everyone turned and stared at the redneck's wife. 'Hey, don't look at me,' she said. 'He makes his own lunch.'

LESSONS FOR THE DAY >>>

No. 1

A crow was sitting on a tree, doing nothing all day. A small rabbit saw the crow and asked him, 'Can I also sit like you and do nothing all day long?'

The crow answered, 'Sure, why not.' So the rabbit sat on the ground below the crow and rested.

All of a sudden, a fox appeared, jumped on the rabbit and ate it.

The moral of the story is: To be sitting and doing nothing, you must be sitting very, very high up.

No. 2

A turkey was chatting with a bull. 'I would love to be able to get to the top of that tree,' sighed the turkey, 'but I haven't got the energy.'

'Well, why don't you nibble on some of my droppings,' replied the bull. 'They're packed with nutrients.'

The turkey pecked at a lump of dung and found that it actually gave him enough strength to reach the first branch of the tree. The next day, after eating some more dung, he reached the second branch. Finally, after a fortnight, there he was proudly perched at the top of the tree. Soon he was promptly spotted by a farmer, who shot the turkey out of the tree.

The moral of the story: Bullshit might get you to the top, but it won't keep you there.

No. 3

When the body was first made, all the parts wanted to be boss. The brain said, 'I should be boss because I control the whole body's responses and functions.'

The feet said, 'We should be boss as we carry the brain about and get him to where he wants to go.'

The hands said, 'We should be the boss because we do all the work and earn all the money.'

And so it went on and on with the heart, the lungs and the eyes until finally the arsehole spoke up. All the parts laughed at the idea of the arsehole being the boss. So the arsehole went on strike, blocked itself up and refused to work.

Within a short time the eyes became crossed, the hands clenched, the feet twitched, the heart and lungs began to panic and the brain fevered.

Eventually they all decided that the arsehole should be the boss, so the motion was passed. All the other parts did all the work, while the boss just sat and passed out the shit.

The moral of the story: You don't need brains to be a boss – any arsehole will do.

LAWYERS AHOY >>>

Two lawyers had been stranded on a desert island for several months. The only other thing on the island was a tall coconut tree that provided them with food. Each day, one of the lawyers climbed to the top of the tree to see if he could see a rescue boat coming.

One day, the lawyer yelled down from the tree, 'Wow! I can't believe my eyes! I don't believe this is true.'

The lawyer on the ground was sceptical and said, 'I think you're hallucinating and you should come down right now.' So the lawyer reluctantly climbed down the tree and told his friend that he had just seen a naked blonde woman floating face up headed toward their island.

The other lawyer started to laugh, thinking his friend had surely lost his mind. But, within a few minutes up to the beach floated a naked blonde woman, face up, totally unconscious. The two lawyers went over to her and one said to the other, 'You know we've been on this island for months now without a woman. It's been a long time... do you think we should, you know, screw her?'

The other lawyer glanced down at the totally naked woman and asked, 'Out of what?'

AN ORIENTAL SLANT >>>

Sony has announced its own computer operating system now available on its hot new portable PC called the Vaio. Instead of producing the cryptic error messages characteristic of Microsoft's Windows 95, 3.1, and DOS operating systems, Sony's chairman, Asai Tawara, said, 'We intend to capture the high ground by putting a human, Japanese face on what has been until now an operating system that reflects Western cultural hegemony. For example, we have replaced the impersonal and unhelpful Microsoft error messages with our own Japanese haiku poetry.' The chairman went on to give examples of Sony's new error messages:

US '90S CHILDREN >>>

New words for the '90s:

Adminisphere: The rarefied organisational layers beginning just above the rank and file. Decisions that fall from the adminisphere are often profoundly inappropriate or irrelevant to the problems they were designed to solve.

Alpha Geek: The most knowledgeable, technically proficient person in an office or work group.

Arsemosis: The process by which some people seem to absorb success by kissing up to the boss rather than working hard.

Blamestorming: Sitting around in a group, discussing why a deadline was missed or a project failed, and who was responsible.

Chainsaw Consultant: An outside expert brought in to reduce the employee headcount, leaving the top brass with clean hands.

Chips and Salsa: Chips = hardware, Salsa = software, eg. 'Well, first we gotta figure out if the problem's in your chips or your salsa.'

CLM, or Career Limiting Move: Used among microserfs to describe ill-advised activity. Trashing your boss while he or she is within earshot is a serious CLM.

Cube Farm: An office filled with cubicles.

Dilberted: To be exploited and oppressed by your boss. Derived from the experiences of Dilbert, the geek-in-hell comic strip character. 'I've been Dilberted again. The old man revised the specs for the fourth time this week.'

Flight Risk: Used to describe employees who are suspected of planning to leave a company or department soon.

Generica: Features of the American landscape that are exactly the same no matter where one is, such as fast food joints, strip malls, subdivisions. Used as in, 'We were so lost in generica that I forgot what city we were in.'

Going Postal: Euphemism for being totally stressed out, or losing it. Makes reference to the unfortunate track record of postal employees who have snapped and gone on shooting rampages.

Good Job: A 'Get-Out-Of-Debt' Job. A well-paying job people take in order to pay off their debts, one that they will quit as soon as they are solvent again.

Idea Hamsters: People who always seem to have their idea generators running.

Irritainment: Entertainment and media spectacles that are annoying but you find yourself unable to stop watching them. The O.J. trials were a prime example. Clinton's shameful video Grand Jury testimony is another.

Mouse Potato: The on-line, wired generation's answer to the couch potato.

Ohnosecond: That minuscule fraction of time in which you realise that you've just made a BIG mistake.

Percussive Maintenance: The fine art of whacking the heck out of an electronic device to get it to work again.

Prairie Dogging: When someone yells or drops something loudly in a cube farm, and people's heads pop up over the walls to see what's going on.

Salmon Day: The experience of spending an entire day swimming upstream only to get screwed and die in the end.

Seagull Manager: A manager who flies in, makes a lot of noise, craps on everything, and then leaves.

Sitcoms: (Single income, two children, oppressive mortgage) What yuppies turn into when they have children and one of them stops working to stay home with the kids.

Squirt the Bird: To transmit a signal to a satellite.

Starter Marriage: A short-lived first marriage that ends in divorce with no kids, no property and no regrets.

Stress Puppy: A person who seems to thrive on being stressed out and whiny.

Swiped Out: An ATM or credit card that has been rendered useless because the magnetic strip is worn away from extensive use.

Treeware: Hacker slang for documentation or printed material.

Tourists: People who take training classes just to get a holiday from their jobs. 'We had three serious students in the class; the rest were just tourists.'

Umfriend: A sexual relation of dubious standing or a concealed intimate relationship, as in, 'This is Dyan, my… um… friend.'

Uninstalled: Euphemism for being fired. Heard on the voice-mail of a vice-president at a downsizing computer firm, 'You have reached the number of an Uninstalled Vice-President. Please dial our main number and ask the operator for assistance.'

Vulcan Nerve Pinch: The taxing hand position required to reach all the appropriate keys for certain commands. For instance, the arm re-boot for a Mac II computer involves simultaneously pressing the Control Key, the Command Key, the Return Key, and the Power On Key.

Xerox Subsidy: Euphemism for swiping free photocopies from one's workplace.

Yuppie Food Stamps: The ubiquitous $20 bills spewed out of ATMs everywhere. Often used when trying to split the bill after a meal. 'We each owe $8, but all anybody's got are yuppie food stamps.'

404, or someone who's clueless: From the World Wide Web error message, '404 Not Found', meaning that the requested document could not be located. 'Don't bother asking him… he's 404, man.'

FORE! >>>

A married man was having an affair with his secretary. One day, their passions overcame them and they took off for her house, where they made passionate love all afternoon. Exhausted from the wild sex, they fell asleep, awakening around 8 pm.

As the man threw on his clothes, he told the woman to take his shoes outside and rub them through some grass and dirt. Mystified, she nonetheless complied. He then slipped into his shoes and drove home.

'Where have you been?' demanded his wife when he entered the house. 'Darling, I can't lie to you. I've been having an affair with my secretary and we've been having sex all afternoon. I fell asleep and didn't wake up until 8 o'clock.'

The wife glanced down at his shoes and said, 'You lying bastard! You've been playing golf.'

ROLL YOUR OWN >>>

The company hires a new man. He was supposed to start work on Monday, but instead of showing up, he calls his boss. 'I'm sick,' he says. The boss excuses him.

The man shows up on Tuesday morning and works throughout the week, greatly impressing everyone with his diligence and ability.

The next Monday, he once again calls his boss. 'I'm sick,' he says. The boss reluctantly excuses him, but notices this is the second Monday in a row.

Again, the man shows up on Tuesday morning and works throughout the week, even faster and better than the previous week.

The following Monday he again calls his boss. 'I'm sick.' The boss excuses him but decides to call the man to task the next day.

'What gives?' asks the boss. 'I can see you're a hard worker, but you've only been here three weeks and you've called in sick every Monday.' The man says, 'Well, my sister is in a bad marriage and I go over to console her every Monday morning before work. One thing leads to another and we end up making love all day long.'

'Your sister?' says the boss. 'That's disgusting.'

The man says, 'I told you I was sick.'

NUMBERS UP FOR NUMBER CRUNCHERS >>>

What's an auditor?
Someone who arrives after the battle and bayonets all the wounded.

What does an accountant use for birth control?
His/her personality.

What's an accountant's idea of trashing his/her hotel room?
Refusing to fill out the guest comment card.

When does a person decide to become an accountant?
When he/she realises that they doesn't have the charisma to succeed as an undertaker.

What's the most wicked thing a group of young accountants can do?
Go into town and gang-audit someone.

What's the definition of an accountant?
Someone who solves a problem you didn't know you had in a way you don't understand.

What's an actuary?
An accountant without a sense of humour.

Why do some accountants decide to become actuaries?
They find bookkeeping too exciting.

What do actuaries do to liven up their office party?
Invite an accountant.

What's an extroverted accountant?
One who looks at your shoes while he/she is talking to you instead of his/her own.

There are three kinds of accountants in the world.
Those who can count and those who can't.

What's a shy and retiring accountant?
An accountant who is half-a-million shy and that's why he/she is retiring.

SOME SHORT STABS >>>

- An accountant is someone who knows the cost of everything and the value of nothing.
- Old accountants never die. They just lose their balance.
- My accountant told me that the only reason why my business is looking up is that it's flat on its back.
- A fellow is walking into a hospital and sees two doctors down

on their hands and knees in one of the flowerbeds. He goes over and says, 'Can I help? Have you lost something?' 'No,' says one of the doctors. 'We're about to do a heart transplant on an accountant and we're looking for a suitable stone.'

- An accountant is having a hard time sleeping and goes to see his doctor. 'Doctor, I just can't get to sleep at night.' 'Have you tried counting sheep?' 'That's the problem – I make a mistake and then spend three hours trying to find it.'
- A businessman tells his friend that his company is looking for a new accountant. His friend asks, 'Didn't your company hire a new accountant a few weeks ago?' The businessman replies, 'That's the accountant we're looking for.'

HAIL ALL THICKOS AND NASTY BASTARDS >>>

Fortune magazine provided us with these actual resumes and cover letters:

'I have lurnt Word Perfect 6.0 computor and spreasheet progroms.'

'Am a perfectionist and rarely if if ever forget details.'

'Received a plague for Salesperson of the Year.'

'Wholly responsible for two (2) failed financial institutions.'

'Reason for leaving last job: maturity leave.'

'Failed bar exam with relatively high grades.'

'It's best for employers that I not work with people.'

'Let's meet, so you can "ooh" and "aah" over my experience.'

'I was working for my mum until she decided to move.'

'Marital status: Single. Unmarried. Unengaged. Uninvolved. No commitments.'

'I have an excellent track record, although I am not a horse.'

'I am loyal to my employer at all costs.... Please feel free to respond to my resume on my office voice mail.'

'My goal is to be a meteorologist. But since I possess no training in meteorology, I suppose I should try stock brokerage.'

'I procrastinate, especially when the task is unpleasant.'

'Personal interests: donating blood. Fourteen gallons so far.'

'Instrumental in ruining entire operation for a Midwest chain store.'

'Note: Please don't misconstrue my 14 jobs as "job-hopping". I have never quit a job.'

'Marital status: often. Children: various.'

'The company made me a scapegoat, just like my three previous employers.'

'Finished eighth in my class of 10.'

'References: none. I've left a path of destruction behind me.'

Quotes from actual performance evaluations. And you thought your boss was nice:
'Since my last report, this employee has reached rock bottom and has started to dig.'

'I would not allow this employee to breed.'

'This associate is really not so much of a has-been, but more of a definitely won't be.'

'This young lady has delusions of adequacy.'

'Works well when under constant supervision and cornered like a rat in a trap.'

'When she opens her mouth, it seems that this is only to change whichever foot was previously in there.'

'He sets low personal standards and then consistently fails to achieve them.'

'This employee is depriving a village somewhere of an idiot.'

'This employee should go far – and the sooner he starts, the better.'

TEN-SHUNN! MILITARY PERFORMANCE APPRAISALS >>>

'Got into the gene pool while the lifeguard wasn't watching.'

'A room-temperature IQ.'

'Got a full six-pack, but lacks the plastic thingy to hold it all together.'

'A gross ignoramus – 144 times worse than an ordinary ignoramus.'

'A photographic memory but with the lens cover glued on.'

'Bright as Alaska in December.'

'Gates are down, the lights are flashing, but the train isn't coming.'

'He's so dense, light bends around him.'

'If he were any more stupid, he'd have to be watered twice a week.'

'It's hard to believe that he beat out 1,000,000 other sperm.'

'Takes him one and a half hours to watch 60 Minutes.'

'Wheel is turning, but the hamster is dead.'

BRING ON THE MILLENNIUM >>>

10 signs that the '90s have been a real pain:

1. You try to enter your password on the microwave.
2. You haven't played patience with real cards in years.
3. You have a list of 15 phone numbers to reach your family of three.
4. You e-mail your work colleague at the desk next to you to ask, 'Do you fancy going down the pub?' and they reply, 'Yeah, give me five minutes.'
5. You chat several times a day with a stranger from South Africa, but you haven't spoken to your next-door neighbour yet this year.
6. You buy a computer and a week later it is out of date.
7. Your reason for not staying in touch with friends is that they do not have e-mail addresses.
8. You consider the old-fashioned Post Office painfully slow.
9. Your idea of being organised is multiple-coloured post-it notes.
10. You hear most of your jokes via e-mail instead of in person.*

*At least that way, if you don't understand it you can go back over it instead of looking like a complete dick!

TALK ABOUT A DICK! >>>

A doctor, a lawyer, a little boy and a priest were out for a Sunday afternoon flight on a small private plane. Suddenly, the plane developed engine trouble. In spite of the best efforts of the pilot, the plane started to go down.

Finally the pilot grabbed a parachute, yelled to the passengers that they had better jump, and bailed out.

Unfortunately there were only three parachutes remaining. The doctor grabbed one and said 'I'm a doctor, I save lives, so I must live,' and jumped out. The lawyer then said, 'I'm a lawyer and lawyers are the smartest people in the world: I deserve to live.' He grabbed a parachute and jumped.

The priest looked at the little boy and said, 'My son, I've lived a long and full life. You are young and have your whole life ahead of you. Take the last parachute and live in peace.'

The little boy handed the parachute back to the priest and said,

'Not to worry, Father. You can have that one back. The "smartest man in the world" just took off with my backpack.'

TALKING DIRTY >>>

Top 10 things that sound dirty at the office but aren't:

10. I need to whip it out by five.
9. Mind if I use your laptop?
8. Just stick it in my box.
7. If I have to lick one more, I'll gag!
6. I want it on my desk, now!
5. Hmmmmmmm… I think it's out of fluid!
4. My equipment is so old, it takes forever to finish.
3. It's an entry-level position.
2. When do you think you'll be getting off today?

And the number one thing that sounds dirty in the office but isn't:

1. It's not fair… I do all the work while she just sits there!

OOH... THAT NAUGHTY JELLYFISH >>>

Next time you think you have had a bad day at work, think about this guy… Brian is a commercial saturation diver for Global Divers out of Louisiana and performs underwater repairs on offshore drilling rigs. He wrote an e-mail to his sister.

Hi Sue,
Just another note from your bottom-dwelling brother. Last week I had a bad day at the office. Before I can tell you what happened to me, I first must bore you with a few technicalities of my job. As you know my office lies at the bottom of the sea. I wear a suit to the office. It's a wetsuit.

This time of year the water is quite cool. So what we do to keep warm is this: we have a diesel-powered industrial water heater. This $20,000 piece of shit sucks water out of the sea. It heats the water to a delightful temperature. It then pumps it down to the diver through a garden hose, which is taped to the air hose.

Now this sounds like a damn good plan, and I've used it several times with no complaints. What I do, when I get to the bottom and start working, is I take the hose and stuff it down the back of my neck. This floods my whole suit with warm water. It's like working in a Jacuzzi.

Everything was going well until all of a sudden, my arse started to itch. So, of course, I scratched it. This only made things worse. Within a few seconds my arse started to burn. I pulled the hose out from my back, but the damage was done. In agony I realised what had happened. The hot water machine had sucked up a jellyfish and pumped it into my suit. This is even worse than the poison ivy you once had under a cast.

Now I had that hose down my back. I don't have any hair on my back, so the jellyfish couldn't get stuck to my back. My arse crack was not as fortunate. When I scratched what I thought was an itch, I was actually grinding the jellyfish into my arse.

I informed the dive supervisor of my dilemma. His instructions were unclear due to the fact that he, along with five other divers, were laughing hysterically. Needless to say, I aborted the dive. I was instructed to make three agonising in-water decompression stops totalling 35 minutes before I could come to the surface for my chamber dry decompression.

I got to the surface wearing nothing but my brass helmet. My suit and gear were tied to the bell. When I got on board the medic, with tears of laughter running down his face, handed me a tube of cream and told me to shove it 'up my arse' when I get in the chamber. The cream put the fire out, but I couldn't shit for two days because my arsehole was swollen shut. I later found out that this could easily have been prevented if the suction hose was placed on the leeward side of the ship.

Anyway, the next time you have a bad day at the office, think of me. Think about how much worse your day would be if you were to shove a jellyfish up your arse. I hope you have no bad days at the office. But if you do, I hope this will make it more tolerable. Take care, and I hope to hear from you soon.

Love, Brian.

CLEVER DOG >>>

Four men were bragging about how smart their dogs were. The first man was an engineer, the second an accountant, the third a chemist and the fourth was a civil servant.

To show off, the engineer called to his dog: 'T-Square, do your stuff.' T-Square trotted over to a desk, took out some paper and a pen and promptly drew a circle, a square and a triangle.

Everyone agreed that was pretty smart. But the accountant said his dog could do better. He called his dog and said, 'Slide Rule, do your stuff.' Slide Rule went out into the kitchen and returned with a dozen cookies. He divided them into four equal piles of three cookies each. Everyone agreed that was good.

The chemist said his dog could top that. He called his dog and said, 'Measure, do your stuff.' Measure got up, walked over to the fridge, took out a quart of milk, got a 20 ml glass from the cupboard and poured exactly 18 ml without spilling a drop. Everyone agreed that was good. Then the three men turned to the civil servant and said, 'What can your dog do?'

The civil servant called to his dog and said, 'Coffee Break, do your stuff.' Coffee Break jumped to his feet, ate the cookies, drank the milk, shat on the paper, sexually assaulted the other three dogs, claimed he injured his back while doing so, filed a grievance report for unsafe working conditions, put in for compensation and went home on sick leave.

Everyone agreed that was awesome...

REALITY CHECK >>>

A real estate salesman had just closed his first deal, only to discover that the piece of land he had sold was completely under water.

'That customer's going to come back here pretty mad,' he said to his boss. 'Should I give him his money back?'

'Money back?' roared the boss. 'What kind of salesman are you? Get out there and sell him a houseboat.'

STAFF TRAINING >>>

In order to assure the highest levels of quality work and productivity from all employees, it will be our policy to keep all employees well trained through our programme of Special High Intensity Training (SHIT). We are attempting to give our employees more SHIT than anyone else does.

If you feel you do not receive your share of SHIT on the job, please see your manager. You will immediately be placed on the top of the SHIT list and our managers are especially skilled to ensure you get all the SHIT you can handle.

Employees who don't take their SHIT will be placed in Departmental Employees Evaluation Programmes (DEEPSHIT). Those who fail to take DEEPSHIT seriously will need to attend Employee Attitude Training (EATSHIT).

Since our managers took SHIT before they were promoted, they don't do SHIT any more. They are full of SHIT already. If you are full of SHIT you may be interested in training others.

We can add your name to our Basic Understanding Lecture List (BULLSHIT).

Those who are full of BULLSHIT will get the SHIT jobs and can apply for promotion to the Director Intensity Programme (DIPSHIT).

If you have further questions, please direct them to our Head of Training Special High Intensity Training (HOTSHIT).

Thank you,

Boss in General Special High Intensity Training (BIGSHIT).

GIFT OF THE GAB >>>

A crowded flight was cancelled. A single agent was re-booking a long line of inconvenienced travellers. Suddenly an angry passenger pushed his way to the desk. He slapped his ticket down on the counter and said, 'I have to be on this flight and it has to be first class.'

The agent replied, 'I'm sorry sir. I'll be happy to try to help you, but I've got to help these folks first, and I'm sure we'll be able to work something out.'

The passenger was unimpressed. He asked loudly, so that the passengers behind him could hear, 'Do you have any idea who I am?'

Without hesitating, the gate agent smiled and grabbed her public address microphone. 'May have your attention please?' she began, her voice bellowing throughout the terminal. 'We have a passenger here at the gate who does not know who he is. If anyone can help him find his identity, please come to the gate.'

With the folks behind him in line laughing hysterically, the man glared at the agent, gritted his teeth and swore, 'F*** you!' Without flinching, she smiled and said, 'I'm sorry, sir, but you'll have to stand in line for that, too.'

We haven't a clue who the hell that tosser was, but he deserved a slap!

GM VS. MS >>>

At a recent computer expo (COMDEX), Bill Gates reportedly compared the computer industry with the auto industry and stated: 'If GM had kept up with technology like the computer industry has, we would all be driving twenty-five dollar cars that got 1000 miles to the gallon.' in response to Bill's comments, General Motors issued a press release stating: 'If GM had developed technology like Microsoft, we would all be driving cars with the following characteristics:

1. For no reason whatsoever your car would crash twice a day.
2. Every time they repainted the lines on the road you would have to buy a new car.
3. Occasionally your car would die on the freeway for no reason and you would just accept this, restart and drive on.
4. Occasionally, executing a maneuver such as a left turn would cause your car to shut down and refuse to restart, in which case you would have to reinstall the engine.
5. Only one person at a time could use the car, unless you bought "Car95" or "CarNT". But then you would have to buy more seats.
6. Macintosh would make a car that was powered by the sun, reliable, five times as fast and twice as easy to drive, but would only run on five percent of the roads.
7. The oil, water temperature and alternator warning lights would be replaced by a single "general car default" warning light.
8. New seats would force everyone to have the same size butt.
9. The airbag system would say "Are you sure?" before going off.
10. Occasionally, for no reason whatsoever, your car would lock you out and refuse to let you in until you simultaneously lifted the door handle, turned the key, and grabbed hold of the radio antenna.
11. GM would require all car buyers to also purchase a deluxe set of Rand McNally road maps (now a GM subsidiary), even though they neither need them nor want them. Attempting to delete this option would immediately cause the car's performance to diminish by 50 percent or more. Moreover, GM would become a target for investigation by the Justice Department.

12. Every time GM introduced a new model car buyers would have to learn how to drive all over again because none of the controls would operate in the same manner as the old car.
13. You'd press the "start" button to shut off the engine.'

SEXUAL HARASSMENT 1 >>>

Office Managers – keep sexual harassment forms in the bottom drawer of your filing cabinet. That way when female staff bend down to get one, you'll get a terrific view of their arse.

SEXUAL HARASSMENT 2 >>>

Due to pressure for increased political correctness, it has been decreed that the term 'wanker' may no longer be used. This term has now been replaced with 'owner operator'.

help from above

Religion deserves a bit of urine extraction. The Irish comedian Dave Allen was among the first to glean plenty of humour out of the Church – in his case the Catholic Church of his boyhood. Again, this chapter must come with a general warning. If you're seriously into Bible-bashing, rosary rubbing and general God-bothering make your apologies to himself (or herself) now or save it for your next confession when you'll have plenty to be contrite about. And you never know, you might get a laugh out of the priest and he'll be lenient with the Hail Marys!

PARROT FASHION >>>

A woman approaches her priest and tells him, 'Father, I have a problem. I have two talking parrots, but they only know how to say one thing.'

'What do they say?' the priest inquires.

'They only know how to say, "Hi, we're prostitutes. Want to have some fun?"'

'That's terrible,' the priest exclaims, 'but I have a solution to your problem. Bring your two female parrots over to my house and I will put them with my two male talking parrots that I taught to pray and recite the *Bible*. My parrots will teach your parrots to stop saying that terrible phrase and your female parrots will learn to praise and worship.'

'Thank you,' the woman responds.

The next day the woman brings her female parrots to the priest's house. His two male parrots are holding rosary beads and praying in their cage. The woman puts her two female parrots in with the male parrots.

Immediately, the female parrots say, 'Hi, we're prostitutes, want to have some fun?'

One of the male parrots looks over at the other male parrot and says, 'Put the beads away, our prayers have been answered.'

LOVE THY NEIGHBOUR >>>

Once upon a time in the kingdom of heaven, God went missing for six days.

Eventually, Michael the Archangel found him. He inquired of God, 'Where were you?'

God sighed a deep sigh of satisfaction and proudly pointed downwards through the clouds; 'Look son, look what I've made.'

Archangel Michael looked puzzled and said, 'What is it?'

God replied, 'It's a planet and I've put LIFE on it. I've named it earth and there is a balance between everything on it. For example, there's North America and South America. North America is going to be rich and South America is going to be poor, and the narrow bit joining them is going to be a hot spot. Now look over here. I've put a continent of white people in the North and another one of black people in the South.'

The archangel then said, 'And what's that long white line there?'

And God said, 'Ah – that is New Zealand – the land of the long white cloud, and that's a very special place. That's going to be the most glorious spot on earth with beautiful mountains, lakes, rivers, streams, and an exquisite coastline. These people here are going to be modest, intelligent and humorous and they're going to be found travelling the world. They'll be extremely sociable, hard working and high achieving. And I'm going to give them this superhuman, invincible rugby team that will be blessed with the most talented, and charismatic specimens on the planet, and who will be admired and feared by all who come across them.'

Michael the Archangel gasped in wonder and admiration but then, seeming startled, proclaimed, 'Hold on a second, what about the balance? You said they're was going to be a balance.'

God replied wisely, 'Wait until you see the utterly irritating loud-mouthed wankers I'm putting next to them.'

ADAM'S NEW MATE >>>

A newly discovered chapter in the Book of Genesis has provided the answer to 'Where do pets come from?'

Adam said, 'Lord, when I was in the garden, you walked with me every day. Now I do not see you any more. I am lonesome here and it is difficult for me to remember how much you love me.'

And God said, 'No problem. I will create a companion for you that will be with you forever and who will be a reflection of my love for you, so that you will love me even when you cannot see me. Regardless of how selfish or childish or unlovable you may be, this new companion will accept you as you are and will love you as I do, in spite of yourself.'

And God created a new animal to be a companion for Adam. And it was a good animal. And God was pleased. And the new animal was pleased to be with Adam and it wagged its tail. And Adam said, 'Lord, I have already named all the animals in the Kingdom and I cannot think of a name for this new animal.' And God said, 'No problem. Because I have created this new animal to be a reflection of my love for you, his name will be a reflection of my own name, and you will call him Dog.'

And Dog lived with Adam and was a companion to him and loved him. And Adam was comforted. And God was pleased. And Dog was content and wagged his tail.

After a while, it came to pass that Adam's guardian angel came to the Lord and said, 'Lord, Adam has become filled with pride. He struts and preens like a peacock and he believes he is worthy of adoration. Dog has indeed taught him that he is loved, but perhaps too well.'

And the Lord said, 'No problem. I will create for him a companion who will be with him forever and who will see him as he is. The companion will remind him of his limitations, so he will know that he is not always worthy of adoration.'

And God created Cat to be a companion to Adam. And Cat would not obey Adam. And when Adam gazed into Cat's eyes, he was reminded that he was not the Supreme Being. And Adam learned humility.

And God was pleased. And Adam was greatly improved. And Dog was happy. And Cat didn't give a shit one way or the other.

GOOD, BAD AND EVIL >>>

One day God was looking down to earth and saw all the evil going on. He decided to send an angel down to earth to check it out. So, he called on a female angel and sent her to earth for a time. When she returned she told God, yes, it was bad on earth – 95 percent of people were bad and only 5 percent were good.

Well, God thought for a moment and said that maybe he had better send down a male angel and so get both points of view. So God called a male angel and sent him down to earth for a time. When the male angel returned, he went to God and told him – yes, the earth was in decline. Ninety-five percent were bad and 5 percent were good.

God said that this was not good. He would send a letter to the 5 percent of people that were good to encourage them and give them something to help keep them going. Do you know what the letter said?

Oh, so you didn't get one either?

A PRAYER FOR THE STRESSED >>>

Grant me the serenity to accept the things I cannot change,
The courage to change the things I cannot accept,

And the wisdom to hide the bodies of those people I had to kill today because they pissed me off.
And also, help me to be careful of the toes I step on today as They may be connected to the arse that I may have to kiss tomorrow.
Help me to always give 100 percent at work…
12 percent on Monday,
23 percent on Tuesday,
40 percent on Wednesday,
20 percent on Thursday and
5 percent on Fridays.
And help me to remember that…
When I'm having a really bad day and it seems that people are trying to piss me off,
That it takes 42 muscles to frown,
And only four to extend my middle finger and tell them to swivel.

DIVINE RETRIBUTION >>>

Two nude statues (one male and one female) had been standing in a beautiful park for 99 years. On their 100th anniversary in the park an angel came down from heaven to talk to the statues.

He said to them, 'God has been watching you for the past 100 years and has been very pleased with the two of you. So pleased in fact that he has decided to make you human for a short time.'

The angel then went on to say that they would be human for 15 minutes and would finally be able to pleasure themselves in a manner in which they have only fantasised about for the last 100 years.

The statues were so excited they could hardly believe it. The second they became human they ran off together behind the bushes. The angel heard the rustling of the bushes and shouts of joy and laughter.

After 10 minutes the statues returned from behind the bushes sweating and laughing. The angel told the statues that they still had five more minutes.

The male statue quickly turned to the female statue and said: 'Cool, this time, you hold down the pigeon and I'll shit on its head.'

NUN'S HABIT >>>

A man is driving down a deserted stretch of highway when he notices a sign out of the corner of his eye. It says, 'Sisters of Mercy House of Prostitution 15 km'. He thinks it was just a figment of his imagination and drives on without a second thought. Soon, he sees another sign that says, 'Sisters of Mercy House of Prostitution 8 km' and realises that these signs are for real. When he drives past a third sign saying, 'Sisters of Mercy House of Prostitution Next Right' his curiosity gets the better of him and he pulls into the drive.

On the far side of the parking lot is a sombre stone building with a small sign next to the door saying, 'Sisters of Mercy'. He climbs the steps and rings the bell. The door is answered by a nun in a long black habit who asks, 'What may we do for you, my son?'

He answers, 'I saw your signs along the highway and was interested in possibly doing business.'

'Very well, my son. Please follow me.'

He is led through many winding passages and is soon quite disoriented. The nun stops at a closed door and tells the man, 'Please knock on this door.'

He does as he is told and this door is answered by another nun in a long habit and holding a tin cup.

This nun instructs, 'Please place $50 in the cup, then go through the large wooden door at the end of this hallway.'

He gets $50 out of his wallet and places it in the second nun's cup. He then trots eagerly down the hall and slips through the door, pulling it shut behind him. As the door locks behind him, he finds himself back in the parking lot facing another small sign.

'Go in Peace. You Have Just Been Screwed by the Sisters of Mercy.'

COOL DUDE >>>

Seventy-year-old George went for his annual physical. All of his tests came back with normal results.

Doctor Smith said, 'George, everything looks great physically. How are you doing mentally and emotionally? Are you at peace with yourself and do you have a good relationship with your God?'

George replied, 'God and me are tight. He knows I have poor eyesight, so he's fixed it so that when I get up in the middle of the night to go to the toilet, poof, the light goes on when I pee and then, poof, the light goes off when I'm done.'

'Wow,' commented Doctor Smith, 'that's incredible!'

A little later in the day Doctor Smith called George's wife. 'Thelma,' he said, 'George is just fine. Physically he's great. But I had to call because I'm in awe of his relationship with God. Is it true that he gets up during the night and, poof, the light goes on in the toilet and then, poof, the light goes off?'

Thelma exclaimed, 'That old fool. He's been peeing in the refrigerator again!'

DOPEY'S BIG FAUX-PAS >>>

The Pope goes to visit the Seven Dwarfs. As he is finishing his speech on comparative religions, Dopey raises his hand to ask a question.

'Mr Pope, are there any dwarf nuns in Rome?'

'No, Dopey,' responds the Pontiff, 'there are not.'

'Mr Pope, are there any dwarf nuns anywhere in Italy?' Dopey questions.

'No, Dopey,' the Pope chuckles, 'there are no dwarf nuns in Italy.'

'Mr Pope,' Dopey asks pleadingly, 'are there any dwarf nuns anywhere in the world?'

'No, Dopey,' the Pope says sadly, 'there are no dwarf nuns anywhere in the world.'

And softly in the background, the six remaining dwarfs start chanting, 'Dopey f***ed a penguin, Dopey f***ed a penguin.'

FINAL CONFESSION >>>

When nuns are admitted to heaven they go through a special gate and are expected to make one last confession before they become angels.

Several nuns are lined up at this gate waiting to be absolved of their last sins before they are made holy.

'And so,' says Saint Peter, 'have you ever had any contact with a man's penis?'

'Well,' said the first nun in line, 'I did see one once.'

'OK,' says Saint Peter, 'rinse your eyes in the Holy Water and pass on into heaven.'

The next nun admits that, 'Well, yes, I did once get carried away and I, you know, sort of massaged one a bit.'

'OK,' says Saint Peter, rinse your hand in the Holy Water and pass on into heaven.'

Suddenly there is some jostling in the line and one of the nuns is trying to cut to the front of the queue. 'Well now, what's going on here?' says Saint Peter.

'Well, Your Excellency,' says the nun, who is trying to improve her position in line, 'if I'm going to have to gargle that Holy Water, I want to do it before Sister Mary Thomas sticks her arse in it.'

SECOND CHANCE SALOON >>>

A Jew, a Greek and an Irishman were killed in a car accident. When they got to heaven, being young men, they asked Saint Peter if there was any way for them to come back to earth.

Saint Peter thought for a minute and then said, 'Well, if you each promise to give up one particular thing, I'll grant your request.'

All jumped at the chance. The Jew had to agree to never touch any money, the Irishman had to agree to never touch even a drop of alcohol and the Greek had to agree to never touch another man.

Later, the three of them are walking together down the street when they came to a bar. The Irishman begins shaking all over. 'Oh boy, could I use a drink,' he says. The other two try to talk him out of it but he goes into the bar anyway.

He returns with a beer and takes a sip. Suddenly, poof, he disappears. The Jew and the Greek continue walking. At the next block the Jew spots a 5c piece on the footpath. He begins shaking and unable to resist, he bends down to pick up the coin. Suddenly, poof, the Greek disappears.

NEW PRIEST ON THE BLOCK >>>

A new priest at his first mass was so nervous he could hardly speak. After mass he asked the Monsignor how he had done.

The Monsignor replied, 'When I am worried about getting nervous on the pulpit, I put a glass of vodka next to the water glass. If I start to get nervous, I take a sip.'

So, next Sunday he took the Monsignor's advice. At the beginning of the sermon, he got so nervous and took a drink. He proceeded to talk up a storm. Upon his return to his office after mass, he found the following note on the door.

1. Sip the vodka; don't gulp.
2. There are 10 commandments, not 12.
3. There are 12 disciples, not 10.
4. Jesus was consecrated, not constipated.
5. Jacob wagered his donkey, he did not beat his ass.
6. We do not refer to Jesus Christ as the late JC.
7. The Father, Son, and Holy Ghost are not referred to as Daddy, Junior and the Spook.
8. David slew Goliath; he did not kick the crap out of him.
9. When David was hit by a rock and knocked off his donkey, don't say he was stoned off his ass.
10. We do not refer to the cross as the Big T.
11. When Jesus broke the bread at the Last Supper he said, 'Take this and eat it for it is my body.' He did not say, 'Eat me.'
12. The Virgin Mary is not called 'Mary with the cherry'.
13. The recommended Grace before a meal is not, 'Rub-a-dub-dub, thanks for the grub, yeah God.'
14. Next Sunday there will be a taffy-pulling contest at Saint Peter's, not a peter-pulling contest at Saint Taffy's.

CAT IN HEAVEN >>>

A cat dies and goes to heaven. God meets him at the gate and says, 'You have been a good cat all these years. You can have anything you desire, all you have to do is ask.'

'Well,' said the cat, 'I lived all my life on a farm and had to sleep on hardwood floors.'

'Say no more,' says God and instantly a fluffy pillow appears.

A few days later, six mice are killed in a tragic accident and they go to heaven. God meets them at the gate with the same offer he made to the cat.

'All our life,' the mice say, 'we've had to run. Cats, dogs, women with brooms have chased us. If we had roller skates, we wouldn't have to run any more.'

God says he can take care of it and, instantly, each mouse is fitted with a beautiful pair of tiny roller skates. A week later God checks on the cat, which is asleep on its pillow. God gently nudges him awake and asks, 'How are you doing? Are you happy here?'

'Never been happier,' says the cat, stretching and yawning. 'And those meals on wheels you've been sending over are great.'

PLAYING SWAPSIES >>>

A priest was called away for an emergency. Not wanting to leave the confessional unattended, he called his rabbi friend from across the street and asked him to cover for him.

The rabbi told him he wouldn't know what to say, but the priest told him to come on over and he'd stay with him for a little bit and show him what to do. The rabbi comes, and he and the priest are in the confessional. In a few minutes, a woman comes in and says, 'Father, forgive me for I have sinned.'

The priest asks, 'What did you do?'

The woman says, 'I committed adultery.'

The priest says, 'How many times?' And the woman replies, 'Three.'

Priest: 'Say two Hail Marys, put $5 in the box, and go and sin no more.'

A few minutes later a man enters the confessional. He says, 'Father forgive me for I have sinned.'

'What did you do?'

I committed adultery.'

'How many times?'

'Three times.'

The priest says, 'Say two Hail Marys, put $5 in the box and go and sin no more.'

The rabbi tells the priest that he thinks he's got it, so the priest leaves. A few minutes later another woman enters and says, 'Father, forgive me for I have sinned.'

The rabbi says, 'What did you do?'

The woman replies, 'I committed adultery.'

The rabbi, getting it off pat, says, 'How many times?'

The woman replies, 'Once.'

The rabbi said, 'Go and do it two more times, We have a special this week, three for $5.'

GOD'S HOLIDAY >>>

God's sitting up in his ivory tower, he's had enough of the pressures and stresses of being number one, so he's decided to go on holiday. He calls all his super-being mates up and they pop round to discuss a few suggestions over a pint and a joint.

'What about Mars?' says one of them.

'Nah, I went there 15,000 years ago,' says God. 'It was shit, no atmosphere and too dusty.'

'What about Pluto?' suggests another.

'Nah I went there about 10,000 years ago,' says God. 'F***ing freezing.'

'What about Mercury then?' says another.

'It's nice but I went there about 5000 years ago. I nearly burnt me bollocks off it was that hot. Never again,' says God.

'Well what about earth then?' suggests another.

'You must be joking,' says God, 'I went there about 2000 years ago, shagged some Israeli bird, and they're still f***ing talking about it.'

CAME DOWN IN THE LAST SHOWER >>>

Two priests are off to the showers late one night. They undress and step in the showers before they realise there is no soap.

Father John says he has soap in his room and goes to get it, not bothering to dress. He grabs two bars of soap in his hands and heads back to the showers. He is halfway down the hall when he sees three nuns heading his way.

Having no place to hide, he stands against the wall and freezes like he's a statue. The nuns stop and comment on how life-like he looks.

The first nun suddenly reaches out and pulls his dick.

Startled, he drops a bar of soap. 'Oh look,' says the second nun, 'a soap dispenser.'

To test her theory she also pulls his dick… and sure enough he drops the last bar of soap.

The third nun then pulls, first once, then twice and three times. Still nothing happens. So she tries once more and to her delight she yells, 'Look, hand cream!'

NUN THE WISER >>>

A nun gets into a cab and the cab driver won't stop staring at her. She asks him why is he staring and he replies, 'I have a question to ask you, but I don't want to offend you.'

She answers, 'My dear son, you cannot offend me. When you're as old as I am and have been a nun as long as I have, you get a chance to see and hear just about everything. I'm sure that there's nothing you could say or ask that I would find offensive.'

'Well,' the cab driver says, 'I've always had a fantasy that a nun performs oral sex on me.'

She responds, 'Well, let's see what we can do about that. First, you have to be single, and secondly, you must be Catholic.'

The cab driver is very excited and says, 'Yes, I am single and I'm Catholic too!' The nun says, 'OK, pull into the next alley.' He does and the nun fulfils his fantasy.

But when they get back on the road, the cab driver starts crying. 'My dear child, why are you crying?' says the nun.

'Forgive me sister, but I have sinned,' says the cabby. 'I lied. I must confess, I'm married and I'm Jewish.'

The nun says, 'That's OK. My name is Kevin and I'm on my way to a Halloween party.'

JOHNNY COME LATELY >>>

Two nuns were in the back of the convent smoking a cigarette, when one said, 'It's bad enough that we have to sneak out here to smoke, but it really is a problem getting rid of the butts so that Mother Superior doesn't find them.'

The second nun said, 'I've found a marvellous invention called a condom which works really well for this problem. You just open the packet up, take out the condom, and put the cigarette butt in, roll it up, and dispose of it all later.'

The first nun was quite impressed and asked where she could find them. 'You get them at a chemist, sister. Just go and ask the pharmacist for them.'

The next day the good sister went to the chemist and walked up to the counter. 'Good morning, sister,' the chemist said, 'what can I do for you today?'

'I'd like some condoms please,' said the nun.

The chemist was a little taken aback, but recovered soon enough and asked, 'How many boxes would you like? There are 12 to a box.'

'I'll take six boxes. That should last about a week,' said the nun.

The pharmacist was truly flabbergasted by this time and was almost afraid to ask any more questions. But his professionalism prevailed and he asked in a clear voice. 'Sister, what size condoms would you like? We have large, extra large, and the big liar size.'

The sister thought for a minute and finally said: 'I'm not certain, perhaps you could recommend a good size for a Camel?'

BILL'S BUMMER >>>

It was getting a little crowded in heaven, so God decided to change the admittance policy. The new law was that, in order to get into heaven, you had to have a real bummer of a day when you died. The policy would go into effect at noon the next day.

The next day at 12:01, the first person comes to the gates of heaven. The angel at the gate, remembering the new policy, promptly says to the man, 'Before I let you in, I need you to tell me how your day was going when you died.'

'No problem,' the man says. 'I came home to my 25th floor apartment in my lunch hour and caught my wife half-naked and appearing to be having an affair, but her lover was nowhere in sight. I immediately began searching for him. My wife was yelling at me as I searched the entire apartment. Just as I was about to give up, I happened to glance out onto the balcony and noticed that there was a man hanging off the edge by his fingertips! The nerve of that guy!

'Well, I ran out onto the balcony and stomped on his fingers until he fell to the ground. But wouldn't you know it, he landed in some trees and bushes that broke his fall and he didn't die. This ticked me off even more. In a rage, I went back inside to get the first thing I could get my hands on to throw at him. Oddly enough, the first thing I thought of was the refrigerator. I unplugged it, pushed it out onto the balcony, and tipped it over the side. It plummeted 25 storeys and crushed him! The excitement of the moment was so great that I had a heart attack and died almost instantly.'

The angel sits back and thinks for a moment. Technically, the guy did have a bad day. It was a crime of passion. So, the angel announces, 'OK sir. Welcome to the Kingdom of Heaven,' and lets him in. A few seconds later the next guy comes up. 'Before I can let you in, I need to hear about what your day was like when you died.'

The man says, 'No problem. But you're not going to believe this. I was on the balcony of my 26th floor apartment doing my daily exercises. I had been under a lot of pressure so I was really pushing hard to relieve my stress. I guess I got a little carried away, slipped, and accidentally fell over the side!

'Luckily, I was able to catch myself by the fingertips on the balcony below mine. But all of a sudden this crazy man comes running out of his apartment, starts cussing, and stomps on my fingers. Well of course I fell. I hit some trees and bushes at the bottom that broke my fall so I didn't die right away. As I'm laying there face up on the ground, unable to move, and in excruciating pain, I see this guy push his refrigerator of all things off the balcony. It falls the 25 floors and lands on top of me, killing me instantly.'

The angel is quietly laughing to himself as the man finishes his story. 'I could get used to this new policy,' he thinks to himself. 'Very well,' the angel announces, 'welcome to the Kingdom of Heaven,' and he lets the man enter.

A few seconds later, a third man comes up to the gate. The angel is warming up to his task. 'OK, please tell me what it was like the day you died.'

The man says, 'OK, picture this. I'm naked inside this refrigerator…'

CHRIST ALMIGHTY! >>>

A burglar broke into a house one night. He shone his torch around looking for valuables. When he picked up a CD player to place in his sack, a strange disembodied voice echoed from the dark, saying, 'Jesus is watching you.' He nearly jumped out of his skin, clicked his flashlight off and froze.

When he heard nothing more after a little while, he shook his head, promised himself a holiday after the next score, and then clicked his light back on and began searching for more valuables.

Just as he pulled the stereo out so he could disconnect the wires, clear as a bell, he heard, 'Jesus is watching you.'

Freaked out, he shone his light around frantically looking for the source of the voice. Finally, in the corner of the room, his torch came to rest on a parrot.

'Did you say that?' he hissed at the parrot.

'Yep,' the parrot confessed, and then squawked, 'I'm trying to warn you.'

The burglar relaxed. 'Warn me, eh? Who are you?'

'Moses,' replied the parrot.

'Moses?' The burglar laughed. 'What kind of stupid people would name a parrot Moses?'

The parrot replied, 'Probably the same kind of people that would name a Rottweiler Jesus.'

PRAYERS FOR BOYS AND GIRLS >>>

The girls' prayer:
Our Cash
Which art on plastic
Hallowed be thy name
Thy Cartier watch
Thy Prada bag
In Myer
As it is in David Jones
Give us each day our Platinum Visa
And forgive us our overdraft
As we forgive those who stop our Mastercard
And lead us not into Katies
And deliver us from Sussans
For thine is the Dinnigan, the Akira and the Armani
For Chanel No.5 and Eternity
Amex.

The boys' prayer:
Our beer
Which art in bottles
Hallowed by thy sport
Thy will be drunk
I will be drunk
At home as it is in the pub
Give us each day our daily schooners
And forgive us our spillage
As we forgive those who spillest against us
And lead us not into the practice of poofy wine tasting
And deliver us from Tequila
For mine is the bitter
The chicks and the footy
Forever and ever
Barmen.

crossing international boundaries

This chapter is designed to offend just about everyone. The poor old Irish cop some flak, the Kiwis and their sheep likewise, the English and the Aussies are made out to be, well, thick, and the Americans seem to have something against people from Alabama. Basically, you're a sad bastard if you can't laugh at yourself, so here's your chance to change.

PLAYING CHICKEN >>>

Scientists at NASA built a gun specifically to launch dead chickens at the windshields of airliners, military jets and the space shuttle, all travelling at maximum velocity.

The idea was to simulate the frequent incidents of collisions with airborne fowl to test the strength of the windshields. British engineers heard about the gun and were eager to test it on the windshields of their new high-speed trains. Arrangements were made, and a gun was sent to the British engineers.

When the gun was fired, the engineers stood shocked as the chicken hurtled out of the barrel, crashed into the shatterproof shield, smashed it to smithereens, blasted through the control console, snapped the train driver's backrest in two and embedded itself in the back wall of the cabin, like an arrow shot from a bow. The horrified Brits sent NASA the disastrous results of the experiment, along with the designs of the windshield, and begged the US scientists for suggestions.

NASA responded with a one-line memo: 'Thaw the chicken.'

ISLAM WISDOM >>>

A married couple were on holiday in Pakistan. They were touring around the marketplace in Karachi looking at the goods and such, when they passed this small sandal shop.

From inside they heard a gentleman with a Pakistani accent say, 'You foreigners! Come in. Come into my humble shop.'

So the married couple walked in. The Pakistani man said to them, 'I have some special sandals I tink you would be interested in. Dey make you wild at sex like a great desert camel.'

Well, the wife was interested in buying the sandals after what the man claimed, but her husband felt he didn't need them, being the sex god he was. The husband asked the man, 'How could sandals make you into a sex freak?' The Pakistani said, 'Just try them on, sahib.'

Well, the husband, after much badgering from his wife, finally conceded to try them on. As soon as he slipped them onto his feet, he got this wild look in his eyes – something his wife hadn't seen in many years – raw sexual power.

In a blink of an eye, the husband grabbed the Pakistani, bent him violently over a table, yanked down his pants and ripped down his own trousers, and grabbed a firm hold of the Pakistani's thighs.

The Pakistani began screaming, 'You have dem on de wrong feet!'

LATENT ORIENT >>>

On a business trip to the Orient, Joe decided to spend his last night having wild sex with a Chinese prostitute in Hong Kong. Upon returning home three weeks later, he noticed a very weird, green, festering sore growing on his penis.

He went to the doctor, Doctor Jones, who, after hearing of his Orient trip and extracurricular activities, told him he had Hong Kong Dong and the only cure was complete amputation. Joe was horrified, and decided to get a second opinion.

Joe contacted Doctor Smith and showed him the green growth. Doctor Smith said, 'I am sorry but Doctor Jones is correct. We must amputate right away.'

Joe could not accept this. His friend suggested that he visit an oriental doctor. They must deal with this all the time. He went to Doctor Chu Wong.

Doctor Wong agreed with the diagnosis of Hong Kong Dong, but said, 'These Western doctors – so quick to Chop Chop Chop. Amputation not necessary.'

Joe was relieved. Doctor Wong said, 'You wait three weeks and it fall off on its own.'

SOMETHING TO OFFEND EVERYONE >>>

How can you tell the Irish guy in the hospital?
He's the one blowing the foam off his bedpan.

Where does an Australian family go on holiday?
A different bar.

Did you hear about the Chinese couple that had a disabled baby?
They named him Sum Ting Wong.

What would you call it when an Italian has one arm shorter than the other?
A speech impediment.

What do toilets, a clitoris, and an anniversary have in common?
Men miss them all.

Why aren't there any Puerto Ricans on Star Trek?
Because they are not going to work in the future either.

What do you call an Australian farmer with a sheep under each arm?
A pimp.

Why do drivers' education classes in Queensland schools use the car only on Mondays, Wednesdays and Fridays?
Because on Tuesday and Thursday the sex education class uses it.

What's the difference between a Southern zoo and a Northern zoo?
A Southern zoo has a description of the animal on the front of the cage, along with a recipe.

*How do you get a sweet little 80-year-old lady to say f***?*
Get another sweet little 80-year-old lady to yell 'Bingo'.

What's the Cuban national anthem?
'Row, row, row, your boat.'

What's the difference between a Northern fairytale and a Southern fairytale?
A Northern fairytale begins, 'Once upon a time...' while a Southern fairytale begins, 'Y'all ain't gonna believe this shit...'

ON AN ISLAND... >>>

On a beautiful deserted island in the middle of nowhere, the following people are stranded:

- Two Italian men and one Italian woman
- Two French men and one French woman
- Two German men and one German woman
- Two Greek men and one Greek woman
- Two English men and one English woman
- Two Polish men and one Polish woman
- Two Japanese men and one Japanese woman
- Two American men and one American woman
- Two Australian men and one Australian woman
- Two New Zealand men and one New Zealand woman
- Two Irish men and one Irish woman

One month later the following things have occurred:

One Italian man killed the other Italian man for the Italian woman. The two French men and the French woman are living happily together having loads of sex. The two German men have a strict weekly schedule of when they alternate with the German woman. The two Greek men are sleeping with each other and the Greek woman is cleaning and cooking for them. The two English men are waiting for someone to introduce them to the English woman. The two Polish men took a long look at the endless ocean and one look at the Polish woman and they started swimming. The two American men are contemplating the virtues of suicide, while the American woman keeps on bitching about her body being her own, the true nature of feminism, how she can do everything that they can do, about the necessity of fulfilment, the equal division of household chores, how her last boyfriend respected her opinion and treated her much nicer and how her relationship with her mother is improving – but at least the taxes are low and it's not raining. The two Japanese men have faxed Tokyo and are waiting for further instructions. The two Australian men beat each other senseless for the Australian woman, who is checking out all the other men after calling them both 'bloody wankers'. Both the New Zealand men are searching the island for sheep. The Irish began by dividing the island into North and South and by setting up a distillery. They do not remember if sex is in the picture because it gets sort of foggy after the first few litres of coconut whisky, but they are satisfied in that at least the English are not getting any.

HI-YO SILVER >>>

The Lone Ranger and Tonto ride into town one dusty, dry, Wild West day and proceed to the first saloon, where they tie up their trusty steeds and head in for a snort.

After a while a stranger walks into the bar and asks, 'Who owns the white horse tied up outside?'

The Lone Ranger said, 'Why, that would be mine. Why do you ask?'

'Because it's collapsed and looks like it's dying,' says the stranger.

So the Lone Ranger and Tonto head out to check on Silver.

'He's probably just suffering from the heat,' says the Lone Ranger, who asks Tonto if he could run around Silver for a while to help keep him cool.

The Lone Ranger returns to the bar and after half an hour another stranger walks in and asks, 'Who owns the white horse outside?'

The Lone Ranger says, 'That's mine, what's the problem this time?'

'Oh, no problem,' says the stranger, 'it's just that you've left your injun running.'

TRAVELLERS' TALES >>>

Signs from hotels and from around the world:

In a Tokyo hotel:
Is forbidden to steal hotel towels please. If you are not a person to do such a thing please not to read notis.

In a Bucharest hotel lobby:
The lift is being fixed for the next day. During that time we regret that you will be unbearable.

In a Leipzig elevator:
Do not enter lift backwards, and only when lit up.

In a Belgrade hotel elevator:
To move the cabin, push button for wishing floor. If the cabin should enter more persons, each one should press a number of wishing floor. Driving is then going alphabetically by national order.

In a Bangkok drycleaners:
Drop your trousers here for best results.

In a Japanese hotel:
You are invited to take advantage of the chambermaid.

In an Austrian hotel catering to skiers:
Not to perambulate the corridors during the hours of repose in the boots of Ascension.

In a Yugoslav hotel:
The flattening of underwear with pleasure is the job of the chambermaid.

On the menu of a Swiss restaurant:
Our wines leave you nothing to hope for.

On the menu of a Polish hotel:
Salad a firm's own make; limpid red beet soup with cheesy dumplings in the form of a finger; roasted duck let loose; beef rashers beaten up in the country people's fashion.

Outside a Hong Kong tailor's shop:
Ladies may have a fit upstairs.

Outside a Paris dress shop:
Dresses for street walking.

OZ AMOUR >>>

A New Zealander, a sheep and a dog were survivors of a terrible shipwreck. They found themselves stranded on a desert island and after being there for a while they got into the habit of going to the beach every evening to watch the sun go down.

One particular evening, the sky was red with beautiful cirrus clouds, the breeze was warm and gentle; a perfect night for romance. As they sat there, the sheep started looking better and better to the Kiwi.

Soon, he leaned over to the sheep and put his arm around it. But the dog got jealous, growling fiercely until the Kiwi took his arm from around the sheep. After that, the three of them continued to enjoy the sunsets together, but there was no more cuddling.

A few weeks passed by and lo, and behold, there was another shipwreck. The only survivor was a beautiful young woman, the most beautiful woman the Kiwi had ever seen. She was in a pretty bad way when they rescued her, and they slowly nursed her back to health.

When the young maiden was well enough, they introduced her to their evening beach ritual.

It was another beautiful evening: red cirrus clouds, a warm and gentle breeze; perfect for a night of romance.

Pretty soon the New Zealander started to get 'those feelings' again. He fought them as long as he could, but he finally gave in and leaned over to the young woman, cautiously, and whispered in her ear…

'Would you mind taking the dog for a walk?'

GOD BLESS THE IRISH >>>

The curfew in Belfast started at 10 pm and at 9.30 pm the British soldiers were leaving their barracks to enforce it. A sergeant in charge of one of the patrols heard a shot ring out at 9.35 pm.

He soon discovered that Private Connolly had shot a man.

'It's only 9.35 pm,' roared the sergeant. 'Why did you shoot him?'

'I know that man,' said Private Connolly, 'I know where he lives. He would never have got home by 10 o'clock.'

CROC OF SHIT >>>

Three hang-glider pilots, one from New Zealand, one from South Africa, and the other from Australia, are sitting around a campfire near Ayers Rock embroiled in a conversation of bravado.

Andy, from Australia, says, 'I must be the meanest an' toughest hang-glider dude there is, maan. Shit, just the other day, I landed in a field on top of a croc who got loose from the swamp an' had ate six men before I wrestled it to the ground an' snapped it's neek with me bare hands.'

Jaapie, from South Africa, couldn't stand to be bettered. While the froth at the corner of Andy's mouth settled, he stood up and said, 'Well you guys leesin' to this. After a 300 km flight, I landed in the middle of the desert and a five-metre Namibian desert snake came at me from under a rock. I grebbed thet bastard with mar bare hands and beet it's head off end sucked its poison down in one go. End I'm still here today.'

The Kiwi remained silent, slowly poking the fire with his dick.

OLD OIRELAND >>>

Why do the Irish call their basic currency the Punt?

Because it rhymes with bank manager, and... did you hear about the Irishman who went to the toilet?

He wiped the chain and pulled himself.

NIPPON-ESE >>>

Three guys, the American captain, an Australian and a Japanese guy are shipwrecked on an island. On reaching shore, the American asks the Australian to find a good spot for a camp. He turns to the Japanese guy and says to go into the bush and get supplies.

'I'll scout the island and we'll meet at the camp at dusk,' said the captain.

The captain returns to find the Australian has set up camp but the Japanese guy hadn't returned.

'Where's that Jap with the supplies?' said the captain.

The night passes and still there is no sign of the Jap with the supplies, so they go looking for him. They scout the whole island but can't find him.

Just as they are returning to camp, the Jap jumps out from behind a tree and shouts, 'Surplize, surplize.'

BAREBACK RIDING >>>

An attractive woman from New York was driving through a remote part of Texas when her car broke down. An Indian on horseback came along and offered her a ride to a nearby town.

She climbed up behind him on the horse and they rode off. The ride was uneventful except that every few minutes the Indian would let out a whoop so loud that it would echo from the surrounding hills.

When they arrived in town, the Indian let her off at the local service station, yelled one final 'yahoo' and rode off.

'What did you do to get that Indian so excited?' asked the service station attendant.

'Nothing,' shrugged the woman, 'I merely sat behind him on the horse, put my arms around his waist, and held onto his saddle horn so I wouldn't fall off.'

'Lady,' the attendant said, 'Indians ride bareback…'

PADDY AND MICK >>>

Paddy was standing at the bar with a Rottweiler at his feet.

'Does your dog bite, Paddy?' asked Mick.

'No,' replied Paddy.

So Mick went to pat the dog and the dog just about tore Mick's arm off.

'I thought you said your dog didn't bite,' screamed Mick.

'That's not my dog,' replied Paddy.

PROVERBIALLY SPEAKING >>>

Confucius says:

- 'Passionate kiss, like spider's web, soon lead to undoing of fly.'
- 'Virginity like bubble. One prick and all gone.'
- 'Man who run in front of car get tyred.'
- 'Man who run behind car get exhausted.'
- 'Man with hand in pocket feel cocky all day.'
- 'Foolish man give wife grand piano. Wise man give wife upright organ.'
- 'Man who walk through airport turnstile sideways is going to Bangkok.'
- 'Man who scratches arse must not bite fingernails.'
- 'Man who eats many prunes gets good run for money.'
- 'Baseball all wrong. Man with four balls not able to walk.'
- 'Panties not best thing on earth, but next to it.'

- 'War doesn't determine who's right. War determines who's left.'
- 'Man who sleep in cathouse by day sleep in doghouse by night.'
- 'Man who fight with wife all day get no piece at night.'
- 'It takes many nails to build crib, but one screw to fill it.'
- 'Man who drive like hell bound to get there.'
- 'Man who stand on toilet is high on pot.'
- 'Man who lives in glasshouse should change in basement.'
- 'He who fishes in other man's well often catches crabs.'
- 'Man who farts in church sits in own pew.'
- 'Man with one chopstick go hungry.'

WICKETS >>>

An Australian cricket fan dies on match day (probably from drinking too much) and goes to heaven in his Australian cricket shirt. He knocks on the old pearly gates and out walks Saint Peter.

'Hello mate,' the Aussie says.

'No Australian cricket fans in heaven,' replies Saint Peter.

'What?' exclaims the man, astonished.

'You heard, no Australian cricket fans.'

'But, but, but, I've been a good man,' replies the Aussie.

'Oh really,' says Saint Peter. 'What have you done then?'

'Well, three weeks before I died I gave $10 to the starving children in Africa.'

'Oh,' says Saint Peter, 'anything else?'

'Well, two weeks before I died I also gave $10 to the homeless.'

'Hmmm, anything else?'

'Yeah. A week before I died I gave $10 to the Albanian orphans.'

'OK,' said Saint Peter, 'you wait here a minute while I have a word with the boss.'

Ten minutes pass before Saint Peter returns. He looks the bloke in the eye and says, 'I've had a word with God and he agrees with me. Here's your $30 back, now f*** off.'

NOW WATCH MY LIPS >>>

A ventriloquist walks into a small town and sees a local sitting on his porch patting his dog and figures he'll have a little fun.

Ventriloquist: *'G'day mate. Good looking dog... mind if I speak to him?'*

Local: *'The dog doesn't talk, you stupid man.'*
Ventriloquist: *'Hey dog, how's it going old mate?'*
Dog: *'Doin' all right.'*
Local: *(Look of extreme shock)*
Ventriloquist (pointing at local): *'Is this man your owner?'*
Dog: *'Yep.'*
Ventriloquist: *'How does he treat you?'*
Dog: *'Real good. He walks me twice a day, feeds me great food and takes me to the river once a week to play.'*
Local: *(Look of utter disbelief)*
Ventriloquist: *'Mind if I talk to your horse?'*
Local: *'Uh, the horse doesn't talk either... I think.'*
Ventriloquist: *'Hey horse, how's it going?'*
Horse: *'Cool.'*
Local: *(Absolutely dumbfounded)*
Ventriloquist (pointing at local): *'Is this your owner?'*
Horse: *'Yep.'*
Ventriloquist: *'How does he treat you?'*
Horse: *'Pretty good, thanks for asking. He rides me regularly, brushes me down often and keeps me in the barn to protect me from the elements.'*
Local: *(Total look of amazement)*
Ventriloquist: *'Mind if I talk to your sheep?'*
Local: *'The sheep's a bloody liar!'*

KIWI-ESE >>>

Have you spent years trying and failing to understand what they're saying? Just by following these easy steps, you too can hold a conversation with a New Zealander. What you hear and what it means:

A MEDGEN: *visualise, conjure up mentally, John Lennon's first solo album Imagine, as if it was a Bug Hut in the Land of the Long White Cloud.*

BETTING: *'Betting Gloves' are worn by 'betsmen' in 'crucket'.*

BRIST: *Part of the human anatomy between the 'nick' and the 'billy'.*

BUGGER: *As in 'mine is bugger then yours'.*

CHULLY BUN: *'Chilly bin' also known as an ESKY.*

COME YOUSE: *Controversial captain of the Australian cricket team who resigned tearfully in favour of Allan Border. Full name: Kimberley John Hughes.*

DIMMER KRETZ: *Those who believe in democracy.*

ERROR BUCK: *Language spoken in countries like 'Surria', 'E-Jupp' and 'Libernon.'*

EKKA DYMOCKS: *University staff.*

GUESS: *Flammable vapour used in stoves.*

CHICK OUT CHUCKS: *Supermarket point of sale operators.*

SENDLES: *Sandles, thongs and open shoes.*

COLOUR: *Terminator, violent forecloser of human life.*

CUSS: *Kiss.*

DUCK HID: *Term of abuse directed mainly at males.*

PHAR LAP: *New Zealand's famous racehorse christened Phillip but was incorrectly written down as 'Phar Lap' by an Australian racing official who was not well versed in Kiwi-ese.*

DUNNESTY: *US television soap opera starred Joan Collins as 'Elixirs Kerrungton.'*

ERROR ROUTE: *Arnott's famous oval-shaped 'mulk error route buskets'.*

FITTER CHENEY: *A type of long flat pasta, not to be confused with 'Rugger Tony' or 'Toll ya. Tilly'.*

ALABAMA BABY BOOM >>>

After having their 11th child, an Alabama couple decided that was enough. So the husband went to his doctor and told him that he and his wife/cousin did not want to have any more children.

The doctor told him that there was a procedure called a vasectomy that could fix the problem. The doctor instructed him to go home, get a cherry bomb (big firework), light it, put it in a beer can, then hold the can up to his ear and count to 10.

The Alabamian said to the doctor, 'I may not be the smartest man, but I don't see how putting a cherry bomb in a beer can next to my ear is going to help me.'

So the couple drove across the state border into Georgia to get a second opinion. The Georgia physician was just about to tell them about the procedure for a vasectomy when he noticed that they were from Alabama. The doctor instead told the man to go home and get a cherry bomb, light it, place it in a beer can, hold it to his ear and count to 10.

Figuring that both learned physicians couldn't be wrong, the man went home, lit a cherry bomb and put it in a beer can. He held the can up to his ear and began to count '1, 2, 3, 4, 5…' at which point he paused, placed the beer can between his legs and resumed counting on his other hand.

HER FAVOURITE MARTIAN >>>

The year is 2222 and Mike and Maureen land on Mars after accumulating enough air points. They meet a Martian couple and are talking about all sorts of things. Mike asks if Mars has a stock market, if they have laptop computers, and all things about how they make money. Finally Maureen brought up the subject of sex. 'Just how do you guys do it?' asks Maureen.

'Pretty much the way you do,' responds the Martian woman.

Discussion ensues and finally the couples decide to swap partners for the night and experience one another. Maureen and the male Martian go off to a bedroom, where the Martian strips. He's got a teeny, weeny member about 2 cm long and 1 cm thick.

'I don't think this is going to work,' says Maureen.

'Why?' he asks, 'What's the matter?'

'Well,' she replies, 'it's just not long enough to reach me!'

'No problem,' he says, and proceeds to slap his forehead with his palm. With each slap of his forehead, his member grows until it's quite impressively long.

'Well,' she says, 'that's quite impressive, but it's still pretty narrow.'

'No problem,' he says and starts pulling his ears. With each pull his member grows wider and wider until the entire measurement is extremely exciting to the woman.

'Wow!' she exclaims, and they fell into bed and make mad, passionate love.

The next day the couples rejoin their normal partners and go their separate ways. As they walk along, Mike asks Maureen, 'Well, was it any good?'

'I hate to say it,' says Maureen, 'but it was pretty wonderful. How about you?'

'It was horrible,' he replies. 'All I got was a headache. All she kept doing the whole time was slapping my forehead and pulling my ears.'

COUNTER-INTELLIGENCE >>>

An Aussie bloke is having a quiet drink in a bar and leans over to the big guy next to him and says, 'Do you wanna hear a Kiwi joke?'

The big guy replies, 'Well, mate, before you tell that joke, you should know something. I'm 1.80 m tall, 105 kg and I played in the forward for the All Blacks. The guy next to me is 1.85 m, weighs 115 kg and he's an ex-All Black lock. Next to him is a bloke who's 2 m tall, weighs 120 kg and he's a current All Black second rower. Now do you still want to tell that Kiwi joke?'

The first bloke says, 'Nah, not if I'm going to have to explain it three times.'

OH LUCKY MEN >>>

Did you hear what the men say in a Muslim strip club?
'Get your face out for the boys…'

QUICK BIRD CATCHES THE WORM >>>

There was a boy who worked in the produce section of the market. A man came in and asked to buy half a head of lettuce. The boy told him that they only sold whole heads of lettuce, but the man replied that he did not need a whole head, but only half a head. The boy said he would ask his manager about the matter.

The boy walked into the back room and said, 'There is some arsehole out there who wants to buy only a half-head of lettuce.'

As he was finishing saying this he turned around to find the man standing right behind him, so he added, 'and this gentleman wants to buy the other'. The manager okayed the deal and the man went on his way.

Later the manager called on the boy and said, 'You almost got yourself in a lot of trouble earlier, but I must say I was impressed with the way you got yourself out of it. You think on your feet and we like that around here. Where are you from son?'

The boy replied, 'Canada sir.'

'Oh really? Why did you leave Canada?' asked the manager.

The boy replied, 'They're all just whores and hockey players up there.'

The manager said, 'My wife is from Canada.'

And the boy replied, 'Really. What team did she play for?'

AUSSIE PRIORITIES >>>

An Aussie student was walking on campus one day when another Aussie rode up on a shiny new bicycle. 'Where did you get such a nice bike?' asked the first.

The second Aussie replied, 'Well, yesterday I was walking along minding my own business when a beautiful woman rode up on this bike. She threw the bike to the ground, took off all her clothes and said, "Take what you want."'

The first Aussie nodded approvingly. 'Good choice, the clothes probably wouldn't have fitted.'

TIGHT FLIGHT >>>

Aer Lingus Flight 101 was flying from Heathrow to Dublin one night, with Paddy the pilot and Gerry the co-pilot. As they approached Dublin Airport, they looked out of the front window. 'By Jeesus,' said Paddy, 'will you look at how fookin short that runway is.'

'Ya not fookin kiddin, Paddy,' replied Gerry.

'This is going to be one of the trickiest landings you are ever gonna see,' said Paddy.

'Ya not fookin kiddin, Paddy,' replied Gerry.

'Roit Gerry, when I give the signal, you put ta engines in reverse,' said Paddy.

'Roit, I'll be doing dat,' replied Gerry.

'And den you put the flaps down straight away,' said Paddy.

'Roit, I'll be doing dat,' replied Gerry.

'And den you stamp on tem brakes as hard as you can,' said Paddy.

'Roit, I'll be doing dat,' replied Gerry.

'And den you pray to Mother Mary with alla you soul,' said Paddy.

'Roit, I'll be doing dat,' replied Gerry.

So they approached the runway with Paddy and Gerry full of nerves and sweaty palms. As soon as the wheels hit the ground, Gerry put the engines in reverse, put the flaps down, rammed the brakes and prayed to Mother Mary with all of his soul.

Amid roaring engines, squealing of tyres and lots of smoke, the plane screeched to a halt 2 cm from the end of the runway, much to the relief of Paddy and Gerry and everyone on board.

As they sat in the cockpit regaining their composure, Paddy looked out the front window and said to Gerry, 'Dat has gotta be ta shortest fookin runway I have ever seen in my whole life.'

Gerry looked out the side window and replied, 'Yeah Paddy, and the fookin widest too.'

SAUERKRAUT >>>

A doctor started having an affair with his nurse. Shortly after their affair began, she announced that she was pregnant.

Not wanting his wife to find out, he gave the nurse a large amount of money and asked her to go out of the country, to Germany, to wait out the pregnancy and have the baby there.

'But how will you know when our baby is born?' she asked.

'Well,' he said, 'after you've had the baby just send me a postcard and write Sauerkraut on the back.'

Not knowing what else to do, she took the money and went off to Germany. Six months went by and then one day the doctor's wife called him at his surgery. 'John, dear,' she said, 'you received a very strange postcard in the mail today and I don't understand what it means.'

'Just wait until I get home and I'll read it,' he replied.

Later that evening, the doctor came home and read his postcard. It said, 'Sauerkraut, Sauerkraut, Sauerkraut – two with wieners, one without.'

MAMA MIA! >>>

Maria just got married and being a traditional Italian she was still a virgin and very inexperienced around men.

So, on her wedding night, while staying at her mother's house, she was nervous. But her mother reassured her. 'Don't worry Maria,' says the mother. 'Tony's a good man. Go upstairs and he'll take care of you.'

So up she went. When she got upstairs, Tony took off his shirt and exposed his hairy chest. Maria ran downstairs to her mother and says, 'Mama, Mama, Tony's got a big hairy chest.'

'Don't worry, Maria,' says his mother. 'All good men have hairy chests. Go upstairs. He'll take good care of you.'

So up she went again. When she got up in the bedroom, Tony took off his pants exposing his hairy legs. Again Maria ran downstairs to her mother. 'Mama, Mama, Tony took off his pants and he's got hairy legs.'

'Don't worry Maria. All good men have hairy legs. Tony's a good man. Go upstairs and he'll take good care of you.'

So, up she went again. When she got up there, Tony took off his socks, and on his left foot he was missing the better part of three toes. When Maria saw this, she ran downstairs. 'Mama, Mama, Tony's got a foot-and-a-half.'

'Stay here and stir the pasta,' says the mother. 'This is a job for Mama!'

STRANGE AUSSIE RADIO QUIZ >>>

The radio show was Queensland FM (QFM) and the host was Jim. The phone-in competition was to give an English word that's not in the *Oxford Dictionary* and put the word in a sentence. The first prize was a fortnight for two in Los Angeles. The show went as follows (don't forget the Aussie accent):

Jim: *'Hi, this is Jim. What's your name and what's your word?'*
Caller: *'This is Bob from the bush and my word is gaan, spelt g.a.a.n.'*

Jim: '*Thanks Bob, my assistants are just checking and they are telling me that the word does not appear in the* Oxford Dictionary, *so for two weeks in Los Angeles, please put your word into a sentence.*'
Bob from the bush: '*Gaan f*** yourself!*'
Jim immediately breaks the call and puts out the following message: '*Ladies and gents, this is a family show and we would appreciate that any future contestants refrain from using such language.*'
Forty-five minutes and many unsuccessful contestants later…
Jim: '*Hi, this is Jim at QFM. What's your name and what's your word?*'
Caller: '*This is Steve from Caloundra and my word is smee, spelt s.m.e.e.*'
Jim: '*Thanks Steve, we're just checking… and… yes, smee does not appear in the* Oxford Dictionary. *Now for two weeks in Los Angeles, please put your word into a sentence.*'
Steve: '*Smee again, gaan f*** yourself!*'

ARSE LICKING >>>

A lion in the London Zoo was lying in the sun licking its arse when a visitor turned to the keeper and said, 'That's a docile old thing, isn't it?'

'No way,' said the keeper, 'it's the most ferocious beast in the zoo. Why just an hour ago it dragged an Australian tourist into the cage and completely devoured him.'

'Hardly seems possible,' said the astonished visitor, 'but why is it lying there licking its arse?'

'The poor thing is trying to get the taste out of its mouth.'

FOREIGN LEGION >>>

Top 10 reasons for being French:

1. When speaking fast, you make yourself sound gay.
2. You own half the world's perfume industry and still never use deodorant.
3. You get to eat insect food like snails and frogs' legs.
4. If there's a war, you can surrender really early.

5. You don't have to read subtitles on late night films on Channel 4.
6. You can test your nuclear weapons in other people's countries.
7. You can be ugly and still become a famous star.
8. You can allow Germans to march up and down your most famous street and humiliate your sense of national pride.
9. You don't have to bother with toilets, just shit in the street.
10. People think you're a great lover even when you're not.

Top 10 reasons for being American:

1. You can have a woman President – without electing her.
2. You can spell colour wrong and get away with it.
3. You can call Budweiser beer.
4. You can be a crook/adulterer and still be President.
5. If you've got enough money you can get elected to do anything.
6. If you can breathe, you can get a gun.
7. You can invent a new public holiday every year.
8. You can play golf in the most hideous clothes ever made and nobody seems to care.
9. You can call everyone you've ever met 'buddy'.
10. You can think you're the greatest nation on earth when you're not at all.

Top 10 reasons for being English:

1. Two World Wars and one World Cup, doo-dah, doo-dah.
2. Warm beer.
3. You get to confuse everyone with the rules of cricket.
4. You get to accept defeat graciously in major sporting events.
5. Union Jack underpants.
6. Water shortages are guaranteed every summer.
7. You can live in the past and imagine you're still a world power.
8. You can bathe once a week – whether you need to or not.
9. Ditto – changing underwear.
10. It beats being Welsh or Scottish.

Top 10 reasons for being Italian:

1. In-depth knowledge of bizarre pasta shapes.
2. You are unembarrassed to wear fur.
3. No need to worry about tax returns.
4. Glorious military history… well, till about 400 AD.
5. You can wear sunglasses inside.
6. Political stability.
7. Flexible working hours.
8. You live near the Pope.
9. You can spend hours braiding your girlfriend's armpit hair.
10. Sicilian murderers run your country.

Top 10 reasons for being Spanish:

1. You have a glorious history of killing South American tribes.
2. The rest of Europe thinks Africa begins at the Pyrenées.
3. You get your beaches invaded by Germans, Danes and Brits.
4. The rest of your country is already invaded by Moroccans.
5. Everybody else makes crap paella and claims it's the real thing.
6. Honesty.
7. The only sure way of bedding a woman is for you to dress up in stupid, tight clothes and risk your life in front of bulls.
8. You get to eat bulls' testicles.
9. Gibraltar.
10. You supported Argentina in the Falklands War.

Top 10 reasons for being Indian:

1. Chicken Madras.
2. Lamb Passanda.
3. Onion Bhaji.
4. Bombay Potato.
5. Chicken Tikka Masala.
6. Rogan Josh.
7. Popadoms.
8. Chicken Dopiaza.
9. Meat Bhuna.
10. Kingfisher Lager.

Top 10 reasons for being Welsh:

1. You've got to be joking haven't you?

Top 10 reasons for being Irish:

1. Guinness.
2. You have 18 children because you can't use contraceptives.
3. You can get into a fight just by marching down someone's road.
4. Your pubs never close.
5. You can use Papal edicts on contraception passed in the second Vatican Council of 1968 to persuade your girlfriend that you can't have sex with a condom on.
6. No one can ever remember the night before.
7. You kill people you don't agree with.
8. Stew.
9. More Guinness.
10. Eating stew and drinking Guinness in an Irish pub at three in the morning after a bout of sectarian violence.

Top 10 reasons for being Australian:

1. You know your great-grandad was a murdering bastard that no civilised nation on earth wanted. You get to live in what was Britain's largest 'open prison'.
2. Foster's Lager.
3. You dispossess Aborigines who have lived in your country for 40,000 years because you think it belongs to you.
4. You get to annihilate England every time you play them at cricket.
5. Your tact and sensitivity.
6. Bondi Beach.
7. Other beaches.
8. Your liberated attitude to homosexuals.
9. You get to drink cold lager on the beach.
10. You get to have a bit of a swim and then drink some cold lager on the beach.

Top 10 reasons for being a Kiwi:

1. You get to shag chicks that resemble Jonah Lomu in a frock.
2. Beer.
3. Rugby.
4. See above.
5. See above.
6. See above.
7. See above.
8. See above.
9. See above.
10. You get to hate everyone else... unless it's their round.

YING AND YANG >>>

Two brothers, Ying and Yang, wandering down a street in America with arms full of purchases and cameras swinging from their necks, one of the brothers slips into the bank to exchange 30,000 yen into dollars.

Ying: *'I wan to change 30,000 yen for dollar, how much I get?'*
Teller: *'Oh, you will get $8000.'*
Ying: *'Fank you very much.'*
Teller: *'You're welcome,' and hands Ying the $8000.*
Ying and Yang carry on doing copious amounts of shopping until Yang says he is a little low on local currency. So Ying told Yang to go to the same bank and get a good deal.
So off Yang goes.
Yang: *'I wan to change 30,000 yen for dollar. How much I get?'*
Teller: *'Oh, you will get $6000.'*
Yang: *'Only $6000! But how cum my broffer, just a few hour ago, get $8000?'*
Teller: *'Fluctuations.'*
Yang: *'Well, fluck you Yankees too!'*

RUDOLPH KNOWS BEST >>>

Back in the old days of the Soviet Union, a Russian couple were walking down the street in Moscow one night when the man felt a drop hit his nose. 'I think it's raining,' he said to his wife.

'No, that felt more like snow to me,' she replied.

'No, I'm sure it was just rain,' he said.

Well, as these things go, they were about to have a major argument about whether it was raining or snowing. Just then they saw a minor Communist Party official walking towards them.

'Let's not fight about it,' the man said. 'Let's ask Comrade Rudolph whether it's officially raining or snowing.'

As the official approached, the man said, 'Tell us, Comrade Rudolph, is it officially raining or snowing?'

'It's raining, of course,' he replied, and walked on.

But the woman insisted, 'I know that felt like snow.'

The man quietly replied, 'Rudolph the Red knows rain, dear!'

ENGLISH WIT >>>

An Englishman was recently asked about the differences between English and American people. He said there were three:

1. We speak English and you don't.
2. When we hold a World Championship for a particular sport, we invite teams from other countries.
3. When you meet the Head of State in England, you only have to go down on one knee.

OR AUCKLAND... OR LONDON... OR NEW YORK... OR CROYDON >>>

You know you're in Sydney, Australia, when...

- Your co-worker tells you they have eight body piercings but none are visible.
- You earn over $100,000 and still can't afford a house.
- You never bother looking at the bus timetable because you know the drivers have never seen it.
- You can't remember... is dope illegal?
- You've been to more than one baby shower (wetting the baby's head) that has two mothers and a sperm donor.
- You have a very strong opinion about where your coffee beans are grown and can taste the difference between Sumatra and Ethiopian.
- A great parking space can move you to tears.

- Your child's Year Three teacher has two pierced ears, a nose ring and is named Breeze. And, after telling that to a friend, they still need to ask if the teacher is male or female.
- You get used to signs at zebra crossings that say, 'Pedestrians give way to traffic'.
- You are thinking of taking an adult class but you can't decide between yoga, aromatherapy, conversational Mandarin or a 'building your own website' class.
- You get used to the fact that drivers have never heard of the road code and start running red lights, not bothering to indicate lane changes and never, ever, giving way to anyone else – especially if the other has the right of way
- A man walks down the main street in full leather regalia and crotchless pants. Nobody takes any notice.
- You keep a list of companies to boycott.
- Your hairdresser is straight, your plumber is gay and your Avon lady is a guy in drag.

BANK ROBBING, AUSTRALIAN STYLE >>>

A group of Aussie gangsters are sitting around deliberating over methods they will employ in robbing a bank. After a lot of thought, they all agree on the way to go about it.

In the wee hours of the following morning they meet and embark on their plans to get rich.

Once inside the bank, efforts at disabling the internal security system get under way immediately. The robbers, expecting to find one or two huge safes filled with cash and valuables, are more than surprised to see hundreds of smaller safes scattered strategically throughout the bank.

The first safe's combination is cracked and inside the robbers find only a bowl of vanilla pudding.

'Well,' says one robber to another, 'at least we get a bit to eat.' They open up the second safe and it also contains nothing but vanilla pudding and the process continues until all the safes are opened and there is not one dollar, a diamond, or an ounce of gold to be found. Instead, all the safes contain containers of pudding.

Disappointed, each of the mobsters makes a quiet exit, leaving with nothing more than queasy, uncomfortably full stomachs.

The following morning, a Sydney newspaper headline reads, 'Australia's largest sperm bank robbed early this morning.'

CURRY ON >>>

The Indian Top 10:

1. *Tears on My Pillau.*
2. *It's my chappatti and I'll cry if I want to.*
3. *Tikka Chance on Me.*
4. *Scatnaan.*
5. *Korma Korma Chameleon.*
6. *What's the Story Morning Tandoori.*
7. *Easy like Sanjay Morning.*
8. *You Can't Curry Love.*
9. *Poppadum Preach.*
10. *Sheikh Your Body.*

All available on the fantastic new album, *Turban Hymns* by Donner Summer.

Bohemian Curry
(sung to the tune of *Bohemian Rhapsody* by Queen)
Naan-aa, just killed a man
Poppadom against his head
Had lime pickle, now he's dead.
Naan-aa, dinner just begun
But now I'm going to crap it all away. Naan-aa, ooh-ooh
Didn't mean to make you cry,
Seen nothin' yet just see the loo tomorrow, Curry on, Curry on,
'cause nothing really madras.
Too late, my dinner's gone
Sends shivers up my spine
Rectum aching all the time.
Goodbye every bhaji, I've got to go
Gotta leave you all behind and use the loo. Naan-aa, ooh ooh,
This Dopiaza's mild,
I sometimes wish we'd never come here at all…

(Guitar solo)

I see a little chicken tikka on the side, Rogan Josh, Rogan Josh
Pass the chutney made of mango.
Vindaloo does nicely
Nery very spicy
ME!
Biryani (Biryani)
Biryani (Biryani)
Biryani and a naan,
(A vindaloo loo looo…)
I've eaten balti, somebody help me
He's eaten balti, get him to a lavatory, Stand you well back
Cause this loo is quarantined.
Here it comes,
There it goes,
Technicolour yawn.
I chunder
No!
It's coming up again
(There he goes) I chunder
It's coming up again
(There he goes) It's coming up again, (Up again) Coming up again (up again)
Here it comes again
(No no no no no no no no no No).
On my knees, I'm on my knees, I'm on my knees, Oh there he goes
This vindaloo is about to wreck my guts
Poor me… Poor me… Poor me!

(Guitar solo)

So you think you can chunder and still it's all right?
So you want to eat curry and drink beer all night?
Ooh maybe, now you'll puke like a baby,
Just had to come out,
Just had to come right out in here…

(Guitar solo)

Korma, saag or bhuna,
Balti, naan, bhaji.

Nothing makes a difference
Nothing makes a difference to me.

SPRING IS IN THE AIR >>>

An elderly Frenchman was slowly walking down a countryside lane, admiring the beautiful spring day, when over a hedgerow he spotted a young couple, naked, making love in a field.

Getting over his initial shock he said to himself, 'Ah ze young love, ze springtime, ze air, ze flowers. C'est magnifique!' and continued to watch, remembering good times.

Suddenly he drew in a gasp and said, 'Mais… Sacre bleu!! Ze woman – she is dead!' and he hurried along as fast as he could to the town to tell Albert, the police chief.

He came, out of breath, to the police station and shouted, 'Albert… Albert zere is zis man zis woman … naked in Farmer Gaston's field making love.'

The police chief smiled and said; 'Come, come, Henri, you are not so old to not remember ze young love, ze springtime, ze air, ze flowers. Ah, L'amour! Zis is okay.'

'Mais non! You do not understand – ze woman she is dead!'

Hearing this Albert leapt from his seat and rushed out of the station and, the police car being serviced, he ran down to the field, confirmed Henri's story, and ran all the way back nonstop to call the doctor.

'Pierre, Pierre… this is Albert. I was in Gaston's field... zere is a young couple naked 'aving sex.'

To which Pierre replied, 'Albert, I am a man of science. You must remember, it is spring, ze air, ze flowers. Ah, L'amour! Zis is very natural.'

Albert, still out of breath gasped in reply, 'Non, you do not understand. Ze woman, she is dead!'

Hearing this Pierre shouted, 'Mon dieu!' grabbed his black medicine bag, stuffed in his thermometer, stethoscope, and other tools and jumped in the car and drove like a madman down to Gaston's field. Upon getting there he gave the couple a full medical exam and drove back to Henri and Albert, who were waiting at the station. He got there, went inside, and smiled patiently at the two French-men and said, 'Ah, mes amis, do not worry. Ze woman, she is not dead. She is English.'

AN IRISHMAN, AN ENGLISHMAN AND CLAUDIA SCHIFFER >>>

There was an Irishman, an Englishman and Claudia Schiffer sitting together in a carriage in a train going through Tasmania. Suddenly the train went through a tunnel, and as it was an old-style train, there were no lights in the carriages and it went completely dark.

Then there was this kissing noise and the sound of a loud slap.

When the train came out of the tunnel, Claudia Schiffer and the Irishman were sitting as if nothing had happened and the Englishman had his hand against his face as he had been slapped there.

The Englishman was thinking, 'The Irish fella must have kissed Claudia Schiffer and she missed him and slapped me instead.'

Claudia Schiffer was thinking, 'The Englishman must have tried to kiss me and actually kissed the Irishman and got slapped for it.'

And the Irishman was thinking, 'This is great. The next time the train goes through a tunnel, I'll make another kissing noise and slap that English bastard again!'

RUM DO IN JAMAICA >>>

There's this guy named Jack, and he has a girlfriend named Wendy. Jack loves Wendy a lot. To prove how much he loves her, he gets 'Wendy' tattooed on his penis. When it's erect, it says her name, and when deflated, it reads 'Wy'.

So, when she sees her name on his masculine member, she is overwhelmed. He pops the question and she accepts. They decide to go to Jamaica for their honeymoon.

Once there, they try out all the local culture, including a nude beach. They are having a great time when Jack decides to get up from sunbathing and get something to drink at the beach bar. He walks over to the bar with his deflated love muscle, trying not to let his eyes wander and end up embarrassing himself.

He orders a drink from the Jamaican guy at the bar, who is also naked. He is surprised to note that the bartender also has 'Wy' tattooed on his penis!

Jack says to the guy, 'Wow, what a coincidence. So, you have a girlfriend named "Wendy" and her name is tattooed on your penis, too?'

The bartender looks slowly down at Jack, back to his and starts laughing. Flashing a wide grin, he says, 'No, mon. Mine says, "Welcome to Jamaica. Have a nice day."'

SWEET MUSIC >>>

A tourist in Vienna is going through a graveyard and all of a sudden he hears some music. No one is around, so he starts searching for the source.

He finally locates the origin and finds it is coming from a grave with a headstone that reads, 'Ludwig van Beethoven, 1770-1827.'

Then he realises that the music is the Ninth Symphony and it is being played backwards. Puzzled, he leaves the graveyard and persuades a friend to return with him. By the time they arrive back at the grave, the music has changed. This time it is the Seventh Symphony, but like the previous piece, it is being played backwards.

Curious, the men agree to consult a music scholar. When they return with the expert, the Fifth Symphony is playing, again backwards. The expert notices that the symphonies are being played in the reverse order in which they were composed, the Ninth, then the Seventh, then the Fifth.

By the next day the word has spread and a throng has gathered around the grave. They are all listening to the Second Symphony being played backwards.

Just then the graveyard's caretaker ambles up to the group. Someone in the group asks him if he has an explanation for the music.

'Don't you get it?' the caretaker says incredulously. 'Beethoven is decomposing!'

HERE'S A SURPRISE! >>>

Several years ago the United States funded a study to determine why the head on a man's penis is larger than the shaft. The study took two years and cost over $180,000. The results of the study concluded that the reason the head of a man's penis is larger than the shaft was to provide the man with more pleasure during sex.

After the results were published, Germany decided to conduct their own study on the same subject. They were convinced that the results of the US study were incorrect. After three years of research and costs in excess of $250,000, they concluded that the head of a man's penis is larger than the shaft to provide the women with more pleasure during sex.

When the results of the German study were released, Australia decided to conduct their own study. The Aussies didn't trust the US or German studies. So after nearly three weeks of intensive research at a cost of around $75, the Aussie study reached a conclusion. They came to the final conclusion that the reason the head on a man's penis is larger than the shaft is to prevent his hand from flying off and hitting him in the forehead.

CHINESE PRIVATE EYE >>>

A man suspected his wife of seeing another man so he hired a famous Chinese detective to watch and report activities while he was gone. A few days later he received this report:

Most Hon'ble Sir,
You leave the house. I watch house. He come to house. I watch. He and she leave house. I follow. He and she get on train. I follow. He and she go in hotel. I climb tree – look in window. He kiss she. She kiss he. He strip she. She strip he. He play with she. She play with he. I play with me. Fall out of tree. Not see. No fee.

LAST AND LEAST >>>

Three leprechauns, Sean, Mick and Kevin, are sitting in the pub getting quietly pissed when Mick shouts out, 'Jaysus, I'm bored wid bein' a feckin' nobody. I'm tinkin' I'll take meself down to de *Guinness Book of Records* office and get meself entered in de book.'

'What de hell are ye talkin' about, ye eejit? You've dun nuttin' to get in de book for,' says Sean.

'Well, it's me hands, Sean,' Mick says, waving them around. 'I tink dey are de smallest in de world and I'm gonna get meself entered into de book and I'll be world famous.'

The other two agree that they are quite small and they all carry on drinking heartily.

A little while later Kevin pipes up, 'Ya know Mick, if ye can get into de *Guinness Book of Records* for yer small hands, so can I.'

The other two smirk at each other and Mick says, 'How can ye have de smallest hands in the world if I've got dem, ya bloody fool?'

Kevin replies, 'It's not me hands, Mick, it's me feet,' and he takes his boots to show them. 'I tink dat dey are de smallest feet in de world and I'm gonna get meself entered into de *Guinness Book of Records* too.'

The other two agree that they are quite small and with that they all go back to their drinking.

Some time later Sean chimes in, 'Well, if youse two can get into de *Guinness Book of Records*, I can too.' The others fall about laughing.

'What de feck have you got dats so feckin' interesting?' cries Sean.

'It's me dick,' he says and pulls down his breeches to show them. They both howl with laughter as Sean pulls out his little willy.

'Jaysus, ye've got the best chance of us all, Sean', says Kevin. 'Dat's the smallest feckin' dick I ever saw,' and with that they all go back to their drinking.

Later on, full to the gills, they are heading home when, out of the corner of his eye, Mick spots the *Guinness Book of Records* office further down the street. 'Jaysus,' he says, 'I'm gonna go into dat office and I'm gonna get me hands measured' and off he staggers.

Ten minutes later he comes out with a big smile on his face, waving his hands in the air. 'I did it. I did it,' he says. 'I'm in de *Guinness Book of Records* for de smallest hands in the world. Nobody's got smaller hands dan me,' he says and with that he pushes Kevin forward. 'Go on, ye eejit. See if ye have de smallest feet in de world. Go on.'

'Feck it. I will,' says Kevin and off he staggers.

Ten minutes later he too comes out with a big smile on his face, kicking his feet in the air. 'Jaysus, I'm famous,' he says. 'I've got de smallest feet in de world. I'm famous, I'm famous.'

With that Sean staggers to the office door. 'I'm gonna get me dick measured,' he says. 'I won't be long.'

The other two are waiting anxiously for Sean to return, but time slips by.

Ten minutes turns into 20 and 20 into 30. No sign of Sean. Forty minutes go by and the office door opens. Sean slouches out looking disconsolate. 'Who de feckin' hell is Bill Gates?' he says.

IRAQI TV GUIDE >>>

Monday
8:00 Husseinfeld.
8:30 Mad About Everything.
9:00 Suddenly Sanctions.
9:30 Allah McBeal.

Tuesday
8:00 Wheel of MisFortune and Terror.
8:30 The Price Is Right if Saddam Says It's Right.
9:00 Children Are Forbidden to Say the Darndest Things.
9:30 Iraq's Funniest Public Execution Bloopers.

Wednesday
8:00 Buffy the Yankee Imperialist Dog Slayer.
8:30 Diagnosis: Heresy.
9:00 Just Shoot Me.
9:30 Veilwatch.

Thursday
8:00 Mahatma Loves Chachi.
8:30 M*U*S*T*A*S*H.
9:00 Veronica's Closet Full of Long, Black, Shapeless Dresses.
9:30 My Two Baghdads.

Friday
8:00 Judge Saddam.
8:30 Captured Iranian Soldiers Say The Darndest Things.
9:00 Achmed's Creek.
9:30 No-witness News.

THIS JUST IN... >>>

Cities of Sjlbvdnzv, Grzny to Be First Recipients

Before an emergency joint session of Congress yesterday, President Clinton announced US plans to deploy over 75,000 vowels to the war-torn region of Bosnia.

The deployment, the largest of its kind in American history, will provide the region with the critically needed letters A,E,I,O and U, and is hoped to render countless Bosnian names more pronounceable.

'For six years, we have stood by while names like Ygrjvslhv and Tzlynhr and Glrm have been horribly butchered by millions around the world,' Clinton said. 'Today, the United States must finally stand up and say "Enough".' It is time the people of Bosnia finally had some vowels in their incomprehensible words. The US is proud to lead the crusade in this noble endeavor.'

The deployment, dubbed Operation Vowel Storm by the State Department, is set for early next week, with the Adriatic port cities of Sjlbvdnzv and Grzny slated to be the first recipients. Two C-130 transport planes, each carrying over 500 24-count boxes of E's, will fly from Andrews Air Force Base across the Atlantic and airdrop the letters over the cities.

Citizens of Grzny and Sjlbvdnzv eagerly await the arrival of the vowels. 'My God, I do not think we can last another day,' Trszg Grzdnjkln, 44, said. 'I have six children and none of them has a name that is understandable to me or to anyone else. Mr. Clinton, please send my poor, wretched family just one E. Please.' Sjlbvdnzv resident Grg Hmphrs, 67, said, 'With just a few key letters, I could be George Humphries. This is my dream.'

If the initial airlift is successful, Clinton said the United States will go ahead with full-scale vowel deployment, with C-130's airdropping thousands more letters over every area of Bosnia. Other nations are expected to pitch in as well, including 10,000 British A's and 6,500 Canadian U's. Japan, rich in A's and O's, was asked to participate, but declined.

'With these valuable letters, the people of war-ravaged Bosnia will be able to make some terrific new words,' Clinton said. 'It should be very exciting for them, and much easier for us to read their maps.'

Linguists praise the US's decision to send the vowels. For decades they have struggled with the hard consonants and difficult pronunciation of most Slavic words. 'Vowels are crucial to construction of all language,' Baylor University linguist Noam Frankel said. 'Without them, it would be difficult to utter a single word, much less organize a coherent sentence. Please, just don't get me started on the moon-man languages they use in those Eastern

European countries.'

According to Frankel, once the Bosnians have vowels, they will be able to construct such valuable sentences as: 'The potatoes are ready' and 'I believe it will rain'. The airdrop represents the largest deployment of any letter to a foreign country since 1984. During the summer of that year, the US shipped 92,000 consonants to Ethiopia, providing cities like Ouaouoaua, Eaoiiuae, and Aao with vital, life-giving supplies of L's, S's and T's. The consonant-relief effort failed, however, when vast quantities of the letters were intercepted and hoarded by violent, gun-toting warlords.

TONGUE TWISTING IN EUROPE >>>

The European Commission has just announced an agreement whereby English will be the official language of the EU rather than German, which was the other possibility. As part of the negotiations, Her Majesty's Government conceded that English spelling had some room for improvement and has accepted a five-year-phase in plan that would be known as 'EuroEnglish':

In the first year, 's' will replace the soft 'c'. Sertainly, this will make the sivil servants jump with joy. The hard 'c' will be dropped in favor of the 'k'. This should klear up konfusion and keyboards kan have 1 less letter.

There will be growing publik enthusiasm in the sekond year, when the troublesome 'ph' will be replaced with the 'f'. This will make words like 'fotograf' 20 percent shorter.

In the 3rd year, publik akseptanse of the new spelling kan be expekted to reach the stage where more komplikated changes are possible. Governments will enkorage the removal of double letters, which have always ben a deterent to akurate speling. Also, al wil agre that the horible mes of the silent 'e' in the language is disgraceful, and it should go away.

By the 4th yar, peopl wil be reseptiv to steps such as replasing 'th' with 'z' and 'w' with 'v'. During ze fifz year, ze unesesary 'o' kan be dropd from vords kontaning 'ou' and similar changes vud of kors be aplid to ozer kombinations of leters.

After zis fifz yer, ve vil hav a reli sensibl riten styl. Zer vil be no mor trubls or difikultis and evrivun vil find it ezi tu understand ech ozer.

Ze drem vil finali kum tru!!

all in the best possible taste

You know how you hear a particularly tasteless joke and you piss yourself laughing. You say to yourself, 'That's dreadful, I shouldn't really be laughing.' But you do anyway. What's so funny about cracking up over the bizarre way some poor bugger gets killed? Or poking the borax at the Kennedy family?

Let's face it, we're a world full of sick puppies... so come on, join the kennel club!

1998 DARWIN AWARDS >>>

The Darwin Awards are an annual honour given to the person who provided the universal human genepool the biggest service by getting killed in the most extraordinarily stupid way. As always, competition in 1998 was keen. Some candidates appear to have trained their whole lives for this event. Entries did not have the *élan* of some previous ones, but are a worthy catalogue of stupidity, incompetence and bad luck.

1. In Detroit, a 41-year-old man got stuck and drowned in 50 cm of water after squeezing headfirst through a 30-cm-wide sewer grate to retrieve his car keys.

2. A 49-year-old San Francisco stockbroker, who 'totally zoned when he ran', according to his wife, accidentally jogged off a 30 m cliff on his daily run.

3. In Buxton, North Carolina, a man died on a beach when a 2.5 m hole he had dug in the sand caved in as he sat inside it. Beachgoers said Daniel Jones, 21, dug the hole for fun, or protection from the wind, and had been sitting in a beach chair at the bottom when it collapsed, burying him. People on the beach used their hands and shovels to get to Jones but failed. It took rescue workers using heavy equipment almost an hour to free him while about 200 people looked on. Jones was pronounced dead at a hospital.

4. Santiago Alvarado, 24, was killed in Lompoc, California, when he fell face-first through the ceiling of a bicycle shop he was robbing. Death was caused by the long flashlight he had placed in his mouth (to keep his hands free) ramming into the base of his skull as he hit the floor.

5. In Dahlongega, Georgia, 20-year-old Nick Berrena was killed when fellow cadet Jeffrey Hoffman, 23, was trying to prove that a knife could not penetrate the flak-vest Berrena was wearing.

6. Sylvester Briddell Jr, 26, was killed in Selbyville, Delaware, as he won a bet with friends who said he would not put a revolver

loaded with four bullets into his mouth and pull the trigger.

7. According to police in Windsor, Ontario, Daniel Kolta, 27, and Randy Taylor, 33, died in a head-on collision, thus earning a tie in the game of chicken they were playing in their snowmobiles.

8. A seven-year-old boy fell off a 30 m bluff near Ozark, Arkansas, after he lost his grip swinging on a cross that marked the spot where another person had fallen to his death in 1990.

Honourable mentions

1. In Guthrie, Oklahoma, Jason Heck tried to kill a millipede with a shot from his 22-calibre rifle, but the bullet ricocheted off a rock and hit pal Anotonio Martinez in the head, fracturing his skull.

2. In Elyria, Ohio, Martyn Eskins was attempting to clean out cobwebs in his basement. He declined to use a broom in favour of a propane torch and caused a fire that burned the first and second floors of his house.

3. Paul Stilter, 47, was hospitalised in Andover, New Jersey, and his wife, Bonnie, was also injured by a quarter-stick of dynamite that blew up in their car. While driving around at 2 am, the bored couple lit the dynamite and tried to toss it out the window to see what would happen, but they apparently failed to notice that the window was closed.

4. In Betulia, Colombia, an annual festival includes five days of amateur bullfighting. No bull was killed, but dozens of amateur matadors were injured, including one gored in the head and one Bobbitised. Said one participant, 'It's just one bull against a town of a thousand morons.'

Some more also-rans

1. Four people were injured in a string of related bizarre

accidents. Jerry Moeller was admitted with a head wound caused by flying masonry, Tim Vegas was diagnosed with a mild case of whiplash and contusions to his chest, arms and face, Bryan Corcoran suffered torn gum tissue and Pamela Klesick's first two fingers of her right hand had been bitten off. Moeller had just dropped her husband off for his first day of work and, in addition to a goodbye kiss, she flashed her breasts at him. 'I'm still not sure why I did it,' she said later. 'I was really close to the car, so I didn't think anyone would see. Besides, it couldn't have been for more than two seconds.' However, cabbie Vegas did see and lost control of his car, running over the kerb and into the corner of the Johnson Medical Building. Inside, Klesick, a dental technician, was cleaning Corcoran's teeth. The crash of the cab against the building made her jump, tearing Corcoran's gums with a cleaning pick. In shock, he bit down severing two fingers from Klesick's hand. Moeller's wound was caused by a falling piece of the medical building.

2. A woman went to a poison control centre after eating three birth-control vaginal inserts. Her English was so bad she had to draw a picture describing how she believed she had poisoned herself. A translator arrived shortly after and confirmed doctors' suspicions. Marie Valishnokov thought the inserts were some kind of candy or gum, being unable to read the foil wrappers. After the third one she realised something was wrong when her throat and mouth began to fill with sour-tasting foam. She ran for the poison control centre, only a few blocks away, where doctors were able to flush the foam from her mouth, throat and stomach with no ill effects.

3. In La Grange, Georgia, attorney Antonio Mendoza was released from a trauma centre after having a cellphone removed from his rectum. 'My dog drags the thing all over the house,' he said later. 'He must have dragged it into the shower. I slipped on the tiles, tripped against the dog and sat down right on the thing.' The extraction took more than three hours due to the fact that the cover to Mr Mendoza's phone had opened during insertion. 'He was a real trooper during the entire episode,' said Dr Dennis Crobe. 'Tony just cracked jokes and really seemed to be

enjoying himself. Three times during the extraction his phone rang and each time he made jokes about it that had us rolling on the floor. By the time he finished, we really did expect to find an answering machine in there.'

4. In Tacoma, Washington, Kerry Bingham had been drinking with several friends when one of them said they knew a person who had bungee-jumped from the Tacoma Narrows Bridge in the middle of traffic. The conversation grew more heated and at least 10 men trooped along the walkway of the bridge at 4.30 am. Upon arrival at the midpoint of the bridge, they discovered that no one had brought a bungee rope. Bingham, who had continued drinking, volunteered and pointed out that a coil of lineman's cable lay nearby. One end of the cable was secured around Bingham's leg and the other end was tied to the bridge. His fall lasted 12 m before the cable tightened and tore his foot off at the ankle. He miraculously survived his fall into the icy river and was rescued by two nearby fishermen. 'All I can say,' said Bingham, 'is that God was watching out for me on that night. There's just no other explanation for it.' Bingham's foot was never located.

5. Also in the state of Washington, a Bremerton couple, Christopher and Emily Coulter, were engaging in bondage games when Christopher suggested spreading peanut butter on his genitals and letting Rudy, their Irish setter, lick them clean. Sadly, Rudy lost control and began tearing at Christopher's penis and testicles. Rudy refused to obey commands and a panicked Emily threw a large bottle of perfume at the dog. The bottle broke, covering the dog and Christopher with perfume. Startled, Rudy leaped back and tore away Christopher's penis. While trying to get her unconscious husband in the car to take him to hospital, Emily fell twice, injuring her wrist and ankle. Christopher's penis was in a Styrofoam ice cooler. 'Chris is just plain lucky,' said the surgeon who spent eight hours reattaching the penis. 'Believe it or not, the perfume turned out to be very fortuitous. The high alcohol content, which must have been excruciatingly painful, helped sterilise the wound. Also, aside from it being removed, the damage cause by the dog's teeth to

the penis is minimal. It's really a very stringy piece of flesh.' Mr Coulter stands an excellent chance of regaining the use of his limb and Washington animal control has no plans to seize Rudy.

The winner

And the overwhelming winner is... Friedrich Riesfeldt. An overzealous zookeeper in Paderborn, Germany, who fed his constipated elephant, Stefan, 22 doses of animal laxative and more than a bushel of berries, figs and prunes before the plugged-up pachyderm finally let fly and suffocated the keeper under 100 kg of excrement. Investigators say the ill-fated Friedrich, 46, was attempting to give the ailing elephant an olive oil enema when the relieved beast unloaded on him like a dump truck full of mud. 'The sheer force of the elephant's unexpected defecation knocked Mr Riesfeldt to the ground where he struck his head on a rock and lay unconscious as the elephant continued to evacuate his bowels on top of him,' said flabbergasted Paderborn police detective Erik Dern. (Cops speak funny in Germany too!) 'With no one there to help him, he lay under all that dung for at least an hour before he was discovered.'

1999 DARWIN AWARDS >>>

Runners-up

1. In Los Angeles, Ani Saduki, 33, and his brother decided to remove a bees' nest from a shed on their property with the aid of a 'pineapple' (an illegal firecracker), which is the explosive equivalent of half a stick of dynamite. They ignited the fuse and retreated to watch from inside their home, behind a window just 3 m away from the hive. The concussion of the explosion shattered the window inwards, seriously lacerating Ani. Deciding Ani needed stitches, the two brothers headed off to a nearby hospital. While walking towards their car, Ani was stung three times by the surviving bees. Unbeknownst to either brother, Ani was allergic to bee venom and died of suffocation en route to the hospital.

2. Derrick L. Richards, 28, was charged in Minneapolis with third-degree murder for his involvement in the death of his beloved cousin Kenneth E. Richards. According to police, Derrick suggested a game of Russian roulette and put a semi-automatic pistol – instead of the more traditional revolver – to Ken's head and fired.

3. In Phillipsburg, New Jersey, an unidentified 29-year-old male choked to death on sequined panties he had orally removed from an exotic dancer at a local establishment. 'I didn't think he was going to eat it,' the dancer identified only as Ginger said, adding, 'He was really drunk.'

4. In Moscow, a drunken security man asked a colleague at the bank they were guarding to stab his bulletproof vest to see if it would protect him against a knife attack. It didn't and the 25-year-old guard died of a heart wound. (It's good to see the Russians getting into the spirit of the Darwin Awards.)

5. In France, Jacques LeFevrier left nothing to chance when he decided to commit suicide. He stood at the top of a tall cliff and tied a noose around his neck. He tied the other end of the rope to a large rock. He drank some poison and set fire to his clothes. He even tried to shoot himself at the last moment. He jumped and fired the pistol. The bullet missed him completely and cut through the rope above him. Free of the threat of hanging, he plunged into the sea. The sudden dunking extinguished the flames and made him vomit the poison. He was dragged out of the water by a fisherman and was taken to hospital, where he died of hypothermia.

6. A Renton, Washington, man tried to commit a robbery. This was probably his first attempt, as he had no previous record of violent crime and made terminally stupid choices. The target was H. & J. Leather & Firearms – yes – a gun shop. The shop was full of customers in a state where a substantial portion of the adult population is licensed to carry concealed handguns in public places. To enter the shop, he had to step around a marked police patrol car parked at the front door. An officer in uniform was standing next to the counter having coffee before

reporting for duty. Upon seeing the officer, the would-be robber announced a hold-up and fired a few wild shots. The officer and a clerk promptly returned fire, removing the robber from the genepool. Several other customers also drew their guns, but didn't fire. No one else was hurt.

The winner

The 1999 Darwin Award Winner is telephone relay company night watchman Edward Baker, 31, of Thompson, Manitoba, Canada. He was killed early Christmas morning by excessive microwave radiation exposure. He was apparently attempting to keep warm next to a telecommunications feed horn. Baker had been suspended on a safety violation once last year, according to Northern Manitoba Signal Relay spokesperson Tanya Cooke. She noted that Baker's earlier infraction was for defeating a safety shut-off switch and entering a restricted maintenance catwalk in order to stand in front of the microwave dish. He had told co-workers that it was the only way he could stay warm during his 12-hour shift at the station where winter temperatures often dip to 40 degrees below freezing. Microwaves can heat water molecules within human tissue in the same way they heat food in microwave ovens.

For his Christmas shift, Baker reputedly brought a 12-pack of beer and a plastic lawn chair, which he positioned directly in line with the strongest microwave beam. Baker had not been told about a 10-fold boost in microwave power planned that night to handle the anticipated increase in holiday long-distance calling traffic. Baker's body was discovered by the daytime watchman, John Burns, who was greeted by an odour he mistook for a Christmas roast that he thought Baker must have prepared as a surprise. Burns also reported to company officials that Baker's unfinished beers had exploded.

CAUGHT IN BAD TASTE JOKE RUSH >>>

Why didn't JFK Jr take a shower before he left for the Vineyard?
He said he'd wash up on shore.

Hear about Kennedy Airlines?
Their motto is 'Your luggage will arrive before you do!'

What do Kennedys miss most about Martha's Vineyard?
The runway.

How did JFK Jr learn to fly?
Crash course.

How are the Kennedys like oil?
They don't mix well with water.

Why aren't there more JFK Jr jokes out there?
They just haven't surfaced yet.

VASELINE ALLEY >>>

This guy has always dreamed of owning a Harley Davidson. One day he has finally saved enough money, so he goes down to the dealer. After he picks up the perfect bike, the dealer tells him about an old biker trick that will keep the chrome on his new bike free from rust.

The dealer tells him that all he has to do is to keep a jar of Vaseline handy and put it on the chrome before it rains and everything will be fine. He happily pays for the bike and leaves.

After a couple of months he meets a lady and she asks him to take her home to meet her parents over dinner. He readily accepts and the date is set. At the appointed time he picks her up on his Harley and they ride to her parents' house. Before they go in, she tells him that they have a family tradition that whoever speaks first after dinner must do the dishes.

After a delicious dinner everyone sits in silence waiting for the first person to speak and get stuck doing the dishes. After a long 15 minutes the young man decides to speed things up, so he reaches over and kisses the girl in front of her family. No one says a word.

Emboldened, he throws her on the table and has sex with her in front of everyone. No one says a word. Now he is getting desperate, so he grabs her mother and throws her on the table. They have even wilder sex. No one says a word.

By now he is thinking of what to do next when he hears thunder in the distance. His first thought is to protect the chrome on his

Harley, so he reaches into his pocket and pulls out his jar of Vaseline.

And the father shouts, 'Okay damn it, I'll do the dishes.'

DEVOTION TO DUTY >>>

Maria is very religious. She gets married and has 17 children, then her husband dies. She remarries a few weeks later and has another 22 children with her second husband. Maria dies. At her wake, the priest looks tenderly at Maria as she lies in her coffin, looks up to the heavens and says, 'At least they are finally together.'

A man standing next to the priest asks, 'Excuse me, but do you mean Maria and her first husband, or Maria and her second husband?'

The priest says, 'I mean her legs.'

PAYBACK TIME >>>

A successful businessman flew to Vegas for a weekend to gamble. He lost the shirt off his back and had nothing left but a quarter and the second half of his round-trip air ticket. If he could just get to the airport he could get himself home. So he went out to the front of the casino where there was a cab waiting.

He got in and explained his situation to the cabbie. He promised to send the driver money from home, offering his credit card numbers, his driver's licence number and his address but to no avail. The cabbie said, 'If you don't have $15, get the hell out of my cab.'

So the businessman was forced to hitchhike to the airport and was barely in time to catch his flight.

One year later the businessman, having worked long and hard to regain his financial success, returned to Vegas and this time he won big. Feeling pretty good about himself, he went out to the front of the casino to get a cab back to the airport. Well, who should he see out there, at the end of a long line of cabs, but his old buddy who had refused to give him a ride when he was down on his luck.

The businessman thought for a moment about how he could make the guy pay for his lack of charity and he hit on a plan. The businessman got in the first cab in the line. 'How much for a ride to the airport?' he asked. 'Fifteen bucks,' came the reply. 'And how much for you to give me a blowjob on the way?' 'What? Get the hell out of my cab you arsehole!'

The businessman got into the back of each cab in the long line and asked the same questions, with the same result. When he got to his old friend at the back of the line, he got in and asked, 'How much for a ride to the airport?' The cabbie replied, 'Fifteen bucks.'

The businessman said 'OK' and off they went. Then, as they drove slowly past the long line of cabs, the businessman gave a big smile and thumbs-up sign to each driver.

UDDERLY TERRIBLE >>>

A farmer is sitting in the village pub getting pissed. A man comes in and asks the farmer, 'Hey, why are you sitting here on this beautiful day getting drunk?'

Farmer: *'Some things you just can't explain.'*

Man: *'So what happened that is so horrible?'*

Farmer: *'Well, if you must know, today I was sitting by my cow milking her. Just as I got the bucket about full, she took her left leg and kicked it over.'*

Man: *'That's not so bad, what's the big deal?'*

Farmer: *'Some things you just can't explain.'*

Man: *'So then what happened?'*

Farmer: *'I took her left leg and tied it to the post on the left with some rope. Then I sat down and continued to milk her. Just as I got the bucket about full she took her right leg and kicked it over.'*

Man: *'Again? So what did you do then?'*

Farmer: *'I took her right leg and tied it to the post on the right.'*

Man: *'And then what?'*

Farmer: *'I sat back down and continued to milk her and just as I got the bucket just about full, the stupid cow knocked over the bucket with her tail.'*

Man: *'Wow, you must have been pretty upset.'*

Farmer: *'Some things you just can't explain.'*

Man: *'So then what did you do?'*

Farmer: *'Well, I didn't have any more rope, so I took off my belt and tied her tail to the rafter. At that moment, my pants fell down and my wife walked in.'*

SENSITIVE KIND OF GUY >>>

Steve, Bob and Jeff are working on very high scaffolding. Suddenly, Steve falls off and is killed instantly. After the ambulance leaves with Steve's body, Bob and Jeff realise they'll have to inform his wife. Bob says he's good at this sort of sensitive stuff, so he volunteers to do the job.

After two hours he returns carrying a six-pack of beer. 'So did you tell her?' asks Jeff.

'Yep,' replies Bob.

'Say, where did you get the six-pack?'

'She gave it to me.'

'What?' exclaims Jeff. 'You just told her that her husband died and she gave you a six-pack?'

'Sure,' Bob says.

'Why?' asks Jeff.

'Well,' Bob continues, 'when she answered the door, I asked her whether she was Steve's widow. "Widow," she said, "no, no, you're mistaken. I'm not a widow." So I said, "I'll bet you a six-pack you are!"'

THE LAST STRAW >>>

A barman is shutting up for the night when there is a knock at the back door of his pub. When he answers, a dirty, scroungy-looking, homeless guy asks him for a toothpick.

The barman is a little surprised, but nonetheless he gives him the toothpick and the guy goes off.

A few minutes later there is a second knock. When he answers, there is a second homeless guy who also asks for a toothpick. He gets the toothpick and off he goes.

There is a third knock at the door and a third homeless guy. The landlord says, 'Don't tell me, let me guess. You want a toothpick too.'

'Actually no, thanks, but can I have a straw please?'

The landlord is kind of confused by this but, being a good-hearted man, gives him the straw. But before the guy takes off, curiosity gets the better of the barman, so he asks the guy. 'Hey, your friends wanted toothpicks... and you wanted a straw. What's going on?'

The man replies, 'Oh, some drunk girl threw up outside, but all the good stuff's already gone.'

INXS OF MICHAEL >>>

What's the difference between Michael Hutchence and Princess Di?
At least Michael Hutchence remembered to put his belt on.

What was Michael Hutchence's last hit?
The door when the chambermaid entered the room.

Why did Paula Yates leave Bob Geldof for Michael Hutchence?
Because Michael was well hung.

How do you reunite INXS?
Get five more leather belts.

What did Michael Hutchence have that Bob Geldof doesn't?
A widow.

Why did Michael Hutchence prefer to stay at the Ritz Carlton, Double Bay, when he is in Sydney?
Because it's a cool place to hang out.

Did you hear Elton John sang at Michael Hutchence's funeral?
Yeah, he rewrote the words to *The Swing* by INXS.

What was the last thing to go through Michael Hutchence's head?
'This belt is too tight.'

Did Michael Hutchence play golf?
No, he was too much of a choker.

LET THE MUSIC PLAY >>>

At a parade, a cop accidentally bumps into an obviously pregnant woman. He feels like shit, apologises and says, 'It's too bad the little guy isn't born yet. He's missing the parade.'

To this, the woman responds, 'Well I don't have any panties on, so at least he can hear the music.'

GORILLA IN HEAT >>>

A certain zoo had acquired a very rare species of gorilla. Within a few weeks, the female gorilla became very horny and difficult to handle and, upon examination, the zoo veterinarian found that the gorilla was in heat. To make matters worse, there was no male gorilla of the species available.

While reflecting on their problem, the zoo administrators noticed Mike, an employee responsible for cleaning the animals' cages. Mike, it was rumoured, possessed ample ability to satisfy a female, but he wasn't very bright. So the zoo administrators thought they might have a solution and Mike was approached with a proposition: would he be willing to have sex with the gorilla for $500?

Mike showed some interest but said he would have to think the matter over carefully. The following day Mike announced that he would accept their offer, but only under three conditions.

'First,' he said, 'I don't want to have to kiss her. Secondly I want nothing to do with any offspring that may result from the union.'

The zoo administration quickly agreed to these conditions, so they asked what his third condition was.

'Well,' said Mike, 'you've gotta give me another week to come up with the $500.'

SOME MORE INCREDIBLY TRUE STORIES >>>

Talk about bad luck – this lot takes the cake!

A fierce gust of wind blew 45-year-old Vittorio Luise's car into a river near Naples, Italy, in 1983. He managed to break a window, climb out and swim to shore – where a tree blew over and killed him.

Mike Stewart, 31, of Dallas, was filming a movie in 1983 on the dangers of low-level bridges when the truck he was standing on passed under a low-level bridge – and killed him.

Walter Hallas, a 26-year-old store clerk in Leeds, England, was so afraid of dentists that in 1979 he asked a fellow worker to try to cure his toothache by punching him in the jaw. The punch caused Hallas to fall down, hitting his head and he died of a fractured skull.

George Schwartz, owner of a factory in Providence, Rhode Island, narrowly escaped death when a 1983 blast flattened his factory except for one wall. After treatment for minor injuries, he returned to the scene to search for files. The remaining wall then collapsed, killing him.

Depressed that he could not find a job, 42-year-old Romolo Ribolla sat in his kitchen near Pisa, Italy, with a gun in his hand threatening to kill himself. His wife pleaded with him not to do it, and after about half an hour he burst into tears and threw the gun to the floor. It went off and killed his wife.

In 1976, a 22-year-old Irishman, Bob Finnegan, was crossing the busy Falls Road in Belfast when he was struck by a taxi and flung over its roof. The taxi drove away and, as Finnegan lay stunned in the road, another car ran into him, rolling him into the gutter. It too drove on. As a lot of gawkers gathered to examine the magnetic Irishman, a delivery van ploughed through the crowd, leaving in its wake three injured bystanders and an even more battered Bob Finnegan. When a fourth vehicle came along, the crowd wisely scattered and only one person was hit – Bob Finnegan. In the space of two minutes, Finnegan suffered a fractured skull, broken pelvis, broken leg, and other assorted injuries, but hospital officials said he would recover.

Hitting on a novel idea that he could end his wife's incessant nagging by giving her a good scare, Hungarian Jake Fen built an elaborate harness to make it look as if he had hanged himself. When his wife came home and saw him she fainted. Hearing a disturbance a neighbour came over and, finding what she thought were two corpses, seized the opportunity to loot the place. As she was leaving the room, her arms laden, the outraged and suspended Mr Fen kicked her stoutly in the backside. This so surprised the lady that she dropped dead of a heart attack. Happily, Mr Fen was acquitted of manslaughter and he and his wife were reconciled.

FLY IN SHIT >>>

There was a fly buzzing around a barn one day when he came across a pile of fresh cow manure. Due to the fact that it had been hours since his last meal, he flew down and began to eat.

He ate and ate and ate. Finally, he decided he had eaten enough and tried to fly away. He had eaten too much though and could not get off the ground.

As he looked around wondering what to do, he spotted a pitchfork leaning up against the wall. He climbed to the top of the handle and jumped off, thinking that once he got airborne, he would be able to take flight.

Unfortunately he was wrong, and dropped like a rock, splatting when he hit the floor. Dead.

The moral to the story is never fly off the handle when you know you're full of shit.

FASTEN YOUR STRAITJACKETS >>>

A transcript of the new answering service recently installed at the Mental Health Institute.

'Hello, and welcome to the Mental Health Hotline.

- If you are obsessive-compulsive, press 1 repeatedly.
- If you are co-dependent, please ask someone to press 2 for you.
- If you have multiple personalities, press 3, 4, 5 and 6.
- If you are paranoid, we know who you are and what you want. Stay on the line so we can trace your call.
- If you are delusional, press 7 and your call will be transferred to the mother ship.
- If you are schizophrenic, listen carefully and a small voice will tell you which number to press.
- If you are a manic-depressive, it doesn't matter which number you press, as no one will answer.
- If you are dyslexic, press 9696969696969.
- If you have a nervous disorder, please fidget with the hash key until a representative comes on the line.
- If you have amnesia press 8 and state your name, address, phone number, date of birth, social security number and your mother's maiden name.
- If you have post-traumatic stress disorder, slowly and carefully press 000.
- If you have bi-polar disorder, please leave a message after the beep or before the beep. Or after the beep. Please wait for the beep.

- If you have short-term memory loss, press 9.
- If you have short-term memory loss, press 9.
- If you have short-term memory loss, press 9.
- If you have short-term memory loss, press 9.
- If you have low self-esteem, please hang up. All our operators are too busy to talk to you.'

PROPOSING TOASTS >>>

Three guys who have just got married are sitting in their hotel bar after all the receptions having a beer. As they talk, it transpires that all three are virgins, and are a bit naive about how many times they can expect to have sex with their new bride that evening.

One devises a plan of how they can relay this information to the others at breakfast without getting a slap.

'All we do is order as many rounds of toast for how many times you had it last night,' he says, and the others readily agree.

At breakfast the next morning, all three guys look very happy with themselves. The first bloke orders cornflakes, and in a loud voice asks for four slices of toast, and the others give him a wink and a thumbs-up.

The next guy orders scrambled eggs, and again in a voice so the others can hear, orders six slices of toast. Again, his mates give him a 'good-on-yer' look.

The next guy orders a full English breakfast, and then asks for eight slices of toast. His mates give a low whistle of approval, and as the waiter walks away, the guy says to the waiter, 'Oh, and could you make two of those brown, please, mate.'

sealed section

In the words of the TV station about to show you a play or movie which might have a bit of bonking, a flash of the odd tit or one or two thrusting arses... discretion is advised with the contents of this section.

Prying young eyes should be averted to halt the inevitable embarrassing questions from those who can't wait to tell their schoolmates a cracking dirty joke but need to understand it first. These jokes are salacious, disgusting, revolting even... but bloody funny. Readers of a nervous disposition be warned.

Jane was a first-time contestant on a $65,000 quiz show. Lady Luck had smiled in her favour, as Jane had gained a substantial lead over her opponents. She even managed to win the game but, unfortunately, time had run out before the show's host could ask her the big question.

Jane agreed to return the following day. She was nervous as her husband drove them home. 'I've just gotta win tomorrow. I wish I knew what the answers were. You know I'm not going to sleep at all tonight. I will probably look like garbage tomorrow.'

'Relax honey,' her husband, Roger, reassured her. 'It will all be OK.'

Ten minutes after they arrived home, Roger grabbed the car keys and started heading out the door. 'Where are you going?' Jane asked. 'I have a little errand to run. I should be back soon.'

After an agonising three-hour absence, Roger returned, sporting a very wide and wicked grin. 'Honey, I managed to get tomorrow's question and answer.'

'What is it?' she cried excitedly.

'OK, the question is, "What are the three main parts of the male anatomy?" And the answer is, "The head, the heart and the penis."'

The couple went to sleep with Jane, now feeling at ease, plummeting into a deep slumber. At 3.30 am, however, Jane was shaken awake by Roger, who was asking her the quiz show question. 'The head, the heart, the penis,' Jane replied groggily before returning to sleep.

Roger asked her again in the morning as Jane was brushing her teeth. Once again she replied correctly.

So it was that Jane was once again on the set of the quiz show. Even though she knew the question and answer, she could feel butterflies. The cameras began running and the host, after reminding the audience of the previous day's events, faced Jane and asked the big question.

'Jane, for $65,000, what are the main parts of the male anatomy? You have ten seconds.'

'Hmmm, uhm, the head? She said nervously.

'Very good. Six seconds.'

'Eh, uh, the heart?

'Very good. Four seconds.'

'I, uhh, oooooooooohh, darn! My husband drilled it into me last night and I had it on the tip of my tongue this morning… '

'That's close enough,' said the game-show host, 'Congratulations!'

HOOKED, LINE AND SINKER >>>

A young boy on his way home from school must pass a group of hookers.

Every day as he passes them, the hookers wave at him with their pinkies and say 'Hi there, little boy.'

One day the boy stops and asks one of the hookers why they always wave at him with their pinkies.

She replies, 'Well, that is what size we imagine your penis to be… it is just a joke.'

The next day on his way home, the hookers repeat the tradition. The young boy stops and drops his school books on the ground, sticks all his fingers in his mouth to stretch his lips very wide and says, 'Hi there ladies!'

COCK-A-DOODLE-DO >>>

A woman walks into her accountant's office and tells him that she needs to file her taxes.

The accountant says, 'Before we begin, I'll need to ask a few questions.'

He gets her name, address and social security number and then asks, 'What is your occupation?'

The woman replies, 'I'm a whore.'

The accountant baulks and says, 'No, no, no. That will never work. That is much too crass. Let's try to rephrase that.'

The woman says, 'OK, I'm a prostitute.'

'No, that is still too crude. Try again.'

They both think for a minute, then the woman says, 'I'm a chicken farmer.'

The accountant asks, 'What does chicken farming have to do with being a whore or a prostitute?'

'Well, I raised over 5000 cocks last year!'

NEW TWIST TO CINDERELLA >>>

Cinderella wants to go to the ball, but her wicked stepmother won't let her.

So, as Cinderella sits crying in the garden, her fairy godmother appears and promises to provide Cinderella with everything she needs to go to the ball, but only on two conditions.

'First, you must wear a diaphragm.'

Cinderella agrees and says, 'What's the second condition?'

'You must be home by 2 am. Any later and your diaphragm will turn into a pumpkin.'

Cinderella agrees to be home by 2 am. The appointed hour comes and goes and Cinderella doesn't show up. Finally, at 5 am, Cinderella shows up looking love-struck and very satisfied.

'Where have you been?' demands the fairy godmother. 'Your diaphragm was supposed to turn into a pumpkin three hours ago!'

'I met a prince, Fairy Godmother. He took care of everything.'

'I know of no prince with that kind of power. Tell me his name.'

'I can't remember exactly, Peter Peter, something or other… '

HE'S WELL HARD >>>

A man is in a hotel lobby. He wants to ask the clerk a question, but as he turns to go to the front desk, he accidentally bumps into a woman beside him and as he does, his elbow goes into her breast.

They are both startled and he says, 'Ma'am, if your heart is as soft as your breast, I know you'll forgive me.'

She replies, 'If your penis is as hard as your elbow, I'm in room 1221.'

IT'S CATCHING ON >>>

A teacher asks her class to use the word contagious. Roland, the class swot, gets up and says, 'Last year I got the measles and my Mum said it was contagious.'

'Well done Roland,' says the teacher. 'Can anyone else try?'

Katie, a sweet little girl with pigtails says, 'My Gran says there's a bug going round and it's contagious.'

'Well done, Katie,' says the teacher. 'Anyone else?'

Little Johnny jumps up and says, 'Our next-door neighbour is painting his house with a 4 cm brush and my Dad says it will take the contagious.'

EXTREMELY POOR TASTE >>>

A young man walks up and sits down at the bar. 'What can I get you?' the barman inquires.

'I want six shots of whisky,' responds the young man.

'Six shots? Are you celebrating something?'

'Yeah, my first blowjob.'

'Well, in that case, let me give you a seventh on the house.'

The young man says, 'No offence sir, but if six shots won't get rid of the taste, nothing will.'

COUNTRY WISE >>>

A businessman boards a flight and is lucky enough to be seated next to an absolutely gorgeous woman. They exchange brief hellos and he notices she is reading a manual about sexual statistics.

He asks her about it and she replies, 'This is a very interesting book about sexual statistics. It identifies that Native Americans have the longest average penis and Polish men have the biggest average diameter. By the way, my name is Jill, what's yours?'

He coolly replies, 'Tonto Kawalski, nice to meet you.'

ON THE TILES >>>

An Irish wife was having a shower and slipped over on the bathroom floor. Instead of slipping over forwards, she slipped over and did the splits and suctioned herself to the floor.

She yelled out for her husband. 'Paddy! Paddy!' she yelled.

Paddy came running in. 'Paddy I've suctioned myself to the floor,' she said.

'Ohhh nooo! Paddy said and tried to pull her up. 'You're just too heavy, love. I'll go across the road and get Shamus.'

Paddy comes back with Shamus and they both tried to pull her up. 'Nope, I can't do it,' Shamus said, 'Let's try plan C.'

'Plan C?' exclaimed Paddy. 'What's that?'

'I'll go home and get my hammer and chisel and we will break the tiles under her.'

'Oh okay,' Paddy said. 'While you're doing that I'll stay here and play with her tits.'

'Play with her tits?' Shamus said. 'Why would you do that? This is hardly the time.'

Paddy replied, 'Well, I figure if I can get her wet enough, we can slide her into the kitchen where the tiles aren't so expensive to replace.'

RUBBING UP THE RIGHT WAY >>>

One night, as a couple lay down for bed, the husband gently taps his wife on the shoulder and starts rubbing her arm.

The wife turns over and says, 'I'm sorry honey, but I've got a gynaecologist's appointment tomorrow and I want to stay fresh.'

The husband, rejected, turns over and tries to sleep. A few minutes later, he rolls back over and taps his wife again. This time he whispers in her ear, 'Do you have a dentist's appointment tomorrow too?'

COME AGAIN? >>>

A small white guy goes into an elevator and the only other passenger is a huge black dude standing next to him. The big black dude looks down upon the small white guy and says, '2.5 m tall, 130 kg, 40 cm dick, 1.5 kg left ball, 1.5 kg right ball, Turner Brown.'

The small white guy faints.

The big black dude picks up the small white guy and brings him to, slapping his face and shaking him and asks the small white guy, 'What's wrong?'

The small white guy says, 'Excuse me, but what did you say?'

The big black dude looks down and says, '2.5 m tall, 130 kg, 40 cm dick, 1.5 kg left ball, 1.5 kg right ball, Turner Brown.'

The small white guy says, 'Thank God. I thought you said, "turn around".'

WILLY 'GATOR >>>

A guy walked into a bar with a pet alligator by his side. He put the alligator up on the bar. He turned to the astonished patrons and said, 'I'll make you a deal. I'll open this alligator's mouth and place my genitals inside. Then the 'gator will close his mouth for one minute. He'll then open his mouth and I'll remove my unit unscathed. In return for witnessing this spectacle, each of you will buy me a drink.'

The crowd murmured their approval. The man stood up on the bar, dropped his trousers, and placed his privates in the alligator's open mouth. The 'gator closed his mouth as the crowd gasped. After a minute, the man grabbed a beer bottle and rapped the alligator hard on the top of its head. The 'gator opened his mouth and the man removed his genitals unscathed as promised.

The crowd cheered and the first of his free drinks were delivered. The man stood up again and made another offer.

'I'll pay anyone $100 who's willing to give it a try.' A hush fell over the crowd. After a while, a hand went up in the back of the bar and a woman timidly spoke up.

'I'll try, but you have to promise not to hit me on the head with a beer bottle.'

IN A PICKLE >>>

Bill worked in a pickle factory. He had been employed there for a number of years when he came home one day to confess to his wife that he had a terrible compulsion. He had an urge to stick his penis into the pickle slicer. His wife suggested that he should see a sex therapist to talk about it, but Bill declined saying that he'd be too embarrassed. He vowed to overcome the compulsion on his own.

One day a few weeks later, Bill came home absolutely ashen. His wife could see at once that something was seriously wrong. 'What's wrong, Bill?' she asked.

Bill said, 'Do you remember that I told you how I had this tremendous urge to put my penis into the pickle slicer?'

'Oh Bill, you didn't,' she said.

'Yes, I did,' said Bill.

'My God, Bill, what happened?'

'I got fired.'

'No, Bill, I mean what happened with the pickle slicer?'

'Oh, she got fired too.'

A REAL CHOKER >>>

A man was visiting his wife in hospital where she had been in a coma for several years. On this visit he decides to rub her left breast instead of just talking to her. On doing this, she lets out a sigh,

The man runs out and tells the doctor, who says this is a good sign and suggests he should try rubbing her right breast to see if there is any reaction. The man goes in and rubs her right breast and this brings a moan.

From this, the doctor suggests that the man should go in and try oral sex, saying he will wait outside as it is a personal act and he doesn't want the man to be embarrassed.

The man goes in and then comes out about five minutes later, white as a sheet and tells the doctor his wife is dead. The doctor asked what happened. The man replied, 'She choked.'

OFF THE RAILS >>>

A man and a woman are riding next to each other in the first-class carriage of a train. The man sneezes, pulls out his penis and wipes the tip. The woman can't believe what she just saw and decides she is hallucinating.

A few minutes pass. The man sneezes again and again he pulls out his penis and wipes the tip.

The woman is about to go nuts. She can't believe that such a rude person exists. A few more minutes pass and the man sneezes again. He again takes his penis out and wipes the tip.

The woman has finally had enough. She turns to the man and says, 'Three times you've sneezed, and three times you've removed your penis from your pants to wipe it. What kind of degenerate are you?'

The man replies, 'I am sorry to have disturbed you, ma'am. I have a very rare condition that means when I sneeze, I have an orgasm.'

The woman, now feeling badly, says, 'Oh, I'm sorry. What are you taking for it?'

The man looks at her and says, 'Pepper.'

FANTASYLAND >>>

Snow White saw Pinocchio through the woods, so she ran up behind him, knocked him flat on his back and then sat on his face crying, 'Lie to me! Lie to me!'

And Mickey Mouse and Minnie Mouse were in the divorce court and the judge said to Mickey, 'You say here that your wife is crazy?'

Mickey replied, 'No I didn't. I said she is f***ing Goofy.'

WHITE WEDDING >>>

A woman getting married for the fourth time visited a tailor to get a wedding dress made. When the tailor inquired about the colour, the bride-to-be said, 'White.'

The tailor was a bit surprised by this, and said, 'Excuse me, I don't mean to pry, but since white is the colour traditionally worn by a virgin on her wedding night, I can't help wondering if you might still be a virgin? How could that be?'

The woman replied, 'I'm sorry to say, but that's the way it is. You see, my first husband was a psychologist. He just wanted to talk about it. My second husband was a gynaecologist. He just wanted to look. My third husband was a stamp collector… God I miss him.'

UNITED NATIONS >>>

A woman is just about to give birth in the hospital when she says to the doctor, 'Doc, do me a favour. Tell me what colour the baby is as it's being born.'

The doctor is understandably a little puzzled at this. 'Why don't you know what colour the child is going to be?'

'Well,' says the woman, 'the problem is that I'm a porno actress and the child was conceived during the making of a film. I have no idea who the father is.'

'OK', says the doctor, 'I'll do it for you, but it's most unusual.'

The baby begins to be born and the doctor says, 'Here comes the head, it seems to have yellow skin and the eyes are slanted. Was one of the actors Chinese?'

'Yes, doctor, he was,' says the woman.

'Wait,' says the doctor, 'the chest and arms are out and they seem to be very dark. Was one of the actors black?'

'Yes doctor, he was.'

'Wait, now the legs are out and they're light brown. Was one of the actors of mixed race?'

'Yes doctor, he was.'

So the doctor pulls the baby free and gives it the traditional slap on the back. The baby lets out a healthy 'waaaaahh' and starts crying.

'Oh, thank God for that!' says the woman, 'for a moment there I thought it might bark.'

PAYMENT IN KIND >>>

One dismal rainy night in Sydney a taxi driver spotted an arm waving from the shadows of an alley. Even before he rolled to a stop at the kerb, a figure leaped into the cab and slammed the door.

Checking his rear view mirror as he pulled away, he was startled to see a dripping wet, naked woman sitting in the back seat.

'Where to?' he stammered.

'Kings Cross,' answered the woman.

'You got it,' he said, taking another long glance in the mirror.

The woman caught him staring at her and asked, 'Just what the hell are you looking at, driver?'

'Well, madam,' he answered, 'I was just wondering how you'll pay your fare.'

The woman spread her legs, put her feet up on the front seat, smiled at the driver and said, 'Does this answer your question?'

Still looking in the mirror, the cabbie asked, 'Got anything smaller?'

DOGGIE FASHION >>>

Three dogs were sitting in the waiting room at the veterinarian's. One of the dogs was hanging its head and sighing. The second dog turned to him and asked, 'What are you in here for, buddy?'

The dog looked depressed. 'I'm in big trouble,' he said. 'My owner has a really nice sports car with leather seats. I just love to go for rides in it. Well, the other day, he took me for a ride and I was so excited, I peed on the nice leather seat. Now he's having me put to sleep.'

'I know how you feel,' said the second dog. 'My owners have a beautiful, expensive oriental rug. The other day they were late getting home from work and I just couldn't help myself. I shit all over their nice carpet and ruined it. They're having me put to sleep too.'

Both dogs turned to the third dog in the waiting room. 'So what are you here for?' they asked.

'Well', said the third dog, 'my owner likes to do her housework in the nude. The other day, she was vacuuming and she knelt down to vacuum under the sofa and I just couldn't help myself. I hopped on her back and had the ride of my life.'

The other dogs nodded in sympathy. 'So she's having you put to sleep too, huh?'

'No,' said the dog, 'I'm having my nails clipped.'

WHALE OF A TIME >>>

A male whale and a female whale were swimming off the coast of Japan when they noticed a whaling ship. The male whale recognised it as the same ship that had harpooned his father many years earlier.

He said to the female whale, 'Let's both swim under the ship and blow out of our air holes at the same time. It should cause the ship to turn over and sink.'

They tried it, and sure enough the ship turned over and quickly sank. Soon, however, the whales realised the sailors had jumped overboard and were swimming to the safety of the shore. The male was enraged that they were going to get away and told the female, 'Let's swim after them and gobble them up before they reach the shore.'

At this point he realised the female was becoming reluctant to follow him. 'Look,' she said. 'I went along with the blowjob, but I absolutely refuse to swallow the seamen.'

REACHING THE HEIGHTS >>>

Height of Patience: *A naked woman lying down with her legs apart under a banana tree.*

Height of Frustration: *A boxer trying to scratch his balls.*

Height of Innocence: *A teenage girl applying Clearasil to her nipples.*

Height of Laziness: *A guy lying on a girl and waiting for an earthquake to do the rest.*

Height of Competition: *A guy peeing beside a waterfall.*

Height of Sophistication: *Sucking nipples with a straw.*

Height of Disgust: *While wiping after a good toilet dump, your finger pokes through the paper.*

Height of Technology: *A condom with a zip.*

Height of Trouble: *A one-handed man hanging from a cliff and his arse is itching.*

CHEMICAL REACTION >>>

A man walks into a chemist and says to the bloke behind the counter, 'Listen, I have three girls coming over tonight. I've never had three girls at once and I need something to keep me horny… keep me potent.'

The chemist reaches under the counter, unlocks the bottom drawer and takes out a small cardboard box marked with the label Viagra-Extra Strength and says, 'If you take this, you'll go mental for 12 hours.'

Very happy and excited, the man says, 'Gimme three boxes.'

The next day the man walks into the same chemist's shop, right up to the same chemist and pulls down his pants. The chemist looks in horror as he notices the man's cock is swollen, black and blue, and the skin is hanging off in some places.

The man says, 'Gimme a tube of Deep Heat.'

The chemist replies, 'Deep Heat? You're not going to put Deep Heat on that are you?'

The man says, 'No, it's for my arms. The girls didn't show up.'

JAPANESE QUEUE JUMPING >>>

A waitress walks up to one of her tables in a New York City restaurant and notices that the three Japanese businessmen seated there are furiously masturbating.

She says, 'What the hell do you guys think you're doing?'

One of the Japanese men says, 'We are all berry hungry.'

The waitress says, 'So how is whacking off in this restaurant going to help that situation?'

Another businessman replies, 'Because menu say, first come first served.'

SCOTTISH LOVE RITES >>>

New research delivers enlightening insight into the sex life of the Scottish male.

Preparation

Friday night is very much love-night for the Scottish man. Arriving back from the pub, having partaken of the traditional Scottish aphrodisiac – 12 pints of heavy, a white pudding supper and three pickled onions – his mind is set on one thing: love.

His lust at fever pitch after the sensuous excitement of a hard night's dominoes, he approaches his beloved wife, enticing her with gentle words of passion, 'Any chance of na nookie?'

The good lady in question, perhaps over-excited by the erotic smell of stale beer or the sensuous vision of pickled onions sticking to his chin, is at first somewhat reluctant. This coy reluctance is expressed with the flirtatious reply, 'Awaity f*** ya bam.'

Foreplay

Foreplay is very important indeed. This basically consists of the male casting off his lightly soiled Y-fronts provocatively at his wife, usually landing skid-mark down, as he approaches the bed and singing the ancient Gaelic fertility chant, 'Here we go, here we go, here we go.' Upon reaching the bed, he comments proudly on his rampant 8 inches. This is a classic example of alcohol-induced double vision.

Initial problems

After 12 pints, sometimes the man's Wee Willie Winkle is a trifle reluctant to extend itself (literally). Impotence is very much a blow to the man's self-esteem and the wife has to be very tactful. She will offer gentle and sensitive words of encouragement such as, 'Ya useless bastard,' or possibly, 'It never happens tae ra milkman.'

Fellatio

Oral sex is a great favourite with the Scotsman. He approaches his wife with a cheeky invitation, 'Howd ya like to put yer teeth roon this?'

The woman nods willingly and points suggestively to her falsies smiling happily in a bedside tumbler. 'Go on yersel,' she says, 'jist dinnae disturb me.'

Down to business

Eventually the moment comes to consummate their tender love. Again, alcohol-induced double vision is an important factor as the man decides which of his willies to use. Sometimes in his excitement, he may suffer from premature ejaculation, a phenomenon he explains to his wife using the poetic phrase, 'F*** me, I've shot ma load.'

If this does occur, it is essential he makes up for disappointing his wife by uttering tender and loving compliments such as informing her she's the nicest woman he's ever come across. An imaginative lover, the Scotsman, possibly having read that women like to be spoken to dirty, says such things as, 'Shite, arsehole.'

The woman is speechless. The man is now thrusting away, his mind a kaleidoscope of jumbled erotic thoughts. The woman wonders if they should repaint the ceiling. Sometimes she utters a word of encouragement such as, 'Are you sure it's in?'

Given his level of sexual expertise, the Scotsman's ideal partner should be a versatile lover specialising in the faked orgasm. This takes the form of a breathless shout, 'Ooyah, ooyah, gallus big man.'

Eventually it's all over. The man rolls over, wipes his dick on her nightie, falls asleep and commences snoring like a pig.

There's no one in the world that performs quite like a Scotsman – a veritable prince in the kingdom of sex.

FLASH HARRY >>>

A young man was showing off his new sportscar to his girlfriend. She was thrilled at the speed. 'If I do 250 kph, will you take off your clothes?' he smirked. 'Yes,' said his adventurous girlfriend. And as he gets up to 250, she peeled off all her clothes.

Unable to keep his eyes on the road, the car skidded onto some gravel and flipped over. The naked girl was thrown clear, but he was jammed beneath the steering wheel.

'Go and get help!' he cried.

'But I can't! I'm naked and my clothes are gone!'

'Take my shoe' he said 'and cover yourself.'

Holding the shoe over her privates, the girl ran down the road and found a service station. Still holding the shoe between her legs, she pleaded to the service station proprietor, 'Please help me! My boyfriend's stuck!'

The proprietor looked at the shoe and said, 'There's nothing I can do. He's in too far.'

BAR TALK >>>

A bloke goes into a pub. The barmaid asks what he wants. 'I want to put my head between your tits, and lick the sweat off,' he replies.

'You dirty bastard!' shouts the barmaid, 'Get out before I get my husband.'

The bloke apologises and says he will never do it again. The barmaid, disgusted, accepts his apology and asks what he wants again.

'I want to pull down your knickers, spread cottage cheese between your arse cheeks and lick it off,' he replies.

'What???' screams the barmaid, 'That's it! You're barred, you dirty, filthy, perverted bastard, get out now.'

Once again the bloke apologises, and says he will never, ever do it again.

'Right. I'll give you one last chance,' says the barmaid. 'Now, what do you want?'

'I want to turn you upside down, fill your pussy with Guinness and drink it all out of you.'

The barmaid starts crying and runs upstairs to her husband, who is sitting down watching the telly. 'What's up, love?' says the husband.

'There's this disgusting bloke downstairs. When I asked him what he wanted, he said that he wanted to put his head between my tits and lick the sweat off,' she says in a flood of tears.

'What? He's a dead man,' shouts the husband getting out of his chair.

'Then he said he wanted to pull down my knickers, spread cottage cheese between my arse cheeks and lick it off,' screams the wife.

'Right, he's going to need a body bag, the bastard,' shouts the husband rolling up his sleeves and picking up a baseball bat.

'Then he said he wanted to turn me upside down, fill my pussy with Guinness and drink it out of me,' she concludes.

When he hears this, the husband puts the baseball bat down and sits back down in his chair.

'Aren't you going to do something?' shouts the wife in hysterics.

'Listen love, I'm not messing with someone who can drink 14 pints of Guinness…'

PICK-UP LINES BOUND TO EARN A SLAP >>>

- 'The word of the day is legs. Let's go back to my place and spread the word…'
- 'Hey baby, can I tickle your belly button – from the inside?'
- 'I like every bone in your body – especially mine… '
- 'My face is leaving in 15 minutes – be on it…'
- 'Why don't you sit on my face and let me eat my way to your heart?'
- 'I may not be Fred Flinstone, but I sure can make your bed rock…'
- 'Is that a mirror in your pants, because I can see myself in them?'
- 'When does your centrefold come out?'
- 'So do ya wanna see something really swell?'
- 'Is your name Gillette? Because you're the best a man can get…'
- 'You're like Pringles – once I pop you, I can't stop you…'
- 'You have great legs, what time do they open?'
- 'If you were a car door, I would slam you all night long…'

COMPARING NOTES >>>

Three ladies all have separate boyfriends named Larry. One evening, while sharing a few drinks at the bar, one of the ladies suggests, 'Let's name our Larrys after a soft drink, because I'm tired of getting my Larry mixed up with your Larry, and her Larry mixed up with your Larry.' The other two ladies agree.

The first lady speaks out, 'Okay then, I'm gonna name my Larry "7-Up" because he has 7" and it's always up!' The three ladies hoot and holler, and slap each other high fives.

Then, the second lady says, 'I'm gonna name my Larry "Mountain Dew" because he can mount and do me any day of the week.' Again, the three ladies hoot and holler, and slap each other more high fives.

The third lady then says, 'You know, those two Larrys were good, but I'm gonna name my Larry "Jack Daniels".'

The other two ladies shout in unison, '"Jack Daniels"? That's not a soft drink… that's a hard liquor!'

The third lady replies, 'That's my Larry!'

MR LIVINGSTONE'S DISCOVERY >>>

This British explorer is in the dark jungle going where no Western man has gone before. Accompanying him is his trusted guide, interpreter, cook and trouble-shooter in one.

One day early in the morning, they arrive at a lake and find a handsome dark young man engaged in 'playful activities' with 10 beautiful, dark, young women – all nude.

The young man had the biggest, strongest penis the Britisher had ever seen, or even imagined. He asked his guide who this man was?

'He is the prince of the tribe that lives on the other side of the lake, sir,' came the reply. 'This is his morning ritual.'

'Ask him,' the awed Brit said to his companion, 'how did his penis get to be this size?' The guide goes to the lake and talks to the man, who seems to get very agitated by the conversation.

'Well, what did he say?' asked our hero to his assistant on his return.

'He said, "There's nothing wrong with my penis. Doesn't the white man's shrink in cold water?"'

by royal appointment

They can't help it. It wasn't their fault they were born into arguably the world's most exclusive family. But then we can't help it either. It is human nature to take a pop at famous or rich people and to a certain extent they help us by being who they are and doing what they do.

There are no tasteless Diana jokes in here – they were funny but they're past their use-by date by now. She does get an honourable mention in a Michael Hutchence jibe – is that all right?

GOING PRIVATE >>>

The Queen is visiting one of Australia's top hospitals and during her tour of the floors she passed a room where a male patient was masturbating. 'Oh my God,' said the Queen. 'That's disgraceful. What is the meaning of this?'

The doctor leading the tour explains, 'I am sorry your Royal Highness, but this man has a very serious condition where the testicles rapidly fill with semen. If he doesn't do that five times a day they'll explode and he would die instantly.'

'Oh I am so sorry,' said the Queen.

On the next floor they passed a room where a young nurse was giving a patient a blowjob. 'Oh my God,' said the Queen, 'what's happening there?'

The doctor replied, 'Same problem, better health cover.'

HELLO SAILOR >>>

On the day of the wedding, Sophie was getting dressed surrounded by all her family when she suddenly realised she had forgotten to get any shoes. Panic! Then her sister remembered she had a pair of white shoes from her wedding, so she lent them to Sophie for the day. Unfortunately they were a bit too small and by the time the festivities were over, Sophie's feet were agony.

When she and Edward withdrew to their room, the only thing she could think of was getting her shoes off.

The rest of the family crowded round the door to the bedroom and they heard roughly what they expected: grunts, straining noises and the occasional muffled scream. Eventually they heard Edward say, 'God, that was tight.'

'There,' whispered the Queen, 'I told you she was a virgin.'

Then, to their surprise, they heard Edward say, 'Right. Now for the other one.' This was followed by more grunting and straining and at last Edward said, 'My God, that was even tighter.'

'That's my boy,' said the Duke. 'Once a sailor, always a sailor.'

DREAM GENIE >>>

Prince Charles was driving around his mother's estate when he accidentally ran over her favourite dog, a corgi, crushing it to a pulp.

He got out of his Range Rover and sat down on the grass totally distraught. The whole world was against him and now his mother would go ballistic. Suddenly he noticed a lamp half-buried in the ground. He dug it up, polished it and immediately a genie appeared.

'You have freed me from thousands of years of imprisonment,' said the genie. 'As a reward I shall grant you one wish.'

'Well,' said the Prince, 'I have all the material things I need, but let me show you this dog.' They walk over to the splattered remains of the dog. 'Do you think you could bring this dog back to life for me?' the Prince asked.

The genie carefully looked at the remains and shook his head. 'This body is too far gone for even me to bring it back to life. Is there something else you would like?'

The Prince thought for a minute, reached into his pocket and pulled out two photos. 'I was married to this beautiful woman called Diana,' said Prince Charles, showing the genie the first photo. 'But now I love this woman called Camilla,' and he showed the genie the second photo. 'You see Camilla isn't beautiful at all, so do you think you can make Camilla as beautiful as Diana?'

The genie studied the two photographs and after a few minutes said, 'Let's have a look at that dog again.'

JOHN PAUL II AND LIZZIE II >>>

The Pope and Queen Elizabeth were standing on a balçony beaming at thousands of people in the forecourt below. The Queen says to the Pope out of the corner of her mouth, 'I bet you a tenner that I can make every English person in the crowd go wild with just a wave of my hand.'

The Pope says, 'No way. You can't do that.' The Queen says, 'Watch this.' So she waves her hand and every English person in the crowd goes crazy, waving their little plastic Union Jacks on sticks and cheering and basically going ballistic.

So the Pope is standing there going, 'Uh oh, what am I going to do? I never thought she'd be able to do it.'

So he thinks for a minute and then he turns to her and says, 'I bet you I can make every Irish person in the crowd go wild, not just now, but for the rest of the week, with just one nod of my head.'

The Queen says, 'No way. It can't be done.' So the Pope headbutts her.

the generation game

This chapter has a poke at things that have moved the earth for different generations and bring on unashamed feelings of nostalgia even when you look back on it all as a load of old bollocks. The decades of the 20th century all seem to have their own expressions that describe them. The '20s were 'roaring'. The '30s were in depression. The '40s were about war and then rationing. The '50s were bloody boring. The '60s were swinging. The '70s were about platform shoes and revolting hairstyles. The '80s were greedy while the '90s were, well, depressingly high-tech and doing a lot of us out of jobs. But they did bring e-mail...

CALLING ALL '70S CHILDREN >>>

You know you're approaching 30 when…

1. You leave gigs before the encore to 'beat the rush'.
2. You own a lawnmower.
3. You stop dreaming of becoming a professional rugby player and start dreaming of having a son who might become one instead.
4. Before throwing the local paper away you look through the property section.
5. You prefer Backch@t with Bill Ralston to Ice TV.
6. All of a sudden, Jenny Shipley is not 47, she's 'only 47'.
7. Before going out anywhere you ask what the parking is like.
8. Flicking through *Pavement* magazine makes you too tired to go out.
9. Rather than throw a knackered pair of trainers out, you keep them because they'll be all right for the garden.
10. You buy your first T-shirt without any writing on it.
11. Instead of laughing at the Innovations catalogue that falls out of the newspaper, you suddenly see both the benefit and money-saving properties of a plastic winter cover for your garden bench, not to mention the plastic man for the car to deter would-be thieves.
12. You start to worry about your parents' health.
13. You complain that Ecstasy's 'not what it used to be' because you know that if you have some it will take about 48 hours to recover and, anyway, you might look a bit of a twat.
14. Sure, you have more disposable income, but everything you want to buy costs between $200 and $300.
15. You don't get funny looks when you buy a Disney video or a Wallace and Gromit bubble bath, as the sales assistant assumes they are for your child.
16. All pop music starts to sound questionable.
17. You opt for Pizza Haven over Pizza Hut because they don't have any pictures on the menus and, anyway, they do a really nice half-bottle of House white.
18. You become powerless to resist the lure of assemble-it-yourself furniture.
19. You always have enough milk in the house.

20. To compensate for the fact that you have little desire to go clubbing, you instead frequent really loud tapas restaurants and pubs with wacky names in the mistaken belief that you have not turned into your parents.
21. The benefits of a pension scheme become clear.
22. You go out of your way to pick up a colour chart from Guthrie Bowron.
23. You wish you had a shed.
24. You have a shed.
25. You actually find yourself saying, 'They don't make 'em like that any more' and, 'I remember when there were only three TV channels' and, 'Of course, in my day.'
26. Instead of tutting at old people who take ages to get off the bus, you tut at schoolchildren whose diction is poor.
27. When sitting outside a pub you become envious of their hanging baskets.
28. You make an effort to be in and out of the local Indian restaurant by 11 pm.

ROLLED OATS OR CREMOATA? >>>

'You know, honey,' the little old lady said. 'My nipples are as hot for you today as they were 50 years ago.'

'I'm not surprised,' replied Gramps. 'One's in your coffee and the other is in your porridge.'

GOOD VIBRATIONS >>>

A mother was walking down the hall when she heard a humming sound coming from her daughter's bedroom. When she opened the door she found her daughter naked on the bed with a vibrator.

'What are you doing?' she exclaimed.

The daughter replied, 'I'm 35 and still living at home with my parents and this is the closest I'll ever get to a husband.'

Later that week the father was in the kitchen and heard a humming sound coming from the basement. When he went downstairs, he found his daughter naked on the sofa with her vibrator.

'What are you doing?' he exclaimed.

The daughter replied, 'I'm 35 and still living at home with my parents and this is the closest I'll ever get to a husband.'

A couple of days later the mother heard the humming sound again, this time in the living room. Upon entering the room, she found her husband watching television with the vibrator buzzing away beside him. She asked, 'What are you doing?'

He replied, 'Watching the game with my son-in-law.'

MOTHER KNOWS BEST >>>

John invited his mother over for dinner. During the meal, his mother couldn't help noticing how beautiful John's flatmate was. She had long been suspicious of a relationship between John and his flatmate and this only made her more curious.

Over the course of the evening, while watching the two interact, she started to wonder if there was more between John and the flatmate than met the eye.

Reading his mum's thoughts, John volunteered, 'I know what you must be thinking, but I assure you, Julie and I are just flatmates.'

About a week later, Julie came to John and said, 'Ever since your mother came to dinner, I've been unable to find the beautiful silver gravy ladle. You don't suppose she took it, do you?'

John said, 'Well, I doubt it but I'll write her a letter just to be sure.'

So he sat down and wrote, *'Dear Mother, I'm not saying you did take a gravy ladle from my house and I'm not saying you did not take a gravy ladle. But the fact remains that one has been missing ever since you were here for dinner.'*

Several days later John received a letter from his mother which read, *'Dear Son, I'm not saying that you do sleep with Julie and I'm not saying that you do not sleep with Julie. But the fact remains that if she were sleeping in her own bed, she would have found the gravy ladle by now. Love, Mum.'*

WILL O' THE WISP >>>

Little Johnny was walking down the road one day and an old man was sitting on his front porch rocking back and forth in his rocking chair. The old man said, 'Whatcha got there, son?'

Johnny said, 'Got me some chicken wire.'

'Whatcha gonna do with that chicken wire, son?' asked the old man.

'Gonna catch me some chickens,' said Johnny.

'You can't catch chickens with chicken wire,' said the oldster.

Johnny just shrugged his shoulders and walked on down the street. About half an hour later, Johnny came back passing the old man's front porch with three chickens entangled in the chicken wire. The old man was shocked and couldn't believe his eyes.

A little later Johnny passed the old man's porch. 'Whatcha got now, son?'

'Got me some duct tape.'

'And whatcha gonna do with that duct tape?' the old man asked.

'Gonna catch me some ducks.'

'You can't catch ducks with duct tape,' said the old man. Johnny just shrugged his shoulders and kept on walking.

About half an hour later, back comes Johnny with three ducks tangled in the duct tape. Again, the old man rubbed his eyes in disbelief.

Half an hour later, Johnny was again passing the old man's porch. 'Whatcha got now, son?' asked the old codger.

'Got me some pussy willow.'

The old man said, 'Wait right there while I get my shoes!'

CHEMICAL REACTIONS >>>

There were four students taking organic chemistry at university. They did so well on all the quizzes, mid-terms, labs and essays that each had an 'A' so far for the semester. These four friends were so confident with the finals approaching that the weekend before they decided to go back to their home town and party with some friends there.

They had a great time. However, after all the hard partying, they slept all day Sunday and didn't make it back to town until early Monday morning – the morning of their final exam.

Rather than taking the final then, they decided to find their professor AFTER the exam and explain to him why they missed it. They explained that they had gone home to do some study for the weekend with the plan to come back in time for the exam. But unfortunately, they had a flat tyre on the way back, didn't have a spare, and couldn't get help for a long time. As a result, they had only just arrived now!

The professor thought it over and then agreed they could make up their final exam the following day. The four were elated and relieved. They studied hard that night – all night – and went in the next day at the time the professor had told them. He placed them in separate rooms and handed each of them a test booklet and told them to begin.

The first problem was worth five points. It was something simple about free radical formation. 'Cool,' they all thought in their separate rooms, 'this is going to be easy.'

Each finished the problem and turned the page. On the second page was written, 'Question 2 (for 95 points): Which tyre?'

PARROT FASHION >>>

A young punk gets on the bus. He's got spiked, multicoloured hair that's green, purple and orange. His clothes are a tattered mix of leather rags. His legs are bare and he's wearing worn-out shoes. His entire face and body are riddled with pierced jewellery and his earrings are big, bright feathers.

He sits down in the only vacant seat, directly across from an old man who glares at him for the next 10 minutes. Finally, the punk gets self-conscious and barks at the old man, 'What are you looking at, you old fart? Didn't you ever do anything wild when you were young?'

Without missing a beat, the old man replies, 'Yeah, back when I was young and in the navy I got really drunk one night in Singapore and had sex with a parrot. I thought that maybe you were my son!'

WHO'RE YOU CALLING OLD? >>>

- As we approach 2000, remember most of the people who started university this year were born in 1981.
- They are too young to remember the space shuttle blowing up.
- They do not remember Australia winning the America's Cup.
- They do not know who Moammar Gaddafi is.
- Their lifetime has always included AIDS.
- They have never had a polio shot and are not likely to know what it is.
- Soft-drink bottle caps have not only always been screw-off, but they have also always been plastic.

- The expression 'You sound like a broken record' means nothing to them.
- They have never owned a record player.
- Star Wars (the original) looks very fake to them and the special effects pathetic.
- The compact disc was introduced before they had turned one.
- As far as they know, stamps have always cost about 40 cents.
- They have always had an answering machine.
- Most have never seen a TV set with only two channels, nor have they seen a black-and-white TV.
- There have always been VCRs, but they have no idea what Beta is.
- They cannot fathom not having a remote control.
- Popcorn has always been cooked in a microwave.
- They never took a swim and thought about *Jaws*.
- The Vietnam War is as ancient history to them as World War II or even World War I.
- They don't know who Mork was or where he was from.
- They do not care who shot J.R. and have no idea who J.R. is.
- The *Titanic* was found. They didn't know it was lost.
- Michael Jackson has always been white.
- McDonalds never came in styrofoam containers.

Do you feel old now? Remember that the people who don't know these things are at university now and get to vote knowledgeably about your future.

CALLING ALL '80S CHILDREN >>>

You might be a child of the '80s if…

- You remember 'Tiger, Tiger, Jellimeat for dinner.'
- You remember the 'Ma-na-ma-na' song of the Muppets.
- Twenty cents worth of mixed lollies could last you hours and 50 cents, well only older kids could afford that much.
- You collected bottles to swap for lollies.
- Popsicles were 20 cents.
- You decided against rushing out and buying a CD player because you objected to the fact that you were being forced to change your collection.

- Picture this… after your nightly bath, dressed in your poncho, ug boots or kung-fu shoes and leg warmers, you sit in a bean bag with your Milo, ready to watch *Ready to Roll*.
- Summers were long and hot.
- Mello Yello made you feel so good so fast.
- Hey, hey, hey, it's Fat Albert time.
- You wondered how the Coke girls and boys got inside that big clear beach ball.
- You remember the advent of AIDS and Ecstasy.
- You remember spending the whole day at the beach with no sunblock at all and what's more, you didn't get burnt – much.
- You wore a leather band around your wrist and believed that any boy or girl that broke it, you had to sleep with.
- Basketball was only played by Americans.
- Sneakers in general were sneakers and not more advanced than your fridge.
- Doctor Who scared you silly.
- You remember the first space invaders. (Someone in your street had an Atari, right?)
- You queued up to see *The Village People Movie*.
- You felt a bit of a thing for Jeannie and Samantha… or better yet Tabitha, or for the girls in Maxwell Smart or Hogan (*Hogan's Heroes*) who were adorable.
- You saw *Grease* and *ET* at the movies.
- The Mickey Mouse Club was soooooo cool – 'M I C etc.'
- You hated missing an episode of *M.A.S.H.*
- You had a $50 Walkman that had fat headphones and chewed tapes after the first three days.
- Matchbox cars or Barbies were essential to your development.
- You had cardboard dolls (or your sisters did) that came with books of paper clothes that you tore out and stuck on the doll.
- The kid with the pool was your best friend… until someone got an in-ground pool.
- The only place you could get a pizza was Pizza Hut and it was expensive.
- You played dress-ups in your parents' funky clothes that you would kill to get your hands on now.
- Floppy disks were actually floppy.
- You actually went through at least one pair of Jandals a year because you wore them so much.

- You remember when the first people in your street got a video machine. It was top loading and there was no such thing as a remote control.
- Beta vs VHS wars.
- You remember a few years later they developed a remote control that was attached by a cord to the video. It was always too short to operate it from the lounge anyway.
- Fags were called 'fags' and nobody batted an eyelid when eight-year-olds walked down the street with a lolly cigarette hanging out their mouth.
- You knew Tommy Lee only for his musical abilities, not the ones shown in the video with Pammy Lee.
- You weren't old enough to go to *Aliens*.
- 'Oh Mickey you're so fine…'
- 'I love rock 'n' roll, so put another dime in the jukebox baby…'
- 'It's the final countdown da na na na…'

Any or all of this rings a bell.

ALL SHOOK UP >>>

Three old men were sitting around complaining about how much their hands shook.

The first geezer said, 'My hands shake so bad that when I shaved this morning I cut my face!'

The second old fogey one-upped him. 'My hands shake so bad that when I trimmed my garden yesterday I sliced all my flowers!'

The third old man laughed and said, 'That's nothing. My hands shake so bad that when I took a piss yesterday, I came three times.'

OBI-WAN FOR THE ROAD >>>

Luke and Obi-Wan are in a Chinese restaurant having a meal. Skilfully using his chopsticks, Obi-Wan deftly dishes himself a large portion of noodles into his bowl, then tops it off with some chicken and cashew nuts.

All this is done with consummate ease – as you might expect from a Jedi Master.

But poor old Luke is having a nightmare, using his chopsticks in both hands, dropping his food all over the table and eventually himself.

Obi-Wan looks at Luke disapprovingly and says, 'Use the forks, Luke.'

HEADS YOU WIN, TAILS I LOSE >>>

A young student reports for a final examination that consists of only true/false-type statements. The student takes a seat in the hall, stares at the question paper for five minutes, removes a coin and starts tossing the coin and marking the answer sheet. Heads means true, tails means false.

The young student is all done in 20 minutes while the rest of the class is sweating it out.

But, suddenly during the last few minutes, the young student is seen desperately throwing the coin, swearing and sweating.

The teacher, alarmed, approaches the student and asks what is going on.

'Well, I finished the exam in half an hour,' says the student, 'but I thought I ought to recheck my answers.'

ADULT NOSTALGIA >>>

I am hereby officially tendering my resignation as an adult. I have decided I would like to accept the responsibilities of an eight-year-old again.

I want to go to McDonald's and think that it's a four-star restaurant.

I want to sail sticks across a fresh mud puddle and make ripples with rocks.

I want to think M & Ms are better than money because you can eat them.

I want to lie under a big oak tree and run a lemonade stand with my friends on a hot summer's day.

I want to return to a time when life was simple. When all you knew were colours, multiplication tables, and nursery rhymes, but that didn't bother you, because you didn't know what you didn't know and you didn't care. All you knew was to be happy because you were blissfully unaware of all the things that should make you worried or upset.

I want to think the world is fair and that everyone is honest and good. I want to believe that anything is possible.

I want to be oblivious to the complexities of life and be overly excited by the little things again.

I want to live simple again. I don't want my day to consist of computer crashes, mountains of paperwork, depressing news, how to survive more days in the month than there is money in the bank, doctor's bills, gossip, illness, and loss of loved ones. I want to believe in the power of smiles, hugs, a kind word, truth, justice, peace, dreams, the imagination, mankind, and making angels in the snow.

So here's my chequebook and my car – keys, my credit card bills and my 401K statements. I am officially resigning from adulthood. And if you want to discuss this further, you'll have to catch me first, 'cause, 'Tag! You're it!'

HORSE SENSE >>>

The aspiring psychiatrists from various colleges were in their first class on emotional extremes. 'Just to establish some parameters,' said the professor, to the student from the University of Houston, 'what is the opposite of joy?'

'Sadness,' said the student.

'And the opposite of depression?' he asked of the young lady from Rice.

'Elation,' she said.

'And you, sir,' he said to the young man from Texas Agricultural, 'how about the opposite of woe?'

The Aggie replied, 'Sir, I believe that would be giddy-up.'

STIFFENED RESOLVE >>>

A man was walking down the street when he noticed his grandpa sitting on the porch, in the rocking chair, with nothing on from the waist down.

'Grandpa, what are you doing?' he exclaimed.

The old man looked off in the distance and did not answer him.

'Grandpa, what are you doing sitting out here with no pants on?' The old man slyly looked at him and said, 'Well, last week I sat out here with no shirt on and I got a stiff neck. This was your Grandma's idea.'

AGEING BODILY FUNCTIONS >>>

Three old men are talking about their aches, pains and bodily functions. One 70-year-old says, 'I have this problem. I wake up every morning at seven and it takes me 20 minutes to pee.'

An 80-year-old says, 'My case is worse. I get up at eight and I sit there and grunt and groan for half an hour before I finally have a bowel movement.'

The 90-year-old says, 'At seven I pee like a horse. At eight I crap like a cow.'

'So what's your problem?' asked the others.

'I don't wake up until nine.'

GOLFING BUDDIES >>>

Sid and Barney head out for a quick round of golf. Since they are short on time, they decide to play only nine holes.

Sid says to Barney, 'Let's say we make the time worth while, at least for one of us, and put $5 on the lowest score for the day.' Barney agrees and they enjoy a great game.

After the eighth hole, Barney is ahead by one stroke, but cuts his ball into the rough on the ninth. 'Help me find my ball. You look over there,' he says to Sid.

After five minutes, neither has had any luck and since a lost ball carries a four-point penalty, Barney pulls a ball from his pocket and tosses it to the ground. 'I've found my ball,' he announces triumphantly.

Sid looks at him forlornly, 'After all the years we've been friends, you'd cheat me on golf for a measly five bucks?'

'What do you mean cheat?' says Barney, 'I found my ball right here.'

'And a liar too,' Sid says with amazement, 'I'll have you know, I've been standing on your ball for the last five minutes.'

AIMING LOW >>>

An 83-year-old woman decided that she's seen and done everything and that the time had come to depart from this world. After considering various methods of doing away with herself, she came to the conclusion that the quickest and surest method would be to shoot herself through the heart.

The trouble was she wasn't certain about exactly where her heart was, so she phoned her doctor and asked him. He told her that her heart was located two inches below her left nipple.

So she shot herself in the left hip.

SNAKES AND LADDERS >>>

A general store owner hires a young female assistant with a penchant for very short skirts. One day, a young man enters the store, glances at the assistant, and glances at the loaves of bread behind the counter.

'I'd like some raisin bread, please,' the man says politely. The assistant nods and climbs up a ladder to reach the raisin bread located on the very top shelf. The man, standing almost directly beneath her, is provided with an excellent view.

As the assistant retrieves the bread, a small group of male customers gather around the young man looking in the same direction.

Pretty soon each person is asking for raisin bread, just to see the assistant climb up and down. After a few trips the assistant is tired and irritated. She stops and fumes at the top of the ladder, glaring at the men standing below.

She notices an elderly man standing among the throng. 'Is yours raisin too?' The assistant yells testily.

'No,' croaks the old man, 'but it's starting to twitch.'

ARSE ABOUT FACE HOPES >>>

'The most unfair thing about life is the way it ends. I mean, life is tough. It takes up a lot of your time and what do you get at the end of it? A death. What's that, a bonus? I think the life cycle is all backwards. You should die first, get it out of the way. Then you live in an old age home. You get kicked out when you're too young, you get a gold watch, you go to work. You work 40 years until you're young enough to enjoy your retirement. You do drugs, alcohol, you party, and you get ready for high school. You go to primary school, you become a kid, you play, you have no responsibilities, you become a little baby, you go back into the womb, you spend your last nine months floating... and you finish off as an orgasm.'

THE ROAD CODE >>>

An old lady in a nursing home is wheeling up and down the halls in her wheelchair making sounds like she's driving a car. As she's going down the hall an old man jumps out of a room and says, 'Excuse me, ma'am, but you were speeding. Can I see your driver's licence?'

She digs around in her purse a little, pulls out a candy wrapper and hands it to him. He looks it over, gives her a warning and sends her on her way.

Up and down the halls she goes again. Then the same old man jumps out of a room and says, 'Excuse me, ma'am, but I saw you cross over the centre line back there. Can I see your registration please?' She digs around in her purse a little, pulls out a store receipt and hands it to him. He looks it over, gives her another warning and sends her on her way.

She zooms off again, up and down the halls, weaving all over. As she comes to the old man's room again he jumps out. He's stark naked and has an erection. The old lady in the wheelchair looks up and says, 'Oh no, not the breathalyser again.'

SIGN LANGUAGE >>>

A mother had three daughters and, on their wedding night, she tells each one to write back about their married life.

To avoid possible embarrassment to their new husbands by openly discussing their love lives, the mother and daughters agree to use newspaper advertisements as a 'code' to let the mother know how their love lives are going.

The first one gets married and the second day the letter arrives with a single message, simply: 'Maxwell House Coffee'.

The mother got the newspaper and checked the Maxwell House advertisement, and it says, 'Satisfaction to the last drop…' So the mother is happy.

Then the second daughter gets married. After a week, there was a message that read: 'Rothman's Mattresses'. So the mother looks at the Rothman's Mattresses ad, and it says, 'Full size, king size'. And the mother is happy.

Then it comes to the third one's wedding. Mother is anxious. After four weeks came the message: 'British Airways'. And the mother looks into the British Airways ad, but this time she fainted.

The ad reads: 'Three times a day, seven days a week, both ways.'

DELAYED REACTION >>>

A 90-year-old man lived in a rest home and got a weekend pass. He stopped in his favourite bar and sat at the end and ordered a drink. He noticed a 70-year-old woman at the other end of the bar and he told the barman to buy the lovely young thing a drink.

As the evening progressed, the old man joined the lady and they went to her apartment, where they got it on.

Four days later, the old man noticed that he was developing a drip, and he headed for the rest home doctor. After careful examination the doctor asked the old man if he had engaged in sex recently.

The old man said, 'Sure!'

The doctor asked if he could remember who the woman was and where she lived. 'Sure, why?'

'Well you'd better get over there, you're about to cum!'

SPEED FREAK >>>

An old man was driving down the Interstate at 22 miles per hour, never going faster or slower. A police officer noticed and followed him for a while, then pulled him over. Before the officer could even get to the car, the man was saying, 'I was not speeding, the speed limit is 22 miles per hour and that is exactly what I was doing, I was not speeding.'

The police officer said, 'I didn't pull you over for speeding, I pulled you over for going too slow.'

'But the sign says 22.' The officer explained that he was on Interstate 22. As the man shook his head, the officer noticed that there were three older ladies in the back of the car. All of them were sitting with their mouths hanging open and spit drooling down the side. Their faces were very white and their hair was completely messy.

The police officer leaned toward the man and asked, 'What's wrong with them?'

'Well, we just came off Interstate 134.'

OH UNLUCKY MAN >>>

When I went to lunch today, I noticed this elderly man about 75 to 80 years old sitting on a bench near the shopping centre sobbing his eyes out.

I stopped and asked him what was wrong. He said, 'I have a 22-year-old wife at home. She makes love to me every morning and then gets up and makes me pancakes, sausage, fresh fruit and freshly brewed coffee.'

I said, 'Well, then why are you crying?'

He said, 'She makes me homemade soup for lunch and my favourite brownies and then makes love to me half the afternoon.'

I asked again, 'So why are you crying?'

He continued, 'For dinner she makes me a gourmet meal with wine and my favourite dessert and then makes love to me until midnight.'

I said, 'Well, why in the world would you be crying?'

He answered, 'I can't remember where I live.'

battle of the blondes

The poor old blondes cop a lot of flak. In Britain it's the Essex girl, but for this book, the global generic blonde does the trick. They're thick and very dizzy, but a lot of fun.

BLUE BLONDE >>>

A depressed young blonde was so desperate that she decided to end her life by throwing herself into the harbour.

When she went down to the docks, a handsome young sailor noticed her tears, took pity on her, and said: 'Look, you've got a lot to live for. I'm off to Europe in the morning, and if you like I can stow you away on my ship. I'll take good care of you and bring you food every day.'

Moving closer, he slipped his arm around her shoulder and added, 'I'll keep you happy, and you'll keep me happy.' The blonde nodded 'Yes.' After all, what did she have to lose?

That night, the sailor brought her aboard and hid her in a lifeboat. From then on, every night he brought her three sandwiches and a piece of fruit, and they made passionate love until dawn.

Three weeks later, during a routine search, the captain discovered her. 'What are you doing here?' the captain asked. 'I have an arrangement with one of the sailors,' she explained, 'He's taking me to Europe, and he's screwing me.'

'He sure is, lady,' said the captain. 'This is the harbour ferry.'

'GOING UP' >>>

A businessman got into an elevator. When he entered, there was a blonde already inside and she greeted him by saying, 'T-G-I-F.'

He smiled at her and replied, 'S-H-I-T.'

She looked at him puzzled and said, 'T-G-I-F' again.

He acknowledged her remark again by answering, 'S-H-I-T.'

The blonde was trying to be friendly, so she smiled her biggest smile and said as sweetly as possible, 'T-G-I-F' another time.

The man smiled back at her and once again replied with a quizzical expression, 'S-H-I-T.'

The blonde finally decided to explain things and this time she said, 'T-G-I-F. Thank Goodness It's Friday, get it?'

The man answered, 'S-H-I-T, Sorry Honey It's Thursday.'

DUMMY RUN >>>

A young ventriloquist is touring the clubs and stops to entertain at a bar. He's going through his usual run of stupid blonde jokes when a big blonde woman in the fourth row stands on her chair and says, 'I've heard just about enough of your denigrating blonde jokes, arsehole. What makes you think you can stereotype women that way? What does a person's physical attributes have to do with their worth as a human being? It's guys like you who keep women like me from being respected at work and in my community, of reaching my full potential as a person… because you and your kind continue to perpetuate discrimination against not only blondes but also women in general, all in the name of humour.'

Flustered, the ventriloquist begins to apologise, when the blonde pipes up, 'You stay out of this mister. I'm talking to that little bastard on your knee.'

FIELD OF DREAMS >>>

This blonde is driving down an old country road when she spots another blonde in a wheat field rowing a boat. She pulls over to the side of the road and stops the car. Staring in disbelief, she stands at the side of the road to watch the woman for a while.

When she can't stand it any more, she calls out to the blonde in the field, 'Why are you rowing a boat in the middle of the field?'

The blonde in the field stops rowing and responds, 'Because it is an ocean of wheat.'

The blonde standing at the side of the road is furious. She yells at the blonde in the field, 'It is dumb blondes like you that give the rest of us a bad name.'

The blonde in the field just shrugs her shoulders and begins rowing again.

The blonde on the side of the road is beside herself and shakes her fist at the blonde in the field yelling, 'If I could swim, I would come out there and kick your arse.'

CARNIVAL WAS OVER >>>

Joe took his blonde blind date to a seaside carnival. 'What would you like to do first, Kim?' asked Joe.

'I want to get weighed,' she said. They ambled over to the weight guesser, who guessed 70 kg. Kim got on the scale and it read 67 kg and she won a prize.

Next the couple went on the ferris wheel. When the ride was over,

Joe again asked Kim what she wanted to do next. 'I want to get weighed,' she said. Back to the weight guesser they went and because she'd been there before the man guessed Kim's correct weight and Joe lost his dollar.

Kim and Joe walked around the carnival and again he asked, 'Where to next?' Kim responded: 'I want to get weighed,' but by this time Joe figured she was really weird and took her home early, dropping her off with a handshake.

Her flatmate, Laura, asked Kim about her blind date, 'How'd it go?' she asked.

Kim said, 'Oh, Waura, it was wousy.'

PUZZLED >>>

One day this blonde calls her friend and says, 'Please come over and help me. I have this killer jigsaw puzzle and I can't even figure out how to start it.'

Her friend asks, 'What is it a puzzle of?' The blonde says, 'From the picture on the box, it's a tiger.'

Well, the friend figures that he's pretty good at puzzles, so he heads over to her place. She lets him in the door and shows him to where she has the pieces spread all over the table. He studies them for a moment, then studies the box.

He turns to her and says, 'Well, no matter what I do, I'm not going to be able to show you how to assemble these to look like the picture of that tiger.'

She asks, 'Oh, how come?'

He says, 'Look, never mind, let's just relax, have a cup of coffee and we'll put all these cornflakes back in the box.'

MILKY WAY >>>

This blonde heard that milk baths would make you beautiful. She left a note for her milkman to leave 30 litres of milk. When the milkman read the note he felt there must be a mistake, and thought she probably meant three litres, so he knocked on the door to clarify the point.

The blonde came to the door and the milkman said, 'I found your note to leave 30 litres of milk. Did you mean 30 litres or three litres?' The blonde said, 'I want 30 litres. I'm going to fill my bath up with milk and take a milk bath.'

The milkman asked, 'Pasteurised?'

The blonde said, 'No. Just up to my tits.'

KEEP ON TRACKING >>>

Two blondes were walking through the woods and they came to some tracks. The first blonde said, 'These look like deer tracks,' and the other one said, 'No they look like moose tracks.'

They argued and argued for a quite while and they were still arguing when the train hit them.

COKEHEAD >>>

A blonde walks up to a Coke machine and puts in a coin. Out pops a coke. The blonde looks amazed and runs away to get some more coins.

She returns and starts feeding the machine madly and, of course, the machine keeps feeding out drinks.

Another woman walks up behind the blonde and watches her antics for a few minutes before asking if someone else could have a go. The blonde spins around and shouts in her face, 'Can't you see I'm winning?'

CHEATED BLONDE >>>

A young blonde woman is distraught because she fears her husband is having an affair, so she goes to a gun shop and buys a handgun.

One day she comes home and finds her husband in bed with a beautiful redhead. She grabs the gun and holds it to her own head.

The husband jumps out of bed, begging and pleading with her not to shoot herself.

Hysterically, the blonde responds to her husband, 'Shut up… you're next.'

ONCE A BLONDE... ALWAYS A BLONDE >>>

A brunette goes to the doctor and as she touches every part of her body with her finger, she says, 'Doctor it hurts everywhere. My leg hurts, my arm hurts, my neck hurts and even my head hurts.'

The doctor asks, 'Were you ever a blonde?'

'Yes I was,' she replies. 'Why do you ask?'

The doctor answers, 'Because your finger is broken.'

SHINY HAPPY PERSON >>>

A blonde woman walks into a store and is immediately curious about a shiny object on sale. She asks the shop assistant, 'What is that?'

The assistant responds, 'It's a thermos.'

The blonde then asks, 'What does it do?'

'It keeps hot things hot and cold things cold.'

So the blonde buys one. The next day she brings the thermos to work with her. Her boss, also a blonde, asks, 'What is the shiny object?'

'It's a thermos.'

'What does it do?'

'It keeps hot things hot and cold things cold.'

Her boss then asks, 'What do you have in there?'

The blonde replies, 'Two cups of coffee and a Popsicle.'

HORSE LAUGH >>>

A blonde decides to try horseback riding even though she has had no lessons or prior experience. She mounts the horse unassisted and the horse immediately springs into motion.

It gallops along at a steady and rhythmic pace, but the blonde begins to slip from the saddle. In terror, she grabs for the horse's mane, but cannot seem to get a firm grip. She tries to throw her arms around the horse's neck, but she slides down the side of the horse anyway. The horse gallops along, seemingly impervious to its slipping rider. Finally, giving up her frail grip, she leaps away from the horse to try to throw herself to safety.

Unfortunately, her foot has become entangled in the stirrup, and she is now at the mercy of the horse's pounding hooves as her head is struck against the ground over and over. As her head is battered against the ground, she is mere moments away from unconsciousness when to her great fortune… the Woolworths manager sees her and shuts the horse off.

EYE CONTACT >>>

A man is eating in a fancy restaurant and there is a gorgeous blonde eating at the next table. He has been checking her out all night, but lacks the nerve to go and talk to her.

Suddenly the woman sneezes and her glass eye comes flying out of its socket towards the man. He reflexively grabs and snatches it out of the air.

'Oh my God, I am sooo sorry,' the woman says as she pops her eye back in place. 'Let me buy you dinner to make it up to you.'

They enjoy a wonderful dinner together and afterwards the woman invites him to the theatre followed by drinks. After paying for everything, she asks him if he would like to come to breakfast the next morning.

When he arrives the next morning, she has cooked a gourmet meal with all the trimmings. The guy is amazed. 'You know you are the perfect woman. Are you this nice to every guy you meet?'

'No,' she replies, 'you just happened to catch my eye.'

QUICK BITES >>>

How do you drown a blonde?
Put a 'scratch and sniff' sticker at the bottom of the pool.

Why does it take longer to build a blonde snowman as opposed to a regular one?
You have to hollow out the head.

How do you get a twinkle in a blonde's eye?
Shine a flashlight in her ear.

Why don't blondes like making Raro juice from sachets?
Because they can't fit eight cups of water in the packet.

Did you hear about the two blondes that were found frozen to death in their car at the drive-in movie theatre?
They went to see 'Closed for Winter'.

Hear about the blonde that got an AM radio?
It took her a month to realise she could play it at night.

What did the blonde say when she saw the sign in front of the YMCA?
'Look! They spelled Macy's wrong.'

Why did the blonde scale the chain-link fence?
To see what was on the other side.

How do you make a blonde laugh on Saturday?
Tell her a joke on Wednesday.

Why do blondes have 'TGIF' written on their shoes?
Toes Go In First.

Why did the blonde stare at the can of frozen orange juice?
Because it said concentrate.

Why do blondes always smile during lightning storms?
They think their picture is being taken.

How can you tell when a blonde sends you a fax?
It has a stamp on it.

What do you do if a blonde throws a pin at you?
Run, she's got a grenade in her mouth.

How can you tell if a blonde has been using your computer?
There is white-out all over the monitor.

Why shouldn't blondes have coffee breaks?
It takes too long to retrain them.

Three blondes were driving to Disneyland. After being in the car for four hours they finally saw a sign that said 'Disneyland Left' so they turned around and went home.

MORE QUICK BITES >>>

She was so blonde…

- She got stabbed in a shoot-out.

- She put lipstick on her forehead because she wanted to make up her mind.
- She told me to meet her at the corner of 'walk' and 'don't walk'.
- She tried to put M&Ms in alphabetical order.
- She tried to drown a fish.
- She thought a quarterback was a refund.
- She got locked in a grocery store and starved to death.
- If you gave her a penny for intelligence, you'd get change back.
- They had to burn the school down to get her out of third grade.
- Under 'education' on her job application, she put 'Hooked On Phonics.'
- She tripped over a cordless phone.
- She took a ruler to bed to see how long she slept.
- At the bottom of the application where it says 'sign here', she put 'Sagittarius.'
- She asked for a price docket at the Dollar Store.
- If she spoke her mind, she'd probably be speechless.
- She studied for a blood test… and failed.
- She thought Boyz II Men was a daycare centre.
- She thought Meow Mix was a record for cats.
- She thought she needed a ticket to get on Soul Train.
- She sold the car for gas money.
- When she saw the 'NC-17' (under 17 not admitted), she went home and got 16 friends.
- When she heard that 90 percent of all crimes occur around the home, she moved.
- She thinks Taco Bell is where you pay your phone bill.
- When she missed the 44 bus, she took the 22 bus twice instead.

BLONDE SUCKER >>>

A brunette, redhead and blonde went to a fitness spa for some fun and relaxation. After a stimulating healthy lunch, all three decided to visit the ladies' room and found a strange-looking woman sitting at the entrance who said, 'Welcome to the ladies' room. Be sure to check out our newest feature: a mirror which, if you look into it and say something truthful, you will be awarded with a wish. But, be warned, if you say something false, you will be sucked into the mirror to live in a void of nothingness for all eternity!'

The three women quickly entered and upon finding the mirror, the brunette said, 'I think I'm the most beautiful of us three' and in an instant she was surrounded by a pile of money.

The redhead stepped up and said, 'I think I'm the most talented of us three,' and she suddenly found the keys to a brand new Jaguar in her hands.

Excited over the possibility of having a wish come true, the blonde looked into the mirror and said, 'I think…' and was promptly sucked into the mirror.

CANINE CLUES >>>

The police department, famous for its superior canine (K-9) unit, was somewhat taken back by a recent incident. Returning home from work, a blonde was shocked to find her house ransacked and burgled. She telephoned the police at once and reported the crime.

The police dispatcher broadcast the call on the channels and a K-9 unit patrolling nearby was the first on the scene.

As the K-9 officer approached the house with his dog on a leash, the blonde ran out onto the porch, clapped a hand to her head and moaned, 'I come home from work to find all my possessions stolen, I call the police for help, and what do they do? They send a blind policeman!'

anonymous alcoholics

The pissheads among us will appreciate this chapter. Most of us have done mad things under the influence and if you're a happy drunk (as opposed to a morose, violent dickhead) the humour will hit a nicely lubricated nerve.

PIANIST ENVY >>>

There is this guy who walks into a bar and notices a man 12 inches tall playing the piano. He asks what it is all about and the barman tells him he'll tell him later. So he asks the barman for a drink and the barman says, 'Before you get your drink you get to rub the magic beer bottle and make a wish.'

'OK,' says the guy. He goes to the bottle and rubs it and, boom, out comes a genie, who says, 'You have one wish.'

The man thinks about it and then wishes for a million bucks. A cloud of smoke fills the room and when the smoke clears there are a million ducks crowding the bar.

He tells the barman, 'Hey, I didn't want a million ducks.'

The barman replies, 'You think I wanted a 12-inch pianist?'

FROTH ESTATE >>>

'You can't be a real country unless you have a beer and an airline. It helps if you have some kind of a football team or some nuclear weapons, but at the very least you need a beer.'
– Frank Zappa.

'Always do sober what you said you'd do drunk. That will teach you to keep your mouth shut.' – Ernest Hemingway.

'Always remember that I have taken more out of alcohol than alcohol has taken out of me.' – Winston Churchill.

'He was a wise man who invented beer.' – Plato.

'Time is never wasted when you're wasted all the time.'
– Catherine Zondonella.

'A woman drove me to drink and I didn't even have the decency to thank her.' – W. C. Fields.

'Sir, if you were my husband, I would poison your drink.'
– Lady Astor to Winston Churchill.
'Madam, if you were my wife I would drink it.'
– Churchill's reply.

'Sir, you're drunk!' – Lady Astor to Winston Churchill.
'Yes madam, and you're ugly. But in the morning I will be sober.' – Churchill's reply.

'If God had intended us to drink beer, He would have given us stomachs.' – David Daye.

'When I read about the evils of drinking, I gave up reading.' – Henny Youngman.

'Beer is proof that God loves us and wants us to be happy.' – Benjamin Franklin.

'If you ever reach total enlightenment while drinking beer, I bet it makes beer shoot out your nose.' – Jack Handy.

'Without question, the greatest invention in the history of mankind is beer. Oh, I grant you that the wheel was also a fine invention, but the wheel does not go nearly as well with pizza.' – Dave Barry.

'The problem with the world is that everyone is a few drinks behind.' – Humphrey Bogart.

'Why is American beer served cold? So you can tell it from urine.' – David Moulton.

'People who drink light beer don't like the taste of beer, they just like to pee a lot.' – Capital Brewery, Middleton, Wisconsin.

'Give me a woman who loves beer and I will conquer the world.' – Kaiser Wilhelm.

'I would kill everyone in this room for a drop of sweet beer.' – Homer Simpson.

'Not all chemicals are bad. Without chemicals such as hydrogen and oxygen, for example, there would be no way to make water, a vital ingredient in beer.' – Unknown

'I drink to make other people interesting.' – George Jean Nathan.

'They who drink beer will think beer.' – Washington Irving.

'An intelligent man is sometimes forced to be drunk to spend time with his fools.' – Ernest Hemingway in For Whom the Bell Tolls.

'You're not drunk if you can lie on the floor without holding on.' – Dean Martin.

'All right, brain, I don't like you and you don't like me – so let's just do this and I'll get back to killing you with beer.' – Homer Simpson.

TRUST A CRUSTACEAN >>>

Once upon a time a humble crab fell in love with Princess Lobster and she with him. They enjoyed an idyllic relationship, but one day Princess Lobster came to Crab in floods of tears saying that King Lobster would not let her see Crab any more.

'But why?' gasped the humble crab.

'Daddy says that crabs are too common,' sobbed the princess. 'You're a lower class of crustacean, and anyway, you walk sideways.' Crab was shattered and scuttled away to drink himself into forgetfulness.

That night was the occasion of the great Lobster Ball and lobsters came from far and near for feasting and merrymaking. Princess Lobster, however, sat by her father's side inconsolable.

Suddenly, the doors flew open. It was the humble crab. Slowly, painstakingly, he made his way to the throne – walking dead straight, one claw after another. A silence gathered around the room. All the lobsters' eyes fell on the intruder. Step by painful straight step he approached until he looked King Lobster in the eye. There was a deadly hush. Finally Crab spoke up:

'F***, I'm pissed!'

TALKING TURKEY >>>

20 Easy Steps to Cook a Turkey

1. Go and buy a turkey.
2. Take a drink of whisky (scotch or bourbon).
3. Put turkey in the oven.
4. Take another two drinks of whisky.
5. Set the degree at 180 ovens.
6. Take three more whiskies of drink.
7. Turn oven the on.
8. Take four whisks of drinky.
9. Turk the bastey.
10. Whisky another bottle of get.
11. Stick a turkey in the thermometer.
12. Glass yourself a pour of whisky.
13. Bake the whisky for four hours.
14. Take the oven out of the turkey.
15. Take the oven out of the turkey.
16. Floor the turkey up off the pick.
17. Turk the carvey.
18. Get yourself another scottle of botch.
19. Tet the sable and pour yourself a glass of turkey.
20. Bless the saying, pass and eat out.

THINGS PISSHEADS REFUSE TO BELIEVE >>>

Due to increasing product liability litigation, wine manufacturers have accepted the Medical Association's suggestion that the following warning labels be placed immediately on all wine bottles:

1. WARNING: Consumption of alcohol may make you think you are whispering when you are not.
2. WARNING: Consumption of alcohol is a major factor in dancing like a moron.
3. WARNING: Consumption of alcohol may cause you to tell the same boring story over and over again until your friends want to smash your head in.

4. WARNING: Consumption of alcohol may cause you to thay shings like thish.
5. WARNING: Consumption of alcohol may lead you to believe that ex-lovers are really dying for you to telephone them at 4 am in the morning!
6. WARNING: Consumption of alcohol may leave you wondering what the hell happened to your trousers.
7. WARNING: Consumption of alcohol may make you think you can logically converse with members of the opposite sex without spitting.
8. WARNING: Consumption of alcohol may make you think you have mystical Kung Fu powers.
9. WARNING: Consumption of alcohol may cause you to roll over in the morning and see something really scary (whose species and/or name you can't remember).
10. WARNING: Consumption of alcohol is the leading cause of inexplicable rug burns on the forehead.
11. WARNING: Consumption of alcohol may create the illusion that you are tougher, handsomer and smarter than some really, really big guy named Frank.
12. WARNING: Consumption of alcohol may lead you to believe you are invisible.
13. WARNING: Consumption of alcohol may lead you to think people are laughing with you.
14. WARNING: Consumption of alcohol may cause an influx in the time-space continuum, whereby small (and sometimes large) gaps of time may seem to literally disappear.

BOOZERS OF THE WORLD UNITE! >>>

The following is an actual excerpt from *Forbes* magazine:

A herd of buffalo can only move as fast as the slowest buffalo, and when the herd is hunted, it is the slowest and weakest ones at the back that are killed first. This natural selection is good for the herd as a whole, because the general speed and health of the whole is maintained or even improved by the regular culling of the weakest members.

In much the same way, the human brain can operate only as fast as the slowest brain cells through which the electrical signals pass.

Recent epidemiological studies have shown that while excessive intake of alcohol kills off brain cells, it attacks the slowest and weakest brain cells first.

Thus, regular consumption of beer helps eliminate the weaker cells, constantly making the brain a faster and more efficient machine.

The result of this in-depth study verifies and validates the causal link between all-weekend parties and job-related performance. It also explains why, after a few short years of leaving university and getting married, most professionals cannot keep up with the performance of the new graduates.

Only those few that stick to the strict regimen of voracious alcoholic consumption can maintain the intellectual levels that they achieved during their university years.

So, this is a call to arms. As our country is losing its technological edge we should not shudder in our homes. Get back into the bars. Quaff that pint.

Your company and country need you to be at your peak, and you shouldn't deny yourself the career that you could have. Take life by the bottle and be all that you can be.

WHEELER DEALER >>>

A man's been drinking at the pub all night. The barman finally says that the bar is closing, so the man stands up to leave and falls flat on his face. He tries to stand one more time, same result.

He figures he'll crawl outside and get some fresh air and that will sober him up. Once outside he stands up and falls flat on his face. So he decides to crawl the four blocks to his home and when he arrives at the door he stands up and falls flat on his face again.

He crawls through the door into his bedroom. When he reaches his bed he tries one more time to stand up. This time he manages to pull himself upright but he quickly falls right into bed and is sound asleep as soon as his head hits the pillow.

He awakens the next morning to his wife standing over him shouting, 'So you've been out drinking again!'

'What makes you say that?' he asks, putting on an innocent look.

His wife said, 'The pub called. You left your wheelchair there again.'

OLD FRIENDS >>>

A man stumbles up to the only other patron in a bar and asks if he could buy him a drink. 'Why, of course,' comes the reply.

The first man then asks, 'Where are you from?'

'I'm from Ireland,' replies the second man.

The first man responds by saying, 'You don't say. I'm from Ireland too. Let's have another round to Ireland.'

'Of course,' replies the second man.

Curious, the first man then asks, 'Where in Ireland are you from?'

'Dublin,' comes the reply.

'I can't believe it,' says the first man, 'I'm from Dublin too. Let's have another drink to Dublin.'

'Of course,' replies the second man.

Curiosity again strikes and the first man asks, 'What school did you go to?'

'St Mary's,' replies the second man, 'I graduated in 1962.'

'This is unbelievable,' the first man says. 'I went to St Mary's and I graduated in 1962 too.'

About that time, one of the regulars comes in and sits down at the bar. 'What's been going on?' he asks the barman.

'Nothing much,' replies the barman. 'The O'Malley twins are drunk again.'

PRAYER FOR BEER >>>

Our lager,
Which art in barrels,
Hallowed be thy drink,
Thy will be drunk (I will be drunk),
At home as it is in the pub.
Give us this day our foamy head,
And forgive us our spillages,
As we will forgive those who spill against us.
And lead us not to incarceration,
But deliver us from hangovers.
For thine is the beer, the bitter and the lager.
For ever and ever.

Barmen.

OFFICIAL DRINKING SCALE >>>

A very British one:

0. Stone cold sober. Brain as sharp as an army bayonet.
1. Still sober. Pleasure senses activated. Feeling of well being.
2. Beer warming up head. Chips are ordered. Barmaid complimented on choice of blouse.
3. Crossword in newspaper is filled in. After a while the blanks are filled with random letters and numbers.
4. Barmaid complimented on choice of bra. Partially visible when bending to get packets of crisps. Try to instigate conversation about bra. Order half a dozen packets of crisps – one by one.
5. Have brilliant discussion with a guy at the bar. Devise a foolproof scheme for winning the lottery. Sort out cricket/tennis/football problems. Agree people are same the world over – except for the bloody French.
6. Feel like a demi-god. Map out rest of life on beer mat. Realise that everybody loves you. Ring up parents and tell them you love them. Ring girlfriend to tell her you love her and she still has an amazing arse.
7. Send drinks over to woman sitting at table with boyfriend. No reaction. Scribble out message of love on five beer mats and frisbee them to her across the room. Boyfriend asks you outside. You buy him a pint.
8. Some slurring. Offer to buy drinks for everyone in room. Lots of people say yes. Go round the pub hugging them one by one. Fall over. Get up.
9. Headache kicks in. Beer tastes off. Send it back. Beer comes back tasting same. Say, 'That's much better.' Fight nausea by trying to play poker machine for 10 minutes before seeing 'out of order' sign.
10. Some doubling of vision. Stand on table shouting abuse at all four barmen. Talked down by barmen's wives, who you offer to give baby to. Fall over. Get up. Fall over. Impale head on corner of table. Fail to notice oozing head wound.
11. Speech no longer possible. Eventually manage to find door. Sit and take stock. Realise you are sitting in pub cellar having taken a wrong turn. Vomit. Pass out.

12. Put in taxi by somebody. Give home address. Taken home. Can't get key in door. Realise you've given address of the local football club. Generally pleased at way evening has gone. Pass out again.

CHEERS, BROTHERS >>>

An Irishman walks into a bar in Dublin, orders three pints of Guinness and sits in the back of the room, drinking a sip out of each one in turn. When he finishes, he comes back to the bar and orders three more.

The barman asks him, 'You know, a pint goes flat after I draw it. It would taste better if you bought one at a time.'

The Irishman replies, 'Well, you see, I have two brothers. One is in America and the other's in Australia and I'm here in Dublin. When we all left home, we promised that we'd drink this way to remember the days when we drank together.'

The barman admits that this is a nice custom and leaves it there.

The Irishman becomes a regular in the bar and always drinks the same way, ordering three pints and drinking them in turn.

One day he comes in and orders only two pints. All the other regulars notice and fall silent. When he comes back to the bar for the second round, the barman says, 'I don't want to intrude on your grief, but I wanted to offer my condolences on your great loss.'

The Irishman looks confused for a moment, then a light dawns in his eye and he laughs. 'Oh no,' he says. 'Everyone's fine. I've just given up drinking.'

A BEAUTIFUL BALLERINA >>>

One day this big, nasty, sweaty woman wearing a raggedy sleeveless sundress walks into a bar. She raises her right arm, revealing a big hairy armpit as she points to all the people sitting at the bar and asks, 'What man out there will buy a lady a drink?'

The whole bar goes dead silent as the patrons try to ignore her. At the end of the bar, a skinny little pisshead slams his hand on the bar and says, 'Barman, I want to buy that ballerina a drink.'

The barman pours the drink and the woman chugs it down. After she's completed the drink, she turns again to the throng and points around at all of them, again revealing the hairy armpit, saying,

'What man out there will buy a lady a drink?'

Once again, the little drunk slaps his hand down on the bar and slurs to the barman, 'Sir, I would like to buy the ballerina another drink.'

After serving the lady her second drink, the barman approaches the little drunkard and says, 'It's your business if you want to buy the lady a drink, but why do you keep calling her a ballerina?'

To which, the drunk replies, 'Sir, in my eyes, any woman who can lift her leg up that high has got to be a ballerina.'

SHOCK HORROR BEER PROBE >>>

This is very upsetting for you guys. Research scientists at Guinness suggested that men should take a look at their beer consumption after considering the results of a recent analysis, which had revealed the presence of female hormones in beer.

The theory is that drinking beer makes men turn into women. To test the finding, 100 men were fed eight pints of beer each. It was then observed that 100 percent of the men gained weight, talked excessively without making sense, became overly emotional, couldn't drive, failed to think rationally, argued over nothing and refused to apologise when wrong.

No further testing is planned.

DEAREST DADDY >>>

Three guys were drinking in a pub when another man comes in and starts drinking at the bar. After a while he approaches the lads and, pointing at the one in the middle shouts, 'I've shagged your mother!'

The guys look bewildered as the man goes back to his place at the bar and resumes drinking.

Ten minutes later he comes back and points to the bloke in the middle of the trio and shouts, 'Did you hear me? I've shagged your mother.' Then he goes back to his drink.

A short time later the man comes up again, jabs his finger at the middle bloke and announces for the pub to hear, 'I've shagged your mother, and it was good.'

By now the trio have had enough and the one in the middle shouts, 'Dad, you're pissed. Bugger off home!'

BREATHING EASY >>>

A cop waited outside a popular pub hoping to nab a drink-driver. At closing time, as everyone came out, he spotted his potential quarry.

The man was so obviously inebriated that he could barely walk. He stumbled around the parking lot for a few minutes looking for his car.

After trying his keys on five others, he finally found his own vehicle. He sat in the car a good 10 minutes as the other pub patrons left.

He turned his lights on, then off. He started to pull forward into the grass, then stopped. Finally, when his was the last car, he pulled out onto the road and started to drive away.

The cop, waiting for this, turned on his lights and pulled the man over. He administered the breathalyser test and, to his great surprise, the man easily passed. The cop was dumbfounded.

'This equipment must be broken,' exclaimed the policeman.

'I doubt it,' said the man. 'Tonight I'm the designated decoy.'

FOR NUTTERS >>>

A guy walks into a bar and hears this voice say, 'Hey, you're a pretty good-looking guy.' Upon, further investigation, he realises that the voice is coming from a bowl of nuts. So he asks the barman, 'What's this?' The bartender replies, 'They're complimentary peanuts.'

HOPS TO IT >>>

At a World Brewing Convention in the United States, the CEOs of various brewing organisations retired to the bar at the end of each day's conferencing.

Bruce, the boss of Fosters, shouted to the barman, 'In 'Strailya, we make the best bloody beer in the world, so pour me a Fosters, cobber.'

Rob, chief of Budweiser, calls out, 'In the States, we brew the finest beers of the world, and I make the king of them all. Give me a pint of Bud.'

Hans steps up next, 'In Germany we invented beer. Give me a Weisen, the real king of beers.'

Up steps Dutchman Jan, chief executive of Grolsch, who states that Grolsch is the ultimate beer and asks for one with two fingers of head on top.

Patrick, the CEO of Guinness, steps forward. 'Barman, give me a coke with ice please.'

The other four stare at him in stunned silence with amazement written all over their faces. Eventually Bruce asks, 'Are you not going to have a Guinness, Pat?'

Patrick replies, 'Well, if you bastards aren't drinking, then neither am I.'

toilet humour

Now these are not to be consumed on a full stomach. Some of them are mild and amusing, while others take the chapter title literally. Be sure to be of strong constitution, but never admit to having anything in common with the subjects of these little stories and imitations of life - unless you know your friends very well!

QUIET IN THE STALLS >>>

Ten ways to annoy the person in the next toilet…

1. Grunt and strain really loudly for 30 seconds and then drop a rock melon into the bowl from a height of 2 m. Release a relaxed sigh.

2. Fill up a large flask with pumpkin soup. Squirt it erratically under the wall of your neighbour while yelling, 'Whoa! Easy big boy!'

3. Cheer and clap loudly every time somebody breaks the silence with a bodily function noise.

4. Using a small squeeze tube, spread peanut butter on a wad of toilet paper and drop the wad under your neighbour's wall. Then say, 'Whoops, could you kick that back over here please?'

5. Say, 'C'mon Mr Happy, don't fall asleep on me!'

6. Drop a D-cup bra on the floor under the stall where the person in the next stall can see it.

7. Say, 'Damn, this water's cold.'

8. Say, 'Hmm, I've never seen that colour before.'

9. Say, 'Interesting… more floaters than sinkers.'

10. Drop a marble and say, 'Oh shit, my glass eye.'

BASHING BUREAUCRACY >>>

A little old lady went to the grocery store to buy cat food. She picked up three cans and took them to the checkout counter. The girl at the cash register said, 'I'm sorry, but we cannot sell cat food without proof that you have a cat. A lot of old people buy cat food to eat and the management wants proof that you are buying the cat food for your cat.'

The little old lady went home, picked up her cat and brought it to the store. They sold her the cat food. The next day she tried to buy three cans of dog food. Again the cashier demanded proof that she had a dog because old people sometimes eat dog food. She went home and brought in her dog. She then bought the dog food.

The next day she brought in a box with a hole in the lid. The old lady asked the cashier to stick her finger in the hole. The cashier said, 'No, you might have a snake in there.'

The little old lady assured her that there was nothing in the box that would harm her. So the cashier put her finger in the box and pulled it out and told the little old lady, 'That smells like shit.'

The little old lady said, 'It is. Now can I buy three rolls of toilet paper?'

SHIT HOT >>>

Many people are at a loss for a response when someone gives them that quaint American phrase, 'You don't know Jack Schitt.' This is how to handle the situation.

Jack is the only son of Awe Schitt and O. Schitt. The fertiliser magnate married O. Schitt, the owner of Knee-Deep Schitt Inc. In turn, Jack Schitt married Noe Schitt and the deeply religious couple produced six children, Holie Schitt, The twins Deep Schitt and Dip Schitt, Fulla Schitt, Giva Schitt and Bull Schitt, a high school dropout.

Noe later married Mr Sherlock and because her kids were living with them, she wanted to keep her previous name. She was known as Noe Schitt-Sherlock.

Dip Schitt married Loda Schitt and they produced a cowardly son, Chicken Schitt. Fulla Schitt and Giva Schitt were inseparable throughout childhood and consequently married the Happens brothers in a dual ceremony.

The Schitt-Happens children are Dawg, Byrd, and Horse. Bull Schitt, the prodigal son, left home to tour the world. He recently returned with his bride, Pisa Schitt.

Now, when someone says, 'You don't know Jack Schitt!' You can correct them.

SILENT BUT VIOLENT >>>

Peter goes to the doctor and says, 'Doctor I have this problem with gas, but it really doesn't bother me too much. They never smell and are always silent. As a matter of fact I've farted at least 20 times since I've been in your office. You didn't know I was farting because they didn't smell and are silent.'

The doctor says, 'I see. Take these pills and come back to see me next week.'

The next week Peter goes back. 'Doctor,' he says, 'I don't know what the hell you gave me, but now my farts, although still silent, stink terribly.'

'Good,' the doctor said. 'Now that we've cleared up your sinuses, let's work on your hearing.'

GRAFFITI RULES >>>

Wit and wisdom on the dunny walls of the world:

Friends don't let friends take home ugly men.
– Women's toilet, Dewey Beach, Delaware.

The best way to a man's heart is to saw his breast plate open.
– Women's toilet, Champaign, Illinois.

Beauty is only a light switch away.
– Perkins Library, Duke University, Durham, North Carolina.

I've decided that to raise my grades I must lower my standards.
– Houghton Library, Harvard, Cambridge, Massachusetts.

God made pot. Man made beer. Who do you trust?
– *The Irish Times*, Washington DC.

Fighting for peace is like screwing for virginity.
– Baton Rouge, Louisiana.

At the feast of ego, everyone leaves hungry.
– Tucson, Arizona.

No matter how good she looks, some other guy is sick and tired of putting up with her shit.
– Men's toilet, Chapel Hill, North Carolina.

A Women's Rule of Thumb – if it has tyres or testicles, you're going to have trouble with it.
– Women's toilet, Dallas, Texas.

Jesus Saves, but wouldn't it be better if he had invested?
– Men's toilet, American University, Washington DC.

Express Lane: Five beers or less.
– Sign over one of the urinals, Phoenix, Arizona.

You're too good for him.
– Sign over mirror in women's toilet, Beverly Hills, California.

No wonder you always go home alone.
– Sign over mirror in men's toilet, Beverly Hills, California.

If life is a waste of time, and time is a waste of life, then let's all get wasted together and have the time of our lives.
— Armand's Pizza, Washington DC.

To do is to be — Descartes
To be is to do — Sartre
Do be do be do — Frank Sinatra
— Men's toilets, Scottsdale, Arizona.

It's hard to make a comeback when you haven't been anywhere.
— Written in dust on back of a bus, Wickenburg, Arizona.

Make love, not war — hell, do both, get married!
— Women's toilet, Bozeman, Montana.

If voting could really change things, it would be illegal.
— Revolution Books, New York.

Every once in a while each of us experiences a perfect crap. It's rare, but a thing of beauty in all respects. You sit down expecting the worst, but what you get is the smooth-sliding, fartless masterpiece that breaks the water with the splashless grace of an expert diver. But that's not the end of it. You use some toilet paper only to find that it was totally unnecessary. It makes you feel that all is right with the world and you are in perfect harmony with it.

On the other hand (so to speak) there is:

The Beer Crap

Talk about nasty craps. Depending on the crapper's tolerance, the beer crap is the result of too many beers. It could have been two or 22, it doesn't matter. What you get is a sinister, lengthy, noisy crap accompanied by a malevolent fog that could close a bathroom for days.

The Chilli Crap

Hot when it goes in and rocket fuel when it leaves. The chilli crap stays with you all day, making your tush feel like a heat shield.

The Cable Crap

Long, curly and perfectly formed like two feet of E13 telephone co-axial cable. It loops lazily around the bowl, like a friendly serpent. You wonder admiringly, 'Did I do that? Where did it come from?' You leave the toilet pleased with yourself.

The Latrine Crap

In case you didn't know, a latrine is a hole in the ground with a tent around it — where soldiers, boy scouts and flies go to crap. Tip: don't ever look down the hole.

The Mona Lisa Crap

This is the masterpiece of craps. It's as perfectly formed as it can be. Delicate and slender with intricacies that would make Da Vinci weep. And just think, you made it yourself. You may even want to break out the Polaroid camera, but maybe that's going too far.

The Empty Roll Crap
You're done… you reach for the toilet paper only to discover that empty cardboard cylinder. A mild panic begins coldly in your throat. You could use the curtains… no, someone would say, 'Where are the curtains?' Then what would you say. The rug? Too cumbersome. Then you must come to the same conclusion that every 'empty roll crapper' must face… pull up your daks, tighten your arse and wriggle yourself to the nearest full roll.

A mate about to run the London Marathon lined up outside the dozens of portaloos on Blackheath to unload a nervous one and discovered when the business was done and he was ready to run a world record race, there was no paper. Panic. The only thing available was a pound note — the last he possessed because they were being replaced by the coin — and he used that, being careful not to use the side with the Queen's head, of course!

The Splash Back Crap
You send the crap on its way; it drops like a depth charge into the bowl creating a column of cold bowl water that washes your bottom with a startlingly unpleasant shock. Now you're wet and embarrassed. Tip: blot instead of wipe.

The Aborted Crap
You are in mid-crap when the phone rings. What do you do? ABORT! Pinch it off; go for the phone and save the rest for later. It isn't pretty, but you've gotta do what you've gotta do.

The Caesarean Crap
Pain, that's what this crap and childbirth have in common. It's simply a case of too much crap trying to go through too small a hole and there's no obstetrician to help.

The Alfresco Crap
Everyone has had to go outdoors from time to time. This can be a rather pleasant experience really. The open air, the nature, and a good bush all contribute to the peaceful ambience that our primitive forefathers must have enjoyed. What can screw up this harmonious interlude is a troop of Brownies or a patch of poison ivy.

The Tijuana Trot Crap (also known as Delhi Belly, Rabat Runs, Seskatchewan Squits, Balsall Heath Balti Bypass)
The phrase 'shit happens' really applies here in a big way. When the ice in your tainted margarita makes contact with your lower intestinal tract, the fun begins. For the next 72 hours you'd be better off if you carried your own portable toilet with you because you will spend most of that time on the pot and the rest of the time in a foetal position.

The Machine Gun Crap
You're just sitting there in a state of sublime peace when all of a sudden you emit a group of noisy gassy bursts that break the silence like machinegun fire. The guy in the next stall hits the floor like a combat veteran — cradling his umbrella like an AK47.

The Sound Effect Crap
You feel a noisy one coming on. Relatives, friends or workmates are within earshot, so you must employ some clever techniques to cover the disgusting sounds you are about to emit. Timing is obviously very important here. At the precise moment of release, try the following sound effects:

1. Flush the toilet.
2. Sing the first two stanzas of your national anthem.
3. Drop a handful of change on the floor.

The Security Crap
You have enough on your mind when you're in the toilet without worrying about a lockless door and someone bursting in to find you in mid-crap mode. So how can you prevent this embarrassing spectacle from taking place? One way is to strategically place your foot against the door. If you can't reach to do this... hum loudly.

The Cling-On Crap
For the most part you've completed your crap, but there's one little morsel that refuses to drop off. You're getting impatient. Someone else wants to use the toilet. So you grip the seat with both hands and wriggle, twist and pump but that last little stubborn piece just hangs there, suspended, clinging like a canned peach between you and the water. Maybe the person pounding impatiently on the door has scissors.

The Houdini Crap

You go, then you stand up to flush and the damn thing has disappeared. Where'd it go? Did it creep down the pipe? Did you dream the whole thing? Is it lurking out of sight? Should you wipe… maybe you should just to make sure you went. Should you flush? You'd better, because if you don't, you know it will reappear and smile at the next person who comes in.

The Hangover Crap

You feel so bad that you don't know which end of you to put down first. You have roaring cramps, so you sit down. Then a wave of nausea rolls over you like a cold fog, so you stand up and cramps squeeze your intestines like a vice so you sit down again… up down, up down. Don't you wish Mum was close by.

The Porta-Pottie Dump

Construction workers and outdoor concertgoers will tell you about going in a portable toilet. My best description would be, 'It's like taking a shit in an upright coffin.' It's claustrophobic and it smells bad. Best advice: go in a paper cup.

The Proctologist Crap

In the beginning, the Lord created the earth, the sky and the firmament, but I hope he didn't create this dump because there is nothing biblical about it. You run out of gas. That's right, you run out of propulsion. The crap is right there at the end of your barrel and refuses to go any further. You grunt, you squeeze, you wriggle but it just stays there like a lump of lead. You've only got two choices here. One is to squeeze the damn thing back up your intestine and wait until next time. The other is to pretend you're a proctologist and go after it yourself. Not a pretty picture is it?

The Whole Roll Crap

No matter how much you wipe, it doesn't seem to be enough. You blow the whole roll and you have to flush 25 times too. The whole episode is consumer waste.

The Graffiti Crap

You flush the crap and the swirling motion of the receding bowl water forces the crap to the porcelain sides, scraping a creative squiggle on its way down. You flush again but the curly-Q hangs there… love it or leave it, it's your choice.

The Encore Crap
'Ahhh!' You're done, so you wipe, put yourself together, wash your hands and are about to vacate the toilet when you feel another crap on its way. You have to return for a curtain call.

The Born Again Crap
This is a dump that's going badly. You say, 'Lord, if I live through this, I'll take up religion.' You always get through it, but seldom keep the promises you made in desperation, because a born-again crap is like childbirth — you forget the pain quickly.

MIDGET TERRORIST >>>

A man is standing at a urinal when he notices that a midget is watching him. Although the little fellow is staring at him intently, the guy doesn't really become uncomfortable until the midget drags a small stepladder up next to him, climbs up, and proceeds to admire his privates at close range.

'Wow,' comments the midget, 'those are the nicest balls I have ever seen!' Surprised, yet flattered, the man thanks the midget and starts to move away.

'Listen, I know this is a rather strange request,' says the little fellow, 'but I wonder if you would mind if I touch them.' Again the man is rather startled, but seeing no real harm in it, he complies with the request.

The midget reaches out, gets a tight grip on the man's balls, and says loudly, 'Okay, hand me your wallet or I'll jump off the ladder.'

BOIL ON A BAG >>>

A woman walks into a doctor's surgery with a huge boil on her arse. The doctor squeezes it, pushes it, and then looks at the hard white pus core.

He says, 'This is too big a job for me.' So he sends her to Gus the pus sucker.

The woman goes to Gus who looks at the bulging, red, inflamed boil festering with pus and says, 'This is no problem.'

Halfway through the operation the woman drops a mammoth fart.

Gus stops what he's doing, looks up and says, 'You know lady, it's people like you that make this job f***ing disgusting.'

GETTING PISSED ON >>>

Responding to a woman who accidentally walked into a men's toilet:

Please don't feel bad. It wasn't you entering the men's washroom that caused that guy to pee on the guy next to him. Hell, we do that all the time. It's rare us guys ever hit what we're aiming for. Sometimes I go into the toilet, start to piss, and then just start spinning around just so I make sure I hit something.

You see something you ladies should understand by now is that men's penises have minds of their own. A guy can go into a toilet stall because all the urinals are being used, take perfect aim at the toilet and his penis will still manage to piss all over the roll of toilet paper, down his left pant leg and onto his shoe. I'm telling you those little buggers can't be trusted.

After being married for 28 years, my wife has me trained. I'm no longer allowed to pee like a man — standing up. I'm required to sit down and piss. She has me convinced that this is a small price to pay. Otherwise if she had gone to the toilet one more time at night and either sat on a piss soaked seat, or fell right into the toilet because I forgot to put the seat down, she was going to kill me in my sleep.

Now there's another thing us guys don't usually like to talk about, but since you and I have become such good friends and you think I'm a classy guy, I might as well be candid with you because it's a real problem and you ladies need to be understanding. It's the dreaded 'morning wood'. Most mornings us guys wake up with two things. A tremendous desire to piss and a penis so hard you could cut diamonds with it. Well, no matter how hard you try, you can't get that thing to bend and if it won't bend you can't aim. Well hell, if you can't aim you have no choice but to piss all over the wallpaper and the damn fuzzy toilet seat cover that you women insist on putting on the toilet.

So that means we have to use one hand to hold up the toilet seat and the other hand to try to control our less than perfect aim. Now sometimes, when you're newly married, you think you can get the toilet seat with the damn fuzzy thing to stay up. You jam it back and compress that fuzzy thing until the seat stays there. OK, so you start to pee, but then that compressed fuzzy starts to decompress and without warning that damn toilet seat comes flying down and tries to whack off your willie. So us guys will not lift a toilet seat with a fuzzy, it's just not safe.

I tried to delicately explain this morning situation to my wife. I told her, 'Look, it won't bend.'

She said, 'So sit down like I told you to do all the rest of the time.'

OK, I tried sitting down on the toilet with 'morning wood'. Well, it's very hard to get it bent under the seat and before I could manage it, I had pissed all over the bath towels hanging on the wall across the room.

Now, even if you are sitting down and you can get it forced down under the seat, when you start to pee it shoots out from the crack between the bottom of the toilet seat and the top of the bowl. You piss all over the back of your knees and it runs down the back of your legs onto that damn matching fuzzy horseshoe rug you keep putting on the floor in front of the toilet.

I have found the only effective manoeuvre to deal with this morning urinary dilemma is to assume the flying Superman position lying over the toilet seat. This takes a great deal of practice, perfect balance, and split-second precision, but it's the only sure way to get all the piss in the bowl during the first morning session. So you ladies have to understand that us men are not totally to blame.

We are sensitive to your concerns about hygiene and bathroom cleanliness, but there are times when things just get beyond our control. It's not our fault; it's Mother Nature. Now if it were Father Nature, there wouldn't have been a problem.

SPOT THE DOG >>>

A young man was delighted to finally be asked home to meet the parents. He was quite nervous about the meeting, though, and by the time he arrived punctually at the doorstep he was in a state of gastric distress.

The problem developed into one of acute flatulence and halfway through canapes the young man realised that he couldn't hold it in one second longer without exploding. A tiny fart escaped.

'Spot,' called out the young woman's mother to the family dog lying at the young man's feet. Relieved at the dog getting the blame, the young man let another slightly larger one go. 'Spot,' she cried out sharply.

I've got it made, thought the fellow to himself. One more and I'll be fine. So he let loose a really big one.

'Spot,' shrieked the mother, 'get over here before he shits on you.'

take me to your leader

President Clinton is understandably the butt of most of this section. The lies, lies and damn lies he told in the wake of the Monica Lewinsky affair defied belief, so the grey-haired one from Arkansas deserves all the piss-taking he gets.

PIG IGNORANT >>>

As the President gets off the helicopter in front of the White House, he has a baby pig under each arm. The Marine guard snaps to attention and says, 'Nice pigs, sir.'

The President replies, 'These are not pigs, these are authentic Arkansas razorback hogs. I got one for Hillary, and I got one for Chelsea.'

The Marine again snaps to attention and replies, 'Nice trade, sir.'

A MOULDY OLD STORY >>>

His name was Fleming and he was a poor Scottish farmer. One day, while trying to make a living for his family, he heard a cry for help coming from a nearby bog. He dropped his tools and ran to the bog. There, mired to his waist in black muck was a terrified boy, screaming and struggling to free himself.

Farmer Fleming saved the lad from what could have been a slow and terrifying death. The next day, a fancy carriage pulled up to the Scotsman's sparse surroundings. An elegantly dressed nobleman stepped out and introduced himself as the father of the boy Farmer Fleming had saved.

'I want to repay you,' said the nobleman. 'You saved my son's life.'

'No, I can't accept payment for what I did,' the Scottish farmer replied, waving off the offer.

At that moment, the farmer's own son came to the door.

'Is that your son?' the nobleman asked.

'Yes,' the farmer replied proudly.

'I'll make you a deal. Let me take him and give him a good education. If the lad is anything like his father, he'll grow to a man you can be proud of.' And that he did.

In time, Farmer Fleming's son graduated from St Mary's Hospital Medical School in London and went on to become known throughout the world as the noted Sir Alexander Fleming, the discoverer of penicillin.

Years afterward, the nobleman's son was stricken with pneumonia. What saved him? Penicillin.

The name of the nobleman? Lord Randolph Churchill. His son's name?

Sir Winston Churchill.

GLAD TO ACCOMMODATE YOU >>>

John Howard called Jenny Shipley with an emergency. 'Our largest condom factory exploded,' the Australian Prime Minister cried. 'My people's favourite form of birth control. This is a true disaster.'

'John, you must know that we Kiwis would be happy to do anything within our power to help you,' replied Jenny.

'I do need your help,' said Howard. 'Could you possibly send a million condoms ASAP to tide us over?'

'Certainly, I'll get right on to it,' said Jenny.

'Oh, and one more small favour, please?' said John. 'Could the condoms be yellow and green in colour, at least 20 cm long and 8 cm in diameter?'

'No problem,' replied Jenny and hung up.

Jenny then called the president of Durex Condoms. 'I need a favour. You've got to make a million condoms right away and send them to Australia.'

'Consider it done,' said the Durex boss.

Shipley said, 'Great. Now listen, they have to be green and yellow, at least 20 cm long and 8 cm in diameter.'

'Easily done, anything else?'

'Yes,' said Jenny, 'and print "MADE IN NEW ZEALAND, SIZE SMALL" on each one.'

DRINK ORDERS >>>

Jerry Falwell was seated next to President Clinton on an aeroplane flight and after the plane was airborne, the flight attendant came around for drink orders.

The President asked for a whisky and soda, which was brought and placed before him. The attendant then asked Mr Falwell if he too would like a drink.

Mr Falwell replied in disgust, 'Madam, I'd rather be savagely raped by a brazen whore than let liquor touch my lips!'

Hearing that, the President handed his drink back to the attendant and said, 'I'm sorry, I didn't realise there was a choice. I'll have what he's having.'

LIFE, STRIFE AND GOOD TIMES OF A PRESIDENT >>>

A musical interlude to the tune of *Summer Loving* from *Grease*:

Bill: *'Summer intern, had me a blast.'*
Monica: *'White House intern, happened so fast.'*
Bill: *'Met a girl, crazy for me.'*
Monica: *'Met the prez, down on my knees.'*
Bill: *'Summer days, sucking away, oh, I, but those summer nights.'*
Investigation Committee: *'Well, ah… well, ah… well, ah… uh. Tell us more, tell us more.'*
Linda Tripp: *'Try to remember your best.'*
Investigation Committee: *'Tell us more, tell us more.'*
Kenneth Starr: *'Did he come on your dress?'*
Bill: *'Wanted to screw her but she had a cramp.'*
Monica: *'The prez is sexy — he makes my panties damp.'*
Bill: *'She gave me h***, right in the White House.'*
Monica: *'I said, OK, just don't come in my mouth.'*
Investigation Committee: *'Well, ah… well, ah… well, ah… uh. Tell us more, tell us more.'*
Linda Tripp: *'He sounds like a swell guy.'*
Kenneth Starr: *'Did he tell you a lie?'*
Bill: *'Press found out, it turned into a mess.'*
Monica: *'He gave me 50 bucks to buy a new dress.'*
Bill: *'She promised to lie, she made a vow.'*
Monica: *'Wonder who is servicing him now.'*
Bill and Monica: *'Sex-filled dreams, ripped at the seams*
But… oh…
Those White House Nights.'

A HORRIBLE MISUNDERSTANDING >>>

Bill Clinton was watching TV one night when he had this craving for pork chops and apple sauce. He rang the chef, who was quite pissed off because the kitchen had been closed for half an hour and he'd just finished cleaning up.

However, the chef had a quick look in the bin and saw a couple of pork chops he'd thrown out earlier in the day. 'Sure thing, Mr

President,' he said cheerfully down the phone. 'I'll have your meal sent up in no time.'

The chef rescued the food from the bin, washed it off, quickly made some apple sauce and sent the food on its way. Clinton was most grateful and rang down specially to thank the chef. 'It's a pleasure, Mr President,' came the cheerful reply.

Clinton downed his meal and, about an hour later, was doubled over in agony with severe food poisoning and could barely move. In desperation, he managed to reach the alarm bell.

Within seconds the room was full of security personnel. Monica Lewinsky also burst in, and saw the President doubled over on the floor. She raced to his side, desperate to help.

'What can I do?' she begged him. By now the pain was so bad Clinton thought he was about to faint.

His last words before he fainted were, 'Sack my cook.'

GOOD HEAVENS! >>>

A man died and went to heaven. When he arrived at the pearly gates, Saint Peter said, 'Come on in. I'll show you around. You'll like it here.'

Walking through the gates, the man noticed clocks everywhere. There were grandfather clocks, wall clocks, watches, and clocks in every corner. It appeared that heaven was nothing more than a giant clock warehouse.

Surprised at how heaven looked, the man asked, 'Saint Peter, what's the deal? Why are all these clocks in heaven?'

Saint Peter replied, 'The clocks keep track of things on earth. There is one clock for each person. Every time the person on earth tells a lie, their clock moves one minute.

'For instance, this clock is for Sam, the used car salesman. If you watch it closely, it will move.' 'Click.' The minute hand on Sam's clock moved one minute. 'Click.' It moved another minute.

'Sam must be closing a deal right now,' said Saint Peter. 'The minute hand on his clock moves all day.'

The man and Saint Peter continued walking. Soon they came to a clock with cobwebs on the minute hand. 'Whose clock is this?' asked the man.

'That clock belongs to Widow Mary. She is one of the finest, God-fearing people on earth. I bet her clock hasn't moved in a year or two.'

They continued walking and touring heaven. The man enjoyed watching the clocks of all his friends. When the tour was finished, the man said, 'I've seen everyone's clock but President Clinton's. Where is his clock?'

Saint Peter smiled, 'Just look up. We use his clock for a ceiling fan.'

MAHATMA'S PLIGHT >>>

Mahatma Gandhi, as you know, walked barefoot most of the time, which produced an impressive set of calluses on his feet. He also ate very little, which made him rather frail and, with his odd diet, he suffered from bad breath. This made him what?

A super callused fragile mystic plagued with halitosis!

POLITICAL ANIMALS >>>

Dictatorship: You have two cows. The government takes both and shoots you.

Singaporean Democracy: You have two cows. The government fines you for illegally keeping two unlicensed farm animals in an apartment.

Pure Democracy: You have two cows. Your neighbours decide who gets the milk.

Representative Democracy: You have two cows. Your neighbours pick someone through a vote to tell you who gets the milk.

American Democracy: The government promises to give you two cows if you vote for it. After the election, the President is impeached for speculating in cow futures. The press dubs the affair 'Cowgate'.

Russian Communism: You have two cows. You have to take care of them but the government takes all the milk.

British Democracy: You have two cows. You feed them sheep's brains and they go mad. The government doesn't do anything.

Bureaucracy: You have two cows. At first the government

regulates what you can feed them and when you can milk them. Then it pays you not to milk them. After that the government takes both, shoots one, milks the other and pours the milk down the drain. Then it requires you to fill out a form to account for the missing cow.

MAIN MAN NELSON >>>

Nelson Mandela is sitting at home watching the telly when he hears a knock at the door. When he opens it, he is confronted by a little Japanese man clutching a clipboard and yelling, 'You sign! You sign!' Behind him is an enormous truck full of car exhausts.

Nelson is standing there in complete amazement when the Japanese man starts to yell louder, 'You sign! You sign!'

Nelson says to him, 'Look mate, you've obviously got the wrong bloke. Please go away!' and shuts the door in the Japanese man's face.

The next day he hears a knock at the door again. When he opens it, the little Japanese man is back, with a huge truck full of brake pads. He thrusts his clipboard under Nelson's nose, yelling, 'You sign! You sign!'

Mr Mandela is getting a bit hacked off by now, so he shoves the little Japanese man back, shouting, 'Look, get lost! You've got the wrong bloke! I don't want them!' then slams the door in the Japanese man's face again.

The following day Nelson is resting and, late in the afternoon, hears a knock on the door again. Upon opening the door, the little Japanese man thrusts the same clipboard under his nose, shouting, 'You sign! You sign!'

Behind him are two large trucks full of wing mirrors. Nelson loses his temper completely, picks the little man up by his shirt front and yells at him, 'Look, I don't want these! Do you understand? You must have the wrong man! Who do you want to give these to?'

The little Japanese man looks at him a bit puzzled, consults his clipboard, and says, 'You not Nissan Main Dealer?'

ABE AND JFK'S PARALLEL LIVES >>>

Abraham Lincoln was elected to Congress in 1846.
John F. Kennedy was elected to Congress in 1946.

Abraham Lincoln was elected President in 1860.
John F. Kennedy was elected President in 1960.

The names Lincoln and Kennedy each contain seven letters.

Both were particularly concerned with civil rights.
Both wives lost children while living in the White House.

Both Presidents were shot on a Friday.
Both Presidents were shot in the head.

Lincoln's secretary was named Kennedy.
Kennedy's secretary was named Lincoln.

Both were assassinated by Southerners.
Both were succeeded by Southerners.

Both successors were named Johnson – Andrew Johnson, who succeeded Lincoln, was born in 1808.
Lyndon Johnson, who succeeded Kennedy, was born in 1908.

John Wilkes Booth, who assassinated Lincoln, was born in 1839.
Lee Harvey Oswald, who assassinated Kennedy, was born in 1939.

Both assassins were known by their three names.
Both names are made up of 15 letters.

Lincoln was shot at the theatre named Kennedy.
Kennedy was shot in a car called Lincoln.

Booth ran from the theatre and was caught in a warehouse.
Oswald ran from a warehouse and was caught in a theatre.

Booth and Oswald were assassinated before their trials.

And here's the kicker…

A week before Lincoln was shot, he was in Monroe, Maryland.
A week before Kennedy was shot, he was in Marilyn Monroe.